Exploring Twentieth-Century Music

In this wide-ranging book, Arnold Whittall considers a group of important composers of the twentieth century, including Debussy, Webern, Schoenberg, Stravinsky, Bartók, Janáček, Britten, Carter, Birtwistle, Andriessen and Adams. He moves skilfully between the cultural and the technical, the general and the particular, to explore the various contexts and critical perspectives which illuminate certain works by these composers. Considering the extent to which place and nationality contribute to the definition of musical character, he investigates the relevance of such images as mirroring and symmetry, the function of genre and the way types of identity may be suggested by such labels as classical, modernist, secular, sacred, radical, traditional. These categories are considered as flexible and interactive and they generate a wide-ranging series of narratives delineating some of the most fundamental forces which affected composers and their works within the complex and challenging world of the twentieth century.

ARNOLD WHITTALL is Professor Emeritus of Music Theory and Analysis at King's College London and he has written widely on twentieth-century music. His recent publications include *The Music of Britten and Tippett* (1990) and *Musical Composition in the Twentieth Century* (1999).

Exploring Twentieth-Century Music

Tradition and Innovation

Arnold Whittall

CAMBRIDGE
UNIVERSITY PRESS

PUBLISHED BY THE PRESS SYNDICATE OF THE UNIVERSITY OF CAMBRIDGE
The Pitt Building, Trumpington Street, Cambridge CB2 1RP, United Kingdom

CAMBRIDGE UNIVERSITY PRESS
The Edinburgh Building, Cambridge CB2 2RU, UK
40 West 20th Street, New York, NY 10011-4211, USA
477 Williamstown Road, Port Melbourne, VIC 3207, Australia
Ruiz de Alarcón 13, 28014 Madrid, Spain
Dock House, The Waterfront, Cape Town 8001, South Africa

http://www.cambridge.org

First published 2003

Printed in the United Kingdom at the University Press, Cambridge

Typefaces Rotis 10/14 pt and Quadraat   *System* LATEX 2$_\varepsilon$ [TB]

A catalogue record for this book is available from the British Library

Library of Congress Cataloguing in Publication data
Whittall, Arnold.
Exploring twentieth-century music : tradition and innovation / Arnold Whittall.
    p.   cm.
Includes bibliographical references and indexes.
ISBN 0 521 81642 4 (hardback) – ISBN 0 521 01668 1 (paperback)
1. Music – 20th century – History and criticism.   I. Title.
ML197 .W54   2003
780′.9′04 – dc21   2002073825

ISBN 0 521 81642 4 hardback
ISBN 0 521 01668 1 paperback

Contents

v

Preface

Exploring Twentieth-Century Music stems from a series of six one-hour lectures
I gave in London between October 2000 and March 2001. I am greatly indebted
to the Society for Music Analysis, and to Royal Holloway, University of London,
for supporting and promoting the lectures. In particular, my warmest thanks go to
John Rink, Robert Pascall and their colleagues for their initiative and generosity,
with respect both to the lectures and to this publication. I also owe a particular debt
to Jonathan Dunsby for his invaluable comments on a draft of the present text.

The form and content of this book has grown out of the form and content of the lectures. Nevertheless, readers with memories of the lectures will find
that differences outweigh similarities. Three of the lectures were fully scripted,
three were improvised, on the basis of short notes and preselected music examples, and all contained an informal autobiographical element which it has not
seemed appropriate to preserve in these pages. There was an inherent incitement
to megalomania in my original title, 'The World of Twentieth-Century Music',
quickly modified in practice to 'My World of Twentieth-Century Music'. That title,
too, has been jettisoned, but it should soon become clear that the text is very
personal – selective, narrow, limited – in the range of composers, commentators,
materials and topics considered. While striving to resist presumptions of absolute
authority, I cannot deny that my chosen materials are the result of value judgements preceding, and therefore influencing, analysis. Despite the use of a very
general title, I have shunned the relative comprehensiveness of my earlier text-
book, *Musical Composition in the Twentieth Century* (Oxford, 1999). But I cannot
claim to have radically transformed my identity since that earlier project, to the
extent of changing all the instincts, interests, predispositions and prejudices which
in the end determine matters of authorial style and content.

What I have attempted here is a discourse, or series of narratives, going
deeper into certain aspects of twentieth-century composition than was possible
in its more introductory predecessor. In essence, twentieth-century composition is
seen as the result of a continuing, intensifying dialogue between modernism and
classicism which began quite early in the nineteenth century, in the wake of the
Enlightenment. Yet I do not propose a simple homology between compositional
techniques and those social, cultural forces and events that can be seen as more or
less direct reflections of developments in the history of ideas: for example, there
is no presumption that late modernism maps tidily onto late capitalism. Matters

of cultural context are certainly not shunned: but they tend to facilitate the high-lighting of the special qualities of artworks as objects for subjective reception, contemplation and aesthetic sustenance, rather than as functional commodities subject to the economic imperatives of the entertainment industry.

Although such aspects as place and nationality, and social or aesthetic be-liefs and practices, are acknowledged and discussed, the book remains focused, first, on compositions as expressive structures and, second – this is especially the case with Chapter 5 – on various critical, musicological commentaries on those compositions. It is not a history of musical life in the twentieth century: in terms of Jim Samson's useful distinction, it is more about music as object and concept – as 'text' – than about music as event: always allowing for the fact that any discus-sion of the genre or style of a composition has the potential to mediate between the status of a musical work as 'object' and its status as 'event'. Moreover, although the discourse is consistently work-centred, the concept of the work it embodies is anything but monolithic, dehumanised or dehistoricised: the autonomy of the mas-terly musical composition and its ability to transcend the limitations of a specific time and place are never as absolute as might initially appear to be the case.

The contexts which feature in the following pages are therefore a reflection of what I term, early in Chapter 1, 'multivalent critical perspectives', which fan out from that elementary binary division between the possible meanings or inter-pretations of a composition and the methods or techniques which have helped to generate it. Other binary pairings follow, among them formalism and hermeneu-tics, modernism and classicism, innovation and conservation, sacred and secular, Dionysian and Apollonian. But all these pairs are viewed less as absolute oppo-sites than as interacting, overlapping tendencies, more mobile than fixed. This mobility extends to the various chapter and section titles, many of which are, to a degree, interchangeable: in addition, several composers and commentators on music appear in more than one location, acknowledging the pervasiveness of their perceived significance or influence. Occasionally the main context is that of other compositions, and these need not belong to the twentieth century: this is particularly so in Chapter 8, where references to Mozart, Tchaikovsky and – most extensively – Wagner range round the central topic of the *Requiem* by Hans Werner Henze.

One primary result of this focus on composed texts is that the quoted music examples can usually only give a hint of the critical and technical perspectives under consideration. A search for the published materials listed in the captions to the music examples is, therefore, strongly recommended. In preparing the text for publication, I have taken the opportunity to include revisions of certain writ-ings already published elsewhere (these materials are identified in the Notes and Bibliography). I am grateful to the Boydell Press, and the publishers of *The Musical Times* and *Music and Letters*, for permission to include these reworked materials.

Acknowledgements

Acknowledgements for music examples are as follows:

Adams, *El Niño*. © Copyright 2000 by Hendon Music, Inc. Reproduced by permission of Boosey & Hawkes Music Publishers Ltd.

Andriessen, *Rosa*. © Copyright 1995 by Boosey & Hawkes Music Publishers Ltd. Reproduced by permission.

Andriessen, *Writing to Vermeer*. © Copyright 1999 by Boosey & Hawkes Music Publishers Ltd. Reproduced by permission.

Andriessen, 'Tao'. © Copyright 1997 by Boosey & Hawkes Music Publishers Ltd. Reproduced by permission.

Bartók, String Quartet No. 4. Copyright by Universal Edition (London) Ltd. Reproduced by permission.

Bartók, String Quartet No. 6. © Copyright 1941 by Hawkes & Son (London) Ltd. Reproduced by permission of Boosey & Hawkes Music Publishers Ltd.

Berg, *Lyric Suite*. Copyright by Universal Edition (London) Ltd. Reproduced by permission.

Berio, *Sequenza XII* for solo bassoon. Copyright by Universal Edition (London) Ltd. Reproduced by permission.

Birtwistle, Celan settings (*Pulse Shadows*), 'Night'. Copyright by Universal Edition (London) Ltd. Reproduced by permission.

Birtwistle, *Pulse Shadows*, 'Todesfuge'. © Copyright 1998 by Boosey & Hawkes Music Publishers Ltd and Universal Edition (London) Ltd. Reproduced by permission.

Boulez, *Incises* (1994 version). Copyright by Universal Edition (London) Ltd. Reproduced by permission.

Boulez, *Sur Incises*. Copyright by Universal Edition (London) Ltd. Reproduced by permission.

Britten, *Variations on a Theme of Frank Bridge*. © 1938 by Hawkes & Son (London) Ltd. Reproduced by permission of Boosey & Hawkes Music Publishers Ltd.

Britten, *Les Illuminations*. © Copyright 1940 by Hawkes & Son (London) Ltd. Reproduced by permission of Boosey & Hawkes Music Publishers Ltd.

Britten, Canticle 1. © Copyright 1949 by Hawkes & Son (London) Ltd. Reproduced by permission of Boosey & Hawkes Music Publishers Ltd.

Britten, *The Turn of the Screw*. © Copyright 1955 by Hawkes & Son (London) Ltd. Reproduced by permission of Boosey & Hawkes Music Publishers Ltd.

Britten, Suite for Cello, No. 1. Copyright 1966 by Faber Music Ltd.

Carter, 'Inner Song'. © Copyright 1992 by Hendon Music, Inc. Reproduced by permission of Boosey & Hawkes Music Publishers Ltd.

Carter, *A Mirror on Which to Dwell*. © Copyright 1976 by Associated Music Publishers, Inc (BMI). International Copyright Secured. All Rights Reserved. Reprinted by permission.

Carter, Piano Sonata. © Theodore Presser Company. Used by permission of the publisher.

Carter, *Syringa*. © Copyright 1980 by Associated Music Publishers, Inc. (BMI). International Copyright Secured. All Rights Reserved. Reprinted by permission.

Henze, *Requiem*. Copyright by Schott & Co. Ltd. Reproduced by permission.

Janácek, String Quartet No. 2, Copyright by Universal Edition (London) Ltd. Reproduced by permission.

Kagel, *A deux mains*, Impromptu for piano. From Edition Peters No. 8896. © 1997 by Henry Litolff's Verlag. Reproduced on behalf of the Publishers by kind permission of Peters Edition Limited, London.

Ligeti, Etude for Piano, No. 15, 'White on White'. Copyright by Schott & Co. Ltd. Reproduced by permission.

Ligeti, Sonata for Viola Solo. Copyright by Schott & Co. Ltd. Reproduced by permission.

Messiaen, *Quatuor pour la fin du Temps*. © 1940–1 Editions Durand.

Schnittke, String Trio. © Copyright 1985 by Universal Edition A.G. Wien, Sole publisher for the UK, British Commonwealth (ex. Canada) Eire and South Africa: Boosey & Hawkes Music Publishers Ltd. Reproduced by permission of Boosey & Hawkes Music Publishers Ltd.

Schoenberg, String Quartet No. 3. Copyright Universal Edition (London) Ltd. Reproduced by permission.

Schoenberg, String Trio. © Copyright 1950 by Bomart Music Publications; assigned 1955 to Boelke-Bomart Inc.; revised edition © Copyright 1977 by Boelke-Bomart, Inc.; used by permission.

Schoenberg, 'Waltz' from Five Piano Pieces, Op. 23. Copyright by Universal Edition (London) Ltd. Reproduced by permission.

Shostakovich, String Quartet No. 3. © Copyright 1992 by Boosey & Hawkes Music Publishers Ltd. Reproduced by permission.

Stravinsky, *Les Noces*. French words by Charles Ferdinand Ramuz. © Copyright for all countries 1922, 1990. Chester Music Limited, 8/9 Frith Street, London W1D 3JB. All Right Reserved. Reproduced by permission.

Stravinsky, *The Rake's Progress*, © 1951 by Hawkes & Son (London) Ltd. Reproduced by permission of Boosey & Hawkes Music Publishers Ltd.

Stravinsky, *Duo concertant*. © Copyright 1933 by Hawkes & Son (London) Ltd. Reproduced by permission of Boosey & Hawkes Music Publishers Ltd.

Webern, Op. 16 No. 2, Canon for voice and clarinet. Copyright by Universal Edition Ltd. Reproduced by permission.

Webern, Variations for Piano, Op. 27, Copyright Universal Edition (London) Ltd. Reproduced by permission.

1 The work in the world

Western orientations

'Cereal music for the weed-killers. Sally Beamish's new Proms piece calls for cleaner farming methods.' This was the punning headline to an article in *The Independent on Sunday* for 22 July 2001 about a BBC Proms commission called *Knotgrass Elegy*. A note in the 2001 Proms brochure elaborated: 'inspired by Graham Harvey's book *The Killing of the Countryside* and set in a latter-day Garden of Eden, the work describes the ravaging of our planet by pesticides and herbicides, with a particular focus on the fate of the humble knotweed grass... and the work describes a catalogue of destruction that results in the demise of both the knotgrass beetle and the partridge'.

While this pressingly contemporary, literally down-to-earth subject-matter was bound to affect the immediate response of audience and critics to *Knotgrass Elegy*, it is safe to predict that Beamish's composition is unlikely to have any great influence or effect on the environmental policies of the British government. It is not to be equated with a series of massive public demonstrations, or with a decisive electoral vote in favour of The Green Party. A composition like *Knotgrass Elegy* takes its place in the world as an art-work making political or other statements of belief. The beliefs in themselves are neither new nor unfamiliar; and in presenting them in the way they do, musical art-works in a modern, serious style demonstrate that their principal purpose is to be aesthetic within a particular cultural context.

Sally Beamish chose, in *Knotgrass Elegy*, to call for cleaner farming methods: yet her artistic and social value as a composer cannot be constrained by the relevance of her compositions to environmental or social topics, even if her musical style can somehow be shown to reflect a life-style consistently committed to 'green' principles. Just as, in the most familiar twentieth-century British examples, the fact that Michael Tippett, Benjamin Britten and several other important composers were homosexuals and pacifists creates a context for their compositions but cannot be said to provide all the useful materials for the critical, technical interpretation of those compositions, so the musical world of Sally Beamish is not determined entirely by her attitude to herbicides and pesticides.

To write in this way might appear to support the belief that 'postwar music scholarship has been particularly prone to the view that an analysis of social and political processes is irrelevant to an understanding of culture', and that while

> much music scholarship has sought to avoid out-and-out formalism by addressing music's various 'contexts'... the very treatment of these contexts as explanatory factors in understanding musical texts can reinforce the tendency to privilege the text itself. What is lost here is any sense of the dialectical relationship between acts of musical communication on the one hand and political, economic, and cultural power-relations on the other.[1]

There can be few musicologists writing about and reading around the subject today who will not be sensitive to the problems and challenges which arise with the concept of the composition, the work, as a text — an object open to infinite interpretation and reinterpretation. Yet to ask 'musical scholarship' — as Georgina Born and David Hesmondhalgh do — to transform itself into a form of cultural history rooted in unease with 'a cultural system than conceals domination and inequality' (p. 21) is to ask a great deal, given 'the multitextuality of music as culture and the irreducible complexity of musical signification' (p. 37).

It is therefore useful to be reminded of the difference between modes of critical and technical interpretation rooted in beliefs about the quality and value of those musical manifestations commonly termed 'compositions', and those more contextual enterprises to which such discriminations are anathema. For example, Peter J. Martin is clear that a proper sociology of music avoids aesthetic judgements, remaining 'indifferent to the arguments of musicians, critics and so on in their various debates and disputes',[2] and while it is not inconceivable for musicology to do the same — depending on the aims and ambitions of particular projects — the present enquiry is not of that kind. But my enquiry does acknowledge what Born and Hesmondhalgh term the 'irreducible complexity of musical signification'. There is no attempt to exclude a formalist stratum from its multivalent critical perspectives, if only because this can act as a check on the temptation to constrain the beliefs and predispositions of composers, in the same way as the aims and requirements of the musical institutions which provide composers with social roles are constrained. For myself, now, I do not accept that privileging the 'text', to the extent of commenting — subjectively — in detail on an object which I can see and contemplate in print as well as hear in real time, inevitably leads to an interpretation that lacks all social, political, cultural content.

The following chapters will be much concerned with the argument that musical compositions exist in, and in some ways reflect, the wider world of politics, society, culture: that even if the nature of musical compositions (as describable in texts like this one) is primarily determined by the relationship between the creating mind of the composer and the interpreting minds of performers and listeners, those minds do not exist in a vacuum. To explore composers and their works from within cultural contexts held to interact significantly with the character and content of those works continues a well-established critical tradition, the composition of twentieth-century music having taken place in constant counterpoint with commentaries on composers and compositions, many by musicologists eager to impose a sense of order, a construction of discipline, on what were often seen by contemporaries as the most chaotic and subversive compositional initiatives. We can trace in many of these writings the assumption that the kind of creativity most relevant to the last century reflected cultural realities as vividly as it resisted absorption into mere parallelism with social, political or military events. From the tension between reflection and resistance comes that sense of discontent commonly aligned with modernism as a form of cultural practice, even if that practice has more to do with alienation from a culture's predominant elements than with acceptance of them. And it should follow, logically, that modernism as discontent should be traceable to another binary tension – between the composer's sense of place (the need for the comforts of home, stability, tradition) and that same composer's resistance to the kind of constraints that are likely to be present in any modern, developed society founded in the uneasy interaction of conservative and radical impulses, and with strong popular preferences for 'escapist' entertainment, short-term gratification, rather than the challenges and deferred rewards of 'high' art.

Progressiveness and place

The argument that the early twentieth-century Viennese environment stimulated Schoenberg and Webern to pursue their radical visions, just as the contemporaneous Parisian environment stimulated Debussy and Stravinsky, says little more than that the larger cities were most likely to offer that institutional variety necessary to ensure an occasional hearing for radical or exotic musics, alongside more mainstream materials. That is not to suggest that composers were driven into radical modernity by cities, or that they were somehow obliged to compose the city into their music. Yet the feeling persists that the kind of opposition found, especially in Mahler and Ives, between the stresses and strains of professional life in the city before 1914 and the escape into the country for idyllic periods of composition was not typical of composers belonging more decisively to the twentieth century than to the nineteenth. Indeed, these composers might have gained strength from being implicated in such explicit interactions between city and nature as Julian Johnson has proposed in writing about early twentieth-century Vienna:

> It is one of Vienna's most remarkable contradictions that it was a city increasingly financed by industrial wealth and yet one which managed largely to disguise the origin of that wealth. It epitomised the bourgeois fantasy of an autonomous culture which denied its economic foundations in industry and the market place. While denying that its cultural life was founded on the domination of nature, it sought to redress that by importing nature into itself.[3]

There is an important distinction to be drawn between the bourgeois 'desire to mask the modernity of their economic life with the archaisms of their aesthetic style' (p. 18) and the ability of a composer like Webern to fulfil the modernist project by means of what Johnson terms 'the transformation of nature'. Webern did this by developing the Mahlerian precept of nature 'not as the "expressive content" of his music but as a formal model, the paradigm of a technical process' (p. 42). It has long been known that Webern's susceptibility to landscape – to mountains, in particular – was associated by him with music that shuns the directly pictorial programmaticism of Strauss's *Eine Alpensinfonie* (1911–15). Yet there is something in the spirit of Webern's music which is equivalent to the character of a location, and the feelings that location inspired in him. Johnson links this 'something' directly to the contrast between country and city:

> It seems reasonable to suggest [that the song, 'Nachtgebet der Braut' (1903),] was a product of his new life in Vienna to the same extent that the majority of the early songs are hymns to the beauties of the landscape surrounding the Preglhof. The majority of these are concerned with landscape as a metaphor of peace and spaciousness. Yet the first song he wrote after moving to Vienna is fast-moving, passionate, anxious, and full of a new, highly erotic longing not evidenced in many of the other songs. (pp. 56–7)

Similarly, Johnson observes that 'modern communications – such as those of a modern metropolis like Vienna or Berlin criss-crossed by transport systems in a world of constant movement which tended to dissolve the sense of solid objects and places – produced the paradox of individually purposive lines accumulating to such an extent that the result, to the bystander, verged on chaos'. Johnson then claims that 'this can be heard quite literally in Schoenberg's Chamber Symphony [No. 1] of 1906', in which 'contrapuntal activity – the combination of subjectively purposive lines – here becomes so dense and so rapid that it risks becoming opaque' (p. 18).

As Johnson notes, significant moments of change and progress in the work of composers can often be illuminatingly associated with conjunctions between location and subject-matter, life and work. In the case of Stravinsky, Richard Taruskin's assertion that *Petrushka* was the work in which 'Stravinsky at last became Stravinsky'[4] can be developed to suggest that *Petrushka* was the first work in which Stravinsky achieved the distance and detachment necessary to embody the specifically national in a potently modernist way. Most notably, its ending provides a paradigm of modernism's concern with disorientation and discontinuity: there is the terror of the Showman at the sudden, unexpected appearance of that most unnatural feature, the ghost of a puppet. And the music responds with superimpositions and juxtapositions that focus intently on the tension between octatonic symmetry and diatonic hierarchy which was one of Stravinsky's best-learned lessons from his Russian precursors.[5] This music evokes a continuing national tradition, and at the same time makes itself acceptable and attractive to radical spirits within a broader Western culture. In 1910, and after, Stravinsky's up-to-date Russian exoticism had a special appeal to the kind of French sensibility that found a sympathetic resonance between the 'otherness' of the octatonic scale (and other modes of limited transposition) and those poetic and pictorial concerns of the French progressives located primarily in Paris. Stravinsky might not have felt encouraged to develop his radical streak so fully and so rapidly had he been writing entirely for and within Russia in the years immediately after *Petrushka*.

So far I have touched on some of the ways in which early twentieth-century music can be perceived in terms of a conjunction between a composer's personal response to place (as nationality and location) and varieties of disorientation and instability as technical characteristics of musical modernism. Another example of this conjunction emerges from Judit Frigyesi's analysis of the conflicting reactions to Bartók's early work – the contrast between the 'hostility and unfair criticism' he received from 'the official cultural establishment in Hungary' and the 'enthusiastic, almost fanatically devoted and supportive audience...that surrounded him in Budapest'.[6] Escaping from city to country, Frigyesi argues, 'gave Bartók the feeling of being one with all – with nature and society – and at the same time above and distanced from everything' (p. 153): and this polarity linked on to a technical practice aiming to express 'the greatest polarisation and underlying unity of the material' (p. 194). This was a practice in which 'unity' meant 'the capacity to make transparent the presence of the inner governing force that unites all elements in spite of their fragmentary nature, even opposition' (p. 297). It was a practice directly relevant to Bartók's later 'classicising' tendency (discussed in Chapter 3), and to his concern to distance himself from fully fledged modernism, even when he was in unhappy exile from Hungary after 1939.

'Genius' can be defined as the ability to develop the most visionary responses to wherever geniuses find themselves: and this supports Julian Johnson's ideas about the link between the hectic polyphony of Schoenberg's First Chamber Symphony and the topography of Vienna and Berlin. There is an obvious but profound process of interaction between the attractions which the physical qualities of locations can exert on strongly creative personalities, and the degree to which the cultural significance of a location is determined by the personality choosing it as somewhere to live and work. It would nevertheless be futile to claim that – for example – Debussy (to be discussed in Chapter 2) did more to imbue France in general and Paris in particular with distinctive musical attributes, than France, and Paris, did to mould Debussy's musical personality. Both sides of the equation are vital, and one side is meaningless without the other. Hence the importance of nationality (as distinct from nationalism) as a factor in culture, and the importance of degrees of pictorialism in twentieth-century composition, contributing to musical identity and character.

City life

Few compositions are likely to have been more directly affected by non-musical events occurring some years after their composition than Steve Reich's *City Life* (1995) for eighteen musicians, including pre-recorded sounds played on two sampling keyboards. Reich writes that 'the desire to include everyday sounds in music has been growing', and gives as examples 'the use of taxi horns in Gershwin's *An American in Paris*…Varèse's sirens, Antheil's airplane propeller' and 'Cage's radio'. With twentieth-century advances in technology, the sampling keyboard now makes such usages 'a practical reality. In *City Life* not only samples of speech but also car horns, door slams, air brakes, subway chimes, pile drivers, car alarms, heart-beats, boat horns, buoys, and fire and police sirens are part of the fabric of the piece.'[7]

Including everyday, predominantly urban sounds in a composition along-side conventional instruments or voices is an obvious way of introducing a doc-umentary, illustrative element into a work. It has long been possible to evoke the everyday by creating a collage of real-life sounds, 'composition' being the process of manipulating materials through editing. Such documentary compilations are the closest music comes to photography, in that the specifics of what is being depicted and evoked are relatively precise and unambiguous. The relationship between work and world is therefore direct, even if the possibility of determining some associated narrative as the collage unfolds in time may still be left to the listener's imagina-tion. The association with musical sounds and structures usually ensures that the work/world relation is less precise. For example, in the fourth of *City Life*'s five movements, called 'Heartbeats/boats and buoys', the musical atmosphere evokes familiar kinds of water music, or riverscapes: but the connection with any partic-ular city can only be arrived at through knowing the work's title, and hearing the movement in the context of other movements which are much more specific in their recreation of a New York environment. Moreover, even the last movement, called 'Heavy smoke', which uses speech samples 'from actual field communica-tions of the New York City Fire Department on February 26, 1993, the day the World Trade Center was bombed', is not so much a documentary recreation – a 'picture in sound' – of the immediate aftermath of that event, as a musical struc-ture which is associated by the composer with that event in that place. After 11 September 2001, it is instructive to reflect on why it will probably prove impossi-ble to treat recordings made on that day as the basis for an art-work, and *City Life* itself will inevitably be affected by these retrospective associations. Yet it remains true – if we can set these associations aside – that of Reich's chosen materials and their treatments, forming something quite close to a kind of chorale prelude, only the speech samples are exclusively and entirely associated with city life. The harmonies, rhythms and tone colours devised by Reich could serve equally well to evoke many quite different situations, locations and states of mind. And if location and situation disappear, a mood of non-place-specific agitation and menace is still likely to survive.

While works like *City Life* are written for live concert performance, or domestic reproduction by way of compact disc, they can still be said to have a function, though not qualifying as functional music like folk dances, wedding marches or national anthems. Their function is to refute any assumption that concert music has no significant connection to the cultural, social world within which the concert in question takes place. Nevertheless, to assert with every sign of confidence that 'musical autonomy... is a chimera: neither music nor anything else can be other than worldly through and through'[8] simply draws attention to the problems inherent in trying to show exactly in what the 'worldliness' of musical works consists. There is, for example, a great difference between the directness of the associations of a music hall song and other 'found' materials with which Charles Ives evokes late nineteenth-century New York in his orchestral piece *Central Park in the Dark* (1906) and the far more allusive network of connections between Brooklyn Bridge, Hart Crane's poem 'The Bridge', and Elliott Carter's *A Symphony of Three Orchestras* (1976). David Schiff describes this as 'a symphonic work whose sounds, textures and form would evoke Crane's life and work in purely abstract terms'.[9] At one extreme, the association is essential − Carter's *Symphony* would not be as it is, we infer, without Crane and his poem. At the other extreme, Crane's (and New York's) specifics have been transformed into 'purely abstract' musical terms, so that even when certain pictorial associations can be proposed − Crane's flight of the seagull, Carter's volatile opening trumpet solo − the assumption is that knowledge of such an association is not only unnecessary to understanding the music; it might even impose an inappropriately literal and restrictive level of connection between source and product. Neither the real Brooklyn Bridge nor Hart Crane's poetic evocation of the bridge is more than a pretext for a composition whose importance to the world represented by the institutions and individuals who value Carter's music must be determined primarily in terms of that composition's quality and status as a musical work of art. This formulation reinforces the aesthetic, evaluative processes at work in my text, and distinguishes its hermeneutics − its assessment of the relations between work and world − from those to be found in sociologies of music.

In its use of distinct, interacting instrumental groupings, *A Symphony of Three Orchestras* does not sound all that different from Carter's earlier Concerto For Orchestra (1969), inspired by a poem by St John Perse which 'describes winds blowing over the American plains destroying old, dried-up forms and sweeping in the new' (Schiff, *Carter*, p. 291). David Schiff accepts that listeners to the concerto – especially those who have prior information about its poetic inspiration – might sense that it evokes 'an entire continent and a vast hetero- geneous society in a state of turmoil', whereas 'for those who prefer their music "absolute", the Concerto can be heard as a four-tiered kaleidoscopic collage of shimmering textures and pulsating rhythms, all in a state of continuous flux'. In fact, there seems no great difference between the relatively literal sense of 'a vast heterogeneous society in a state of turmoil' and the more abstract 'shimmering tex- tures and pulsating rhythms, all in a state of continuous flux'. The first response scarcely depends on the matching vision of a precise location: the work's worldli- ness is assured by the truth of its musical character, its ability to convince listeners that this turmoil, this flux, is an experience of substance and significance, a real experience of value to real people. When as searching a commentator as Roger Scruton declares that Carter's Concerto is 'a life-affirming work...which succeeds in turning an uncompromising modernism to the service of joy'[10] his account of his response makes no reference to landscapes or weather systems, even though terms like 'life-affirming' and 'uncompromising' identify qualities of human personality whose interaction offers one possible construction of a modernist aesthetic.

Place, personality and Sibelius

Carter avoids pictorial titles, like Messiaen's *Des canyons aux étoiles*, or Tippett's *The Rose Lake*, which seem to promise a direct connection between ge- ographical location and musical sound. If we have visited Bryce Canyon, Utah, or Senegal's Rose Lake, we might believe that our experience of these places (as monumental, numinous) matches our experience of the music – that the music represents and embodies the essence of the place. At the same time, we might recognise that other titles for the same music are not inconceivable.

The identity of a musical composition results from the conjunction of a personal tone of voice – the composer's style – and the particular form or genre chosen for the work in question, which under normal circumstances will not be the sole creation of that composer. In listening to, and thinking about, Sibelius's last orchestral work, *Tapiola* (1926), we may find it difficult to avoid notions of nationality on the one hand and of genre – the orchestral tone poem – on the other. This is a work with an illustrative title and a poetic epigraph, referring to a Finnish forest region,[11] and the title creates expectations about the meaning of the music, to the extent that, we presume, the composer intended the one to refer to and to evoke the other. Although the distinctiveness and distinction of Sibelius's style might seem to matter more than the specifics of its Finnishness, it is pointless to try to divorce the Sibelian musical identity from all national qualities, even when there is little if any direct input from folk-music. It is inconceivable that Sibelius's musical personality would be as distinctive as it is without the sense of place which *Tapiola* and other works convey. Yet it is an essential aspect of

Sibelius's achievement that this distinctive voice should find expression in all his mature works, not just in those with titles evoking Finnish legend and landscape.

If location is one aspect of music's world, the life-history of the composer is another. In recent musicology, Sibelius's identity has been reconstructed from a variety of source materials, of which his diaries and the annotations on his musical manuscripts have proved especially fruitful. In particular, James Hepokoski's notion of the composer as a 'modern classicist'[12] underlines his distance from Germanic late romanticism and expressionism, as well as from the more exotic, even primitive forms of nationality contemporarily evident in Stravinsky, Bartók or Janáček. On its own, the concept of modern classicism could suggest a composer concerned to avoid treating music solely as a means of self-expression, or self-representation, preferring 'objective' forms and a general air of detachment. Such detachment need not imply bloodless music, as the powerful climaxes of Sibelius's Fifth and Seventh Symphonies show. But the familiar comparisons with Mahler – or Strauss – reinforce this characterisation of Sibelius as the reviver of disciplined attitudes to composition which are at odds with more progressive contemporary practices – attitudes which required him not simply to turn away from his leading contemporaries but to resist the open emotionalism and expansive expressiveness of his own earlier style, linked as this was to nineteenth-century Russian romanticism.

On the basis of sketchbook evidence for the common elements shared by *Tapiola* with Sibelius's last three symphonies, James Hepokoski comments that 'it may be argued that "Tapiola" or "The forest" (literally, "The place where the god Tapio dwells") – may be regarded as the implied overarching title of Symphonies 5, 6 and 7 as well' (Hepokoski, *Symphony*, p. 36). Hepokoski also refers to Sibelius's 'separate, redemptive world of symphonic composition' (p. 54) as a kind of escape from a world of 'harsh external events' (the explosion of Finland into Civil War as a consequence of the 1917 Russian Revolution): and it is surely a legitimate response to the 'affirmation' of E♭ major at the end of the Fifth Symphony to interpret this as a triumph *over* society, rather than a triumph with or for society. That 'vital rise' to the symphony's forceful conclusion was not simply the Ode to Joy of a Finnish patriot, since by temperament the older Sibelius was not so much organically at one with the metropolitan, political world as self-consciously distanced from its ideals and practices.

Such an evaluation makes it all the more appropriate that Sibelius's 'last word' as a composer should have been music which portrays a landscape embodying nature as both indifferent and threatening. *Tapiola* depicts both storm and calm, but the calm is less that of contemplative humanity than of sublimely indifferent natural forces to which humanity is irrelevant. It is therefore more appropriate to speak of *Tapiola*, rather than the Seventh Symphony, as a work in which '"resurrection" becomes ambiguous if not tragically precluded'.[13]

The world into which James Hepokoski places *Tapiola* is unambiguously anti-urban. Starting from the argument that all the works after the Symphony No. 4 are the result of 'an increasing flight from cosmopolitan fashion into near-solitary contemplation' (Hepokoski, 'Sibelius', p. 333), Hepokoski declares that Sibelius's later compositions

> are inseparable from his day-to-day existence at his forest retreat, Ainola, outside Järvenpää: its towering, resinous pines, its crystalline lakes, its boreal plants and wildlife, including its majestic migrating birds...its dramatic and pitiless change of seasons, its utter separation from anything urban.

There is a close connection between this very specific environment and compositional objectives and processes: Hepokoski claims that from 1912 Sibelius envisaged 'an enormous final project: bringing the nineteenth century ideal of organic form to a culmination'; and he also argues that Sibelius's 'aesthetic pantheism' was supplemented by

> his growing belief in the potential reuniting of music with nature. He now sought to bring the palpable, grainy textures of musical sound and the processes of musical elaboration into alignment with the magisterial spontaneity of nature's cries, rustles, splashes, storms, cyclical course and the like. Thus the act of composition became a neo-pantheist spiritual exercise. The resultant work of art was intended to invite a complementarily mystical, reverential or poetic listening – not to be captured by rational analysis or chalkboard explanation. (p. 334)

Hepokoski's powerful rhetoric allows little room for 'mere humankind' in this world, as his comments on *Tapiola* itself reveal. He claims that 'the entire work, seeking an identity with the dark and ancient pine forests, harbouring their hidden god, Tapio, is produced from the ramifying growth of a single, brief motive', and he links 'the gathering up and climactic double-discharging' of that basic motive with 'the self-disclosure of the animated forest-god', as the result of a musical form and atmosphere governed by 'impersonal, elemental natural processes before which mere humankind fades into insignificance' (p. 338).

My immediate response to Hepokoski's reading is to try to bring Sibelius himself, and with him 'mere humankind', back into the world of *Tapiola*. Hepokoski has also suggested that Sibelius was a 'nature-mystic' who 'may have been inviting us to brood on the elemental cycles that structure our own lives',[14] and the composer's own comment that works like the Sixth Symphony are 'more confessions of faith than are my other works' encourages the argument that – even if that 'faith' is pantheistic – it is the relationship between the human and the divine which is central, not the implacable, awe-inspiring existence of the divine alone. From this it could follow that the music of *Tapiola* attempts an interaction between

Ex. 1.1   Sibelius, *Tapiola*, bars 353–8

those 'impersonal, elemental natural processes' and human awareness of them –
even if that 'awareness' involves resistance as well as acceptance. An analysis pursuing this understanding would therefore interpret the work's basic motive not as
a representation of the forest god Tapio but as the human response to perceptions
about the god. Thus that 'climactic double-discharging' in bars 356 (Ex. 1.1) and
569 can be felt as embodying troubled humanity's terror and despair in face of the
god's 'self-disclosure' – a sense of the human contemplating an intimidating form
of otherness that can then be read back into *Tapiola*'s opening contrast between a
short, pleading melodic phrase and a sustained, swelling and dying chord.

In proposing this interpretation, I am aligning *Tapiola* with a rather different
single-movement orchestral composition, Webern's Variations for Orchestra Op. 30
(1940), if only because thinking about the nature of the Sibelius brought aspects of
my Webern interpretation to mind. These issues concern the principle of dialogue
between lyric and dramatic qualities as they promote 'a spiritual conflict between
vulnerability (seeking serenity) and assertiveness (a tendency to violence)', and the
associations of this with the placing of pastoral, as 'the pantheistic sense of God
in Nature', in a tragic perspective.[15] For me, the claims of a tragic perspective in
Tapiola are focused on what happens after bar 569, the second of Hepokoski's
shattering points of divine self-disclosure. Here it could appear that 'mere humankind' has faded into insignificance – although, as suggested above, this need
not be so if human terror rather than divine fist-shaking is heard. But in any case
Tapiola does not end with this gesture, and the subsequent melodic statements,
high and (initially) loud in the strings, sound less like a gentler, more humanly
tolerant statement from the forest god than pleading and ultimately accepting, if
not quite serene, human responses. As for the final juxtaposition of chords, the
first unstable, animated by swelling and dying away, the second consonant, un-
inflected: a hermeneutic reading cannot ignore the dramatic contrast which these
chords embody, even though it is as absurd to claim that the first stands for divine
grandeur and the second for human acquiescence as it is to argue that the chords
somehow combine to represent the absorption of human into divine, the mortal
into the timeless.

Writing of the first movement of Beethoven's Piano Sonata Op. 101, Robert
S. Hatten argues that 'the mixing of tragic elements endows the pastoral with

greater seriousness, and the elevation of style in turn supports the interpretation of the pastoral as a poetic conceit for a spiritual state of innocence (or serenity) subject to the disturbances of tragic experience (or remembrance)'.[16] While it might be easy to align a multitude of musical compositions with the image of innocence disturbed by tragedy, I believe that the conjunction, and the human focus it involves, is of special significance for *Tapiola*. There is 'tragic' separation here as well as structural interdependence. The 'purely musical' gesture, and drama, have an inevitability and a necessity that leave semantic interpretation opaque and ambiguous. Sibelius's own presence is nevertheless still evident, as is his admonition to his interpreting listeners 'to brood on the elemental cycles that structure our lives',[17] and which do so in cities as well as in forests.

Environmental sensibilities

In the later twentieth century, it was easier for artists and politicians to think in terms of man's self-destructive indifference to, or abuse of, nature than of nature's *Tapiola*-like indifference to mere humanity. As the threat of nuclear disaster receded, and the Cold War waned, the dangers of pollution and global warming advanced to become more pressing threats to life on earth. During the first half of the twentieth century, the literary and visual arts had responded liberally to the killing-fields imagery of the First World War, and even musical compositions were able to find analogies for bleak, stark scenes of despoiled nature. For example, the possibility of connecting representations of landscape with lament, or elegy, is explored in Vaughan Williams's Third, 'Pastoral' Symphony (1916–21), and even though Gustav Holst's austere tone poem *Egdon Heath* (1927) was inspired by Thomas Hardy's description of a bleak English landscape in his novel *The Return of the Native* (1878), it has never been difficult to regard that specific location as a metaphor – prophetic, in Hardy's case – for Flanders and the Somme.

There is always the possibility of linking perceptions about a composer's sense of place, or feeling for location, with generic adaptations or mutations of pastoral, whether openly embraced or in some sense evaded. As the genre most directly connected to place, pastoral is a tempting recourse for critics and commentators eager to avoid accusations of reifying the alleged 'autonomy' of musical compositions: and the possible linkage of pastoral with notions of nationality and nationalism makes it even more seductive as a potential means of finding somewhere in the world for a musical work to belong. The rewards of connecting modernist challenges to synthesis with aspects of pastoral theory have been well demonstrated in Geoffrey Chew's study of *The Rake's Progress*, centring on the argument that 'Stravinsky's neoclassicism, with the differing degrees of "defamiliarisation" it offers of familiar materials, is ideally suited to symbolise and project the fluid ambiguities of Auden's pastoral fable'.[18] But the open-ended relevance of pastoral associations makes it all the more important to avoid implying that there is an invariable connection between technical 'defamiliarisation' and pastoral as a genre. Nor, for that matter, are works of art which deal with the natural world, or with threats to the environment (up to and including Sally Beamish's *Knotgrass Elegy* of 2001), necessarily best thought of as aligned with pastoral, even though in its broadest definition this is 'a literary, dramatic or musical genre that depicts the characters and scenes of rural life or is expressive of its atmosphere'.[19] There is, after all, a distinction between the concept of 'rural life' and an understanding of the natural world as something which impinges on all life, rural and urban alike.

Discussing *Tapiola*'s impact on later twentieth-century composition, Tim Howell notes the particular significance of Sibelius's later style for Peter Maxwell Davies. The comment by Maxwell Davies which Howell quotes – 'What I find particularly interesting is the way he articulates his time and the way he transforms his material'[20] – seems to allude to the way first movement is transformed into scherzo in Sibelius's Fifth, a 'confusion' of formal prototypes which is attractive to Maxwell Davies, concerned as he is to bring out the ambivalence and multiplicity that comes from reworking traditional genres and formal templates. Yet it is in the musical language itself, and how this relates to a feeling for place, that Davies appears to learn most from Sibelius.

Timothy L. Jackson's concept of crystallisation and entropy[21] is in essence an organic, even biological metaphor for musical process, using the opposition between coming to birth (or into focus) and dissolution (or death). The main reason why I prefer Hepokoski's interpretation of Sibelius's language in terms of modern classicism to Jackson's rather underdeveloped notion of modernism is because (as I understand it) modern classicism seeks to re-establish synthesis as the main technical and structural factor in music. For Sibelius, the 'synthesis' represented by traditional tonal structuring had been inherent in all music in his early years, and so for him it was less a question of re-establishing it than of reaffirming it while exploring the tensions between it and forces seeking to destroy it. The case of Peter Maxwell Davies, whose first work called symphony dates from the 1970s, is very different, and although Davies insists that he uses 'tonality' consistently and coherently throughout his symphonic music, he has acknowledged that there are far-reaching differences between tonality as he conceives it and the tonality found in Sibelius. Those differences, as I have argued in detail elsewhere,[22] are substantial enough to enforce a basic distinction between the modern-classic Sibelius and the modernist Maxwell Davies, and I have therefore used a different metaphor, invoking a spatial rather than an organic continuum, and represented by the terms 'fixed' and 'floating' with respect to the presence of tonal centres (or 'rooted' and 'symmetric' with respect to harmonic structuring).

It is possible to demonstrate the parallels and differences between Sibelius and Maxwell Davies in varying degrees of analytical depth – for example, comparing the single-movement design of Davies's Fifth with Sibelius's Seventh: the role of B as principal tonality, or tonal centre, in *Tapiola*, Davies's Second Symphony (1980) and the 'choreographic poem' *The Beltane Fire* (1995). To summarise an intricate technical topic, a world of difference exists between the ultimate consonant, major triad orientation at the end of *Tapiola* (and allowing for the extent to which Sibelius's harmony is far from straightforwardly diatonic in every respect), and the ending of *The Beltane Fire*, in which the principal harmonic factor is not a major triad but a diminished seventh, and the tension, within that seventh, between B and F♮ is enhanced by the way in which the F has a (minor) triad built onto it. Davies's harmony is more post-tonal than tonal as these terms are normally understood, and it might therefore be argued that any alignment between him and Sibelius is pointless. I would nevertheless suggest that placing these works in the world reveals aspects of affinity that speak very directly across the technical barriers of style and structure. As far as the world of this book is concerned, the next step is from the observation of such expressive affinities to the examining of reflection, mirroring, as context and technique.

2 Reflections, reactions

Debussy in the mirror

Roger Nichols's *Life of Debussy* paints a persuasive portrait of 'a deeply divided composer', for whom 'the pull between privacy and publicity is mirrored in his struggles to balance the claims of solitude and friendship, and of simplicity and complication'. Nichols identifies a compositional duality in the opposition between 'the delightful surfaces of the music' and 'its rough, dangerous, even cruel undercurrents',[1] and argues that Debussy's importance in his own time has to do with the music's 'moral dimension' as well as its dedication to a 'feeling of transience' (p. 164). Rather more radically, Craig Ayrey has used his view of Debussy as a 'deconstructive composer' to argue for an analytical method 'that offers systematic procedures but is predicated on ambiguity', and on awareness that 'opposition itself is a relation, a mode of connection between disparate units'.[2] This chapter takes cues about context from both these sources, in keeping with the perception that, just as opposition is also relation, so the reverse can be the case. As a familiar compositional procedure in post-tonal as well as tonal music, imitation, mirroring, can generate the tensions of debate and dispute as much if not more than the complementary balancings inherent in the principle of 'the same yet in a different manner'.[3]

The mirroring metaphor is often used in writing about music, in ways extending from generalised notions of cultural practice – Pierre Boulez declaring that *Pelléas et Mélisande* belongs to that 'highest class' of work that serves 'as a kind of mirror in which a whole culture can see itself transfigured'[4] – to the technical concepts of inversion, reversion and canonic, contrapuntal combination. The image of the composer, like Hamlet, gazing into a mirror with a mixture of self-absorbed fascination and distaste can stand for the instabilities attendant on the creator's subjective sense of identity: but it is easy for such apparent introversion to seem decadent, the unhealthy obsession of a Narcissus failing to engage cheerfully and fruitfully with society. Christophe Charle's assessment of how Debussy succumbed to the bourgeois 'trap' – 'just when the success of *Pelléas et Mélisande* seemed to pry loose the financial vise of his first forty years, Debussy himself walked into a new trap by acquiescing to the fallacious prestige of a life too bourgeois for his real income'[5] – fits well with Nichols's point about a Debussy 'deeply divided', as man and composer, between private and public, simple and complex, delightful and dangerous. Equally, however, the process of mirroring does not require a simple transference or mapping of the personal or psychological onto the musical. Mirroring draws attention to the space between different spheres of existence which the composer can work with and within: 'opposition is itself a relation', but interactions between the two are ambiguous, multiple.

Contrapuntal techniques which involve elements of mirroring are not inherently destabilising, still less deconstructive, as the richly integrated canons by Bach and other tonal composers make clear. Mirroring can nevertheless serve as a means of disorientating the music, if, by exploring inversional relationships between upper and lower strands of texture, it undermines the function of a bass line as the primary means of achieving tonal identity and stability. At issue here is the interplay between hierarchic and symmetrical modes of construction, found as early as Beethoven's 'Waldstein' sonata (1803–4), when the division of the octave into equal intervallic parts (major thirds – C/E/Ab /C) interacts with the more 'natural' inequality of the division into fifth and fourth (C/G/C).

Such dialogues between hierarchy and symmetry are often found in nineteenth-century music, and – particularly in the case of the use of the symmetrical octatonic scale by Russian composers from Glinka to Stravinsky, noted briefly in Chapter 1 – their capacity to enrich rather than merely undermine tonality is clear. 'Pure' modal music of this kind, in which the source mode, being symmetrical, has the same sequence of intervals whether ascending or descending, can demonstrate the explicit mirroring of material: a simple example is Debussy's almost entirely whole-tone piano prelude, 'Voiles' (1909), where, in bar 15, two types of material which have been previously stated separately are superimposed, and their common span, the upper line descending in four whole tones from G♯ to C, the lower ascending in two whole tones from Ab to C, is underlined (Ex. 2.1). Even here, however, Debussy avoids literal rhythmic and registral mirroring for the right hand's descending echo of the left hand's ascent from Ab through Bb to C. This material is particularly significant in the context of this prelude, since the focal tone, Bb, serves as a bass pedal, grounding the texture for much of the piece, and functioning briefly as a dominant of Eb minor (bars 42–7). 'Voiles' does not compose-out a simplistic mirror-opposition between ascending and descending, centred and rooted, but explores the continuum between the extremes which these oppositions represent.

Such a continuum is fundamental to Debussy's mature compositional style, and is deployed with supreme subtlety time and again. In the piano piece 'Reflets dans l'eau' (written before 1905), the title generates inevitable expectations of mirroring, and this can be found at places like bars 16–17, with the spatial convergence and divergence of the hands, even though the intervals are not literally the same in both strata (Ex. 2.2). Nevertheless, as already suggested, Debussy resisted the mechanistic use of such devices: 'Reflets dans l'eau' is more about the refractions of what is reflected (degrees of wave-like motion) than about the static

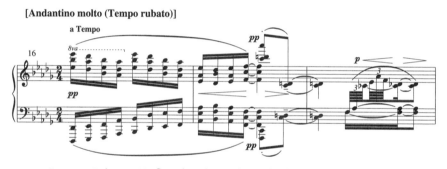

[Modéré (♪ = 88)]

(dans un rythme sans rigueur et caressant)

Ex. 2.1   Debussy, 'Voiles', bars 15–21

[Andantino molto (Tempo rubato)]

a Tempo

Ex. 2.2   Debussy, 'Reflets dans l'eau', bars 16–18

symmetry between reflected and reflection. Mirroring – being mirrored – is a sequence of events affected by space and time, not something fixed and unchanging. And just as the face seen in the water can appear a quite different entity from the face seen bending over the water, so it is impossible to separate the notion of mirroring from that of polarity, the other extreme of another continuum stretching between similarity (identity, even) and difference.

In the opening bars of 'Voiles', the fact that the two types of material use the same whole-tone scale is offset by different modes of characterisation – high/low, relatively flexible/relatively fixed in rhythm: the kind of contrasts that suggest an equilibrium between polarity and mirroring. In principle, such balancing is no different from the balancing of subject and countersubject in fugue, and composers can emphasise – dramatise – difference or similarity as they choose. Since expressionistic extravagance was alien to Debussy, sharp juxtapositions and dis-concerting superimpositions are unlikely. Yet what of those 'rough, dangerous, even cruel undercurrents' which Nichols detects beneath the 'delightful surfaces'? Overt menace and turbulence, such as explode during the storm in *La Mer*,[6] are relatively rare: and when, in the tenth Etude for piano, 'Pour les sonorités op-posées' (1915) Debussy creates the expectation of sustained and explicit opposi-tion, the conflict is tempered rather than extreme, not least because Debussy keeps an extended but persistent tonality of C♯ in view. Here, too, refraction rather than mirroring (or polarity) is the principal quality, in keeping with Debussy's wish that music should not be 'tied to a more or less exact reproduction of Nature but to the mysterious correspondence between Nature and Imagination'.[7]

In his short but penetrating analysis of the tenth Etude Richard S. Parks approaches the idea of 'opposition' through the way Debussy sets a single pitch-class (G♯/A♭) 'in (or, more properly, against) harmonies'.[8] Up to a point, Parks's description of the Prelude 'Feuilles mortes' could serve for the Etude as well: 'the role of harmony and voice leading as tonal determinants is conspicuously weak, and although the key signature implies either E major or C♯ minor, the evi-dence is insufficient to support a tonic ascription for either' (p. 83). The difference is that, in the Etude, not even the key signature is constant, and Parks develops his interpretation by observing that 'the only conventional sonority' to embrace G♯ is the E major triad, while 'all other sonorities "oppose" pc8 [G♯] with dis-sonances' (p. 37). Parks's unease with this formulation is suggested by the quotes round 'oppose', and this unease is wise, since the music has little of the simple con-trast between consonant inclusion and dissonant opposition that Parks's formula seems to describe. He soon concedes that 'the composition's vitality derives from the *constant shifts* in the nature of this opposition...and in settings that range from the E major triad...to sonorities that exclude pc8 altogether' (p. 37, empha-sis added). Although Parks seems to remain committed to the notion of opposition between consonant and dissonant contextualisation of the central pitch and the various, competing tonal allusions, his observation that 'the enigmatic nature of tonality...leaves open the way for pc8 to assert its special kind of primacy, not as a tonal center in the usual sense, but as a solitary constant in an ever-changing pc field' (p. 37) hints at the degree to which the normal sense of 'opposition' is under-mined by a flexible dialogue between the complementary principles of constancy and change.

It would be unfair to continue criticism of Parks's analysis, since it is a small part of a very substantial and comprehensive taxonomy of Debussy's work. But the following interpretation complements Parks's relatively abstract concerns with form and content, beginning with the consequences of Debussy's apparent lack of interest in the more centrifugal connotations of 'opposition', and his treatment of dialogue as understated and ambiguous.

Might the tenth Etude be interpreted as a 'colloque' — and, if not a 'colloque sentimentale', then a 'colloque spatiale'? This possibility arises because the most concrete opposition notated by the composer is verbal — between the terms applied to the music of the first thirty bars — 'dolente, expressif et profond' — and those introduced at bar 31 — 'lointain, mais clair et joyeux' — terms which suggest a quasi-spatial contrast between an initial foreground, and a contrasting, relatively distant background (neither term implying Schenkerian structures). In the first, 37-bar part of the piece, this contrast is presented as one in which the foreground dominates, with the background present in only seven bars — or only five if bars 34–5 are designated a foreground response. And even if bars 15–30, a typically sober Debussian dance — minuet, slow waltz or sarabande — are regarded as transitional, they are closer in character to foreground than to background. In the second, 38-bar part of the Etude (bars 38–75), the balance is more even, with fifteen foreground bars, and a six-bar transition ('calmato') followed by seventeen bars in which the dialogue between the two types of material comes fully into focus.

With this rather elementary contrast goes a sense of two distinct tones of voice, the foreground rather eloquent and solemn, the background lighter, more capricious: and the piece's final section (from bar 59) seems to embody a degree of interlock, even synthesis,[9] between them, as the initial rising fifth of the background voice blends with the more stately parallel triads of the foreground (Ex. 2.3). The prospect of such an accommodation has been acknowledged from the moment when descending triads contribute to the initial background section (bars 34–6), and while it remains an open question as to which of the two voices is most strongly represented in the final cadence, there is a definite sense of the foreground having moved towards the background: 'de loin...de plus loin...'.

This kind of spatial imagery easily extends into the particular tensions between public and private which Roger Nichols and Christophe Charle single out as archetypal for Debussy. The 'public' voice in Etude 10 suggests the burdens imposed on the artist in society, who 'sings' passionately and profoundly of things which 'really' matter. The 'private' voice is more playful, innocent, escaping from the burden of those public expectations, hinting at qualities which Messiaen would later assign to birdsong. There is a sense of that irreconcilability between 'civilised' maturity and childlike naturalness which made Debussy's one completed opera such a powerful and innovative cultural document. The composer commented that 'the drama of *Pelléas*...despite its dreamlike atmosphere, contains far more humanity than those so-called "real-life documents"'.[10] Small wonder, then, that the social, emotional world embodied in the differences between Golaud and Mélisande should have continued to resonate to varying degrees in most of his later works, the subtle interplay between the human and the dreamlike, the portentous and the

Ex. 2.3   Debussy, Etude 10, 'Pour les sonorités opposées', bars 59–75

playful, a rich source of inspiration. In Etude 10, the foreground, public material, with its restless, trudging motion intensified in the first transitional passage (from bar 15), initially has an uneasy encounter with the playful background ('calando'): and the persistence of that low G♯, fitting consonantly with the skipping figure but also a framing reference from the earlier music which is then carried over into the renewed, newly intense foreground material from bar 38, seems to signify the common humanity of these voices, so different in their respective associations with experience and innocence, but equally vulnerable in space and time.

Leon Botstein's argument that Debussy's sympathies with the kind of radicalism found in the paintings of James McNeill Whistler promoted 'an all-encompassing, grand, and unifying continuity' interprets the composer's aesthetic as centring on technical priorities of the kind that Elliott Carter's observations about 'a fluid, changeable continuity' encapsulate more convincingly than attempts to emphasise those discontinuities that imply a more radical modernism.[11] Such discontinuities and juxtapositions are more evident in the late sonatas, but Debussy died before the full implications of these new formal techniques could be explored. As a result, David Lewin's demonstration of 'transformational networks' in the Prélude 'Feux d'artifice' (1913)[12] is a more persuasive way of reflecting Debussy's typical mode of construction, as well as his reservations about modernism. No less persuasive, in the emphasis they give to coherence and continuity, are the Schenkerian readings of Matthew Brown and the subtle, text-based analyses of Marie Rolf.[13] Nevertheless, those 'all-encompassing, grand, and unifying continuities' are usually a good deal less *stable* than those found in more traditional tonal composition. One of Pierre Boulez's comments on his own priorities seems especially appropriate for Debussy: 'I need, or work, with a lot of accidents, but within a structure that has an overall trajectory – and that, for me, is the definition of what is organic.'[14] Yet Boulez's implicit acknowledgement of tension between what he terms the 'spiral' and the 'mosaic' in his music – the complementary tendencies to connect and to disconnect – warns against the easy embrace of singularity at the expense of multiplicity, and this is just as relevant for Debussy – and Webern – as for Boulez himself.

Webern's tribute to perfection

Boulez has argued that 'Varèse and Webern were the first to learn the lesson of Debussy's last works and to "think forms" arising from a process that is primarily spatial and rhythmic, linking "a succession of alternative, contrasting or correlated states"':[15] and Webern, having seen *Pelléas* in Berlin in 1908, wrote to Schoenberg that it was 'very fine, often very strange, in places wonderfully beautiful. The ending is one of the loveliest that exists.'[16]

The strangeness in Debussy's music that Webern admired was, no doubt, its capacity for understatement, for achieving supreme intensity and focus in the most concentrated manner. Yet Webern could not exist in a musical world devoid of links with the Christian religion and the no less awe-inspiring Alpine landscapes whose importance to him was noted in Chapter 1. There one of Webern's later works, the Variations for Orchestra Op. 30, was discussed in terms of a dialogue, between a purely human vulnerability and a sense of security, as well as qualities of certainty and assertiveness, which can obviously be mapped onto the governing, complementary images of human and divine, of someone 'in' the world acknowledging something which transcends yet 'governs' the world. Because Op. 30 is not an overtly religious composition, the 'divine' component can also be interpreted more mundanely – for example, as an element of active tension or drama. This is not to assume that the religious Webern was as 'deeply divided' a personality as the unbelieving Debussy. But study of Webern's life suggests that his religious faith did not give him the kind of ease and confidence that would ensure a trouble-free existence in the professional world of music.

In Webern's case 'the pull between privacy and publicity' took the form of conflict, contentment within the family and, to a degree, with his creative work set against his obvious difficulties in functioning in the public realm, in particular, as a professional conductor. Kathryn Bailey has eloquently summarised those 'unresolvable contradictions' in Webern's life:

> A man who was at the same time complex and naïve, whose ardent German nationalism led him to make the most aggressive militaristic statements, yet who was happiest in the peaceful solitude of a mountain plateau surrounded by gentians and wild narcissus...A man who could demonstrate a fervour of embarrassing intensity for both Schoenberg and Hitler, who throughout his life was given to vitriolic outbursts on the subject of the vulgarity and insensitivity of audiences yet whose entire professional life was spent conducting concerts for 'the people' in socialist Vienna. A man who was described by nearly everyone whose path he crossed as a truly good and honest human being, a devoted husband and father, a loyal friend, a teacher who gave free lessons to gifted students who were too poor to pay when he himself was almost destitute.[17]

Musicologists dabble in human psychology at their peril, and it is certainly possible, as Julian Johnson implies, that Webern's governing ideology was a utopianism which lent an air of unreality to all his attempts to deal with the real world.[18] Yet it is impossible to ignore a significant change of musical character during the 1920s, in which a progression from 'free' atonality to twelve-note technique parallels a shift from an expressionistic mode of utterance, in which lament-like gestures feature strongly, to something much less turbulent, more serene. Even though any such 'shift' is far from absolute, there is a marked difference between the febrile instability of much of the music from Op. 5 to Op. 20 and the less hectic, more poised quality of the last eleven works. To introduce one of the dominant *topoi* of this book, this difference suggests an analogy – deriving from Nietzsche – of great importance to the evolution of twentieth-century music, and alluded to explicitly by both Schoenberg and Stravinsky, with the aesthetic counterpoles of Apollo and Dionysus: 'When the Dionysian element rules, ecstasy and inchoateness threaten; when the Apolline predominates, the tragic feeling recedes.'[19]

Bailey selects 1923, when the composer was forty, as a decisive date in 'the settling of Webern', and links this to the support of his growing family, which 'must have given his life a new dimension and indeed, a core of stability and happiness that it had not previously had. In addition, he derived tremendous emotional and spiritual satisfaction from the alpine excursions, made so easily from Mödling, in which he indulged whenever he had the time' (Bailey, *Life*, pp. 105–6). Then, in 1926, Webern met the writer Hildegard Jone, 'who was to be not only one of his dearest friends and a soulmate for the rest of his life but in a very real sense his muse as well' (pp. 104–5). Family support, Jone as muse, and Schoenberg – by way of the twelve-note technique – as teacher provided a 'core of stability' able to compensate Webern for continuing professional and financial stresses and strains, and to promote a form of musical expression in which the transcendence if not the dissolution of sorrow and anxiety could be realised in sound.

Of all Webern's compositions before Op. 21 none anticipates the atmosphere of his later works more closely than the second of the *Five Canons on Latin Texts* Op. 16 (1924). This is a lullaby, portraying the Mother of God at her most tender, with melodic phrases that seem to float in musical space in an exquisite (rocking) balance of rising and falling, around the symmetrical centre of G above middle C – a pitch given no particular emphasis on the musical surface itself (Ex. 2.4).

Webern chose a folklike text, from *Des Knaben Wunderhorn*, whose structure of two stanzas with four syllables per line (the final three-syllable lines apart) is directly reflected in the musical design. The crucial pre-compositional decision must have been to design the setting as a canon by inversion at the tritone (interval-class [ic] 6) and a time distance of four crotchets.[20] Could Webern have then made a connection between the overall ic 6 space between the lines, and the ic 6 span of all the 4-pc collections which are used in the setting of the first verse? Some conscious principle seems likely to have determined that choice, given that of the twenty-nine possible 4-pc sets, only six span ic 6, and Webern uses five of the six: [0236], [0156], [0126], [0146] and [0136] – see annotations on Ex. 2.4. A further question then arises. If Webern chose ic-6-spanning sets for Verse 1 (the three-syllable last line apart) to reflect the ic 6 relation between the canonic voices, why did he change that principle in Verse 2, where the overall ic 6 canonic relation is preserved, but the four-note collections (save for the final trichord) all span ic 5: [0125] – three times – [0145] and [0135]? Was it, for example, Webern's predilection for – often hidden – octatonic relations, explored by Allen Forte, which prompted a shift from a spanning interval-class that bisected the

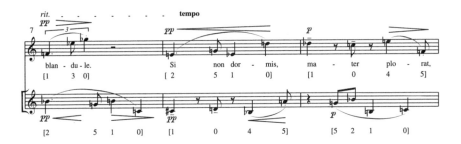

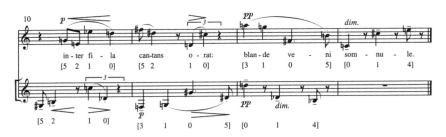

Ex. 2.4   Webern, Op. 16 no. 2, 'Dormi Jesu', Canon for voice and clarinet

symmetrical octatonic connection, to the ic that spans that collection's two component trichords?

   Another possible reason for the technical device is the composer's wish to respond to the text by means of a contrast that was more formal than expressive. Given that the two stanzas of the poem embody basic differences between the image of the mother smiling with joy and weeping with sorrow (to match the corresponding images of the child asleep and the child awake), it could have seemed appropriate for the music to embody an essential change of perspective, even though its basic character as a lullaby is not changed.

There remains the no less fundamental matter of the actual pitch classes chosen by Webern to fill out his ic-6- and ic-5-spanning four-note sets, which, when represented in integer notation, make no prescription as to the pitch identity of any '0'. The pre-twelve-note atonal world was still one of immense – possibly excessive – freedom in this respect, and no attempt is made here to offer a consistent principle for pitch choice in 'Dormi Jesu'. Forte has noted certain patterns of repetition and variation, and has suggested possible textual allusions by way of ciphers and other connections. Yet it seems no less important to argue that the modernist essence of this otherwise highly consistent and gentle piece is embedded not just in the polarity of joy and sorrow which is present despite the retention of the lullaby genre in Verse 2, but also in the opposition between those aspects which Webern aligns with discipline – with fixity, rules, constraints – and those he sees as the preserve of freedom.

The twelve-note method extended the role of discipline over the compositional process, making the challenge to composers who sought to balance this against some necessary freedoms the more stimulating and rewarding. The canon by inversion at ic 2 which underpins the second movement of Webern's Variations for Piano Op. 27 (1936) defends itself against the dangers of mindless mechanistic constructivism by the unpredictable ordering of its motivic events. Of course, this 'unpredictability' is inherent in the fact that each of the transposed forms of the set pairs used by Webern inevitably presents its component dyads, and the thirty-one distinct motivic statements they comprise, in different orders.[21] But if all the composer is doing here is to go along with what his chosen system makes available, many of his other twelve-note canons – a good example is the first movement of the String Quartet Op. 28 – are more complex, and involve a greater degree of intervention on Webern's part to alter the rhythmic relationships between the lines as well as to modify the constituent motivic shapes. The work of Kathryn Bailey has been particularly valuable in describing these techniques in ways which balance out the amounts of strictness and freedom involved.[22] But the brief, explosive scherzo of Op. 27 can make do with a pattern of contrasts that needs no further reshaping or realigning to make its aesthetic effect.

Form and content: Webern's Op. 27/iii

As seen in Chapter 1, Julian Johnson has offered a thought-provoking interpretation of Webern's music in the light of his belief that, because 'Webern's career, like Mahler's, was always shaped by the cultural politics of large cities', it 'tells us a good deal about the predominantly urban society in which it was composed' (p. 9).

At the same time, Johnson acknowledges that 'art and reality are not coterminous. The mediation of art is constituted by a reformulation of social materials, not by their reproduction' (p. 141). Johnson never loses sight of the aesthetic dimension of Webern's world – to 'the equivalence of the idea of nature as organic proliferation and development and the idea of a music that fulfils the same "natural" pattern' (p. 77). This explains why the purely instrumental, twelve-note pieces written after 1926 make frequent use of 'quite specific programmatic associations' centring on 'the gravesites of his parents, in particular that of his mother', in Schwabegg. As Johnson points out,

> the village of Schwabegg is explicitly mentioned in three out of the four extant outlines we have from the sketchbooks (for Opp. 22, 24 and 28). In every case the extra-musical association is tied to the same structural function, to the idea for a second slow movement which will serve as the introduction to the third and final movement. The gravesite of Webern's father, at Annabichl, is also mentioned in the outlines of the same three works...(p. 186)

along with other locations, aspects of landscape, and the members of the composer's close family.

Johnson discusses the non-texted twelve-note works, including the third movement of Op. 27, in relation to these associations, and to extend the 'topical' references beyond those sanctioned by the composer's annotations in his sketches. His argument is that 'Webern's landscapes of the mind are profoundly shaped by a way of seeing real landscapes' (p. 211): that 'Webern's serial music is resonant with ideas of death, memory and landscape, and a process of transformation in which elements of the outward, material world become symbols of a luminous interiority and a celestial, spiritual landscape.' As a result 'his music resists abstraction through the persistence, albeit in transformed versions, of representational topics of late Romanticism' (p. 215).

Kathryn Bailey's discussion of the third movement of Op. 27 could hardly be more different from Johnson's, not least because it seems, on the face of it, to reveal not the slightest of hermeneutic chinks in its formalist armour. Yet her narrative's interpretative thrust balances comments about the movement's symmetrical aspects with an approach which acknowledges the kind of challenge to listeners and analysts having immediate expressive consequences. One example of this is Bailey's statement that 'the only thing' the first two sections of the movement 'can be said to have in common is a confusing multiplicity of sometimes contradictory relationships between constituent parts' (Bailey, *Twelve-Note Music*, pp. 208–9). In the first section, or variation (bars 1–11), twelve-note analysis demonstrates a degree of symmetry in the tripartite row structure, P0, I0 and R0 (Ex. 2.5), and Bailey draws attention to the rhythmic correspondences between the distinct cells of material, identical between the statements of P0 and I0, even to

Ex. 2.5   Webern, Variations for Piano Op. 27, 3rd mvt, bars 1–12

the rests which separate the three cells in each. Bailey continues to stress matters
of relationship – similarity – and ends her analysis with the comment that the
eight dynamic markings used by Webern in the section form a palindrome: *p f*
p f f p f p. In this way the composer's reliance on symmetrical frameworks is
reinforced.

The picture grows less stable when we begin to look for this third movement
to continue the kind of textural mirrorings found in the first and second movements, both of which are canonic, and use paired chains of row forms throughout. But, as already noted, the third movement begins with a sequence of three
single rows, and although abstract, interval-class analysis can point to certain
correspondences (as in the parallel pairs of ic 1 in bars 1–2 and 5–6), Webern
responds to the absence of canonic relations, and the corresponding unavailabil-
ity of the kinds of mirroring used in the first two movements. Rather, he relishes
the freedom, the 'looseness' (a term Webern himself used in 1939 when describing
the Op. 29 Cantata to Hildegard Jone[23]), and composes a relatively fragmented

Ex. 2.6   Webern, Variations for Piano, Op. 27, 3rd mvt, bars 56–66

texture. A particularly striking example of the balance of fixity and freedom is the contrast between the fixed register of the section's highest note – the F which occurs in bars 4, 7 and 10 – and the non-mirroring of this fixity with the lowest note: the C♯ in bar 2 migrates up three octaves in bar 8 and up two octaves in bar 11.

Since this movement of Op. 27 was the first to be written, it might be that Webern intended the more literal symmetrical and canonic textures of the other two movements to balance their absence here. The relatively fragmented character of the third movement's first eleven bars could therefore be a consciously devised complement to the symmetrically parallel final section (bars 56–66), in which registral fixity – in particular, the five low E♭s – are prominent (Ex. 2.6: the pitches in boxes are shared between the ending of one set-form and the beginning of the next – for example, the E♭ in bar 64 functions simultaneously as the last note of R0 and the first of I0). Tensions persist, however: not only is this final section far from a mirror image of the first, but it is asymmetrical in many respects within itself, with freedom countering fixity – uncertainty, or flexibility, standing against security and a sense of peace. As Bailey interprets it, the last variation refers to the first also in its use of imperfect palindromes. The rows are those used in Variation 1, with the addition of I1 and RI1 [that is, five rows, not 3]. These are arranged into two phrases with identical rhythm, plus a third that is unique – exactly the situation in Variation 1 (aab). The pitches of both first and second phrases form palindromes (though the manner in which P0 and R0 are elided in bar 58 makes the centre of this one inexact); the durations do not...Excluding the final bar, there are eight dynamic indications here, as there were in Variation 1, and, as there, they are arranged symmetrically.

But Bailey also observes that although 'Variations 1 and 6 are similar in numerous ways', 'Variation 5 is definitely the climax of the movement and Variation 6 the dénouement/coda, thereby giving the work an asymmetrical (and rather classical) dramatic structure that is quite at odds with its arched form' (Bailey, *Twelve-Note Music*, pp. 211–12).

A reading of this final section complementary to Bailey's would note that, while P0 is followed immediately by its retrograde, with all twelve pitch-classes in the same octave positions, the same vertical combinations are avoided (another aspect of variation). R0 does not mirror P0, but rather refracts it, reacts to it. As the section evolves into its new set forms (with a typically cunning formal duality at bar 60, where the ritardando suggesting a binary division comes during the first of the new set forms, I1), new and old registral groupings briefly occur (bars 60–2), only to be 'corrected' with the return of R0 (bars 63–4) and changed again for the final, and only use here of I0. In this situation, the Ebs do not so much underpin the harmony, as Johnson claims (p. 203), as aspire to a stabilising role which is ultimately denied, and even if we sense that the predominant tone of the music is elegaic, the elegy is tinged with a very human unease. The 'subject' has not been silenced, and that characteristic which Johnson defines as Webern's essential utopianism, coupled with an exorcising of the heterogeneous, remains compromised.

Like all significant commentators on Webern, Julian Johnson strives to avoid reductiveness. Noting the general view that 'global formal patterns like canon and palindrome...seem to take precedence over the particularity of the musical detail', he argues that Webern's music 'resists abstraction through the persistence, albeit in transformed versions, of representational topics of late Romanticism' (p. 215). At the same time, however, Johnson's Adorno-inspired argument about the importance of 'the poetics of the angelic presence', and the need to understand 'the silencing of the subject...in terms of a supra-individual or spiritual process' (p. 127) does not do full justice to the music's materiality, the extent to which 'the particularity of the musical detail' demonstrates the vulnerability of those utopian aspirations to 'global formal patterning'.

In an analysis of the canonic second movement of the String Quartet Op. 28, I asked:

could it be that Webern actually arranged his set-superimpositions to ensure certain fundamental contrasts, not of pitch-content, but of musical character? To compensate, with vertical chordal disorder, and with potentially disruptive pitch or pitch-class repetitions between chords, for the high degree of internal, linear invariance possessed by his row structures and their resultant motives?...Did he find in composing without the safety set of hexachordal complementation a powerful demonstration of the truth that atonality (especially when traditional forms and textures are preserved) can only function properly in making diversities precariously cohere, rather than in aping tonality and diversifying unities?[24]

What I defined as 'Webern's precarious synthesis' was 'not literally a synthesis of old and new but one of unity and diversity within the twelve-note system itself, a synthesis which a canonic surface can help to shape' (p. 352). As the third movement of Op. 27 shows, however, this precariousness was not confined to canonic structures, or to textures employing at least four simultaneous set forms. So, rather than adopting Johnson's interpretation, that, because Webern's music 'denies the listener an affirmation that utopia is already realised. Instead it creates a tension in the listener between what is given and what it suggests, between its material disposition and the reflective thought it provokes' (p. 224), I would argue that the music's 'material disposition' itself resists the exorcising of heterogeneity by moving unity into a background from which it can only be reconstituted by detailed and often complex technical analysis. The tragedy-sensing human presence in Webern is therefore as salient as the idyllic, pastoral response to nature and belief in the angelic maternal presence, because the human subject focuses on the unstable, fallible complement to authority and purity. Humanity does not vanish into the divine but remains distinct. Webern's music holds up a mirror to living, mortal humanity, and even if it is a humanity desiring above all to dissolve itself in the divine radiance, the music does not confine its appeal – its comprehensibility – to those who share such beliefs. Even those apparently Apollonian later works embody a natural unease and sense of transience in sound and time.

Canonic resonances

In the chapter of his book on Conlon Nancarrow called 'Beyond counterpoint: the sound-mass canons', Kyle Gann makes a distinction between those earlier canons 'in which keeping the voices distinct was a concern of paramount importance' and those later sound-mass canons (from No. 24), whose 'very point was that no one could *possibly* hear a discrete difference' between the tempos of the different voices:

here Nancarrow is not illustrating tempo differences, he is using subtleties of tempo to create forms and textures that had never been heard before, and which could have been created no other way. Webern has often received credit for the creation of *diagonal texture*, texture in which harmony and counterpoint merge and cease to oppose each other as horizontal and vertical. Nancarrow not only recreated diagonal texture in a new and vivid way which owed Webern nothing, he created a continuum through which the horizontal could flow through the diagonal to become vertical, then flow back again. In the final few notes of Study No. 32, or the opening notes of No. 37, one hears the horizontal melt into the vertical (or vice versa), with the diagonal as a poignantly ephemeral intermediary stage. To fret about tempo perception during such an illusion is to miss the ocean through wondering which wave is which.[25]

The 'material disposition' of Nancarrow's Studies for Player Piano might deprive individual sonorities of resonance – reverberation is not the point – but what in isolation can seem a dry, even desiccated type of sound becomes exuberant and vivacious through textures and forms designed to project strong human emotions, while transcending the capabilities of individual human performers. Nancarrow's celebration of the human through the mechanical – the subject through the object – is paralleled by the infinitely more 'resonant' music emanating from composers who use electro-acoustic manipulation of live sound to create counterpoints and commentaries diversifying the unity provided by the material to be diversified. Such compositions may have strong spiritual concerns, or be entirely secular in their associations. In Jonathan Harvey's *Ricercare una Melodia* (1984) and *Ritual Melodies* (1989–90) the relationship to traditional canonic techniques is consciously preserved, but extended and elaborated into a language of many different echoes and resonances. Similarly, in later electro-acoustic works by Pierre Boulez – from *Répons* (1981–4) to *Dialogue de l'ombre double* (1982–5) and *Anthèmes 2* (1995–7) – the concept of related yet different commentary, stemming from the procedures of *Le Marteau sans maître* (1953–5; 1957) and the Piano Sonata No. 3 (1956–7), is the basis for complex simultaneities which seem to shatter the integrity of a single line while controlling the ripples of reflection to ensure an inexorably evolving coherence.

The adaptability of canonic technique, and its attractiveness, representing a continuing, modernistic dialogue of freedom and flexibility, is shown in Ligeti's Piano Study no. 15 (1995), called 'White on White', but demonstrating the vulnerability of such a self-contained and apparently serene concept as 'white-note' music to erosion and final decay. Like many of his later compositions, this study has moved away from turbulent expressionism, relishing the contrast between the initial, Apollonian poise of a canonic chant and the subsequent exuberant dance, which eventually admits occasional black notes as if to voice some scepticism about disciplinary constraints. This scepticism causes a rapid dissolution, and in the final chord the stable 'while on white' principle remains subverted by three black notes in the right hand (F♯, C♯ and G♯) shadowing three white notes

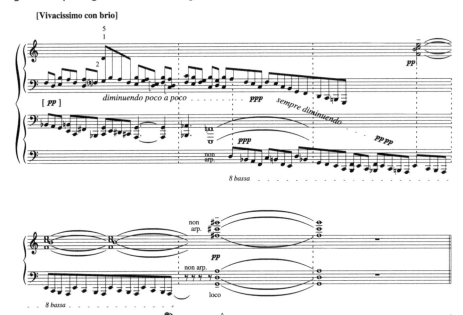

Ex. 2.7   Ligeti, Etude for Piano no. 15, 'White on White', ending

(G, D and A) in the left (Ex. 2.7). Ligeti's study is 'very twentieth-century' in being music about other music – Satie, perhaps, and also Nancarrow – and the distance of both these composers from the modernist mainstream, with its predominantly expressionistic aesthetic, has evidently stimulated Ligeti's search for a more restrained, disciplined, classicising tone.

Roger Scruton would probably dismiss 'White on White' as 'put together from a repertoire of formulae'.[26] But I do not feel that its reliance on repetitive patterning prevents it from serving as an example of the quality Scruton so admires in Janáček – 'sincere human utterance' (see Chapter 3). Ligeti's study is sincere not least in its recognition that it is still difficult in the era of late modernism for music to regard the progression from stable to less stable as any less natural than the opposite. The alignment of 'White on White' with tintinnabular minimalism also evokes the argument – put cogently by David Clarke – about the irreconcilability of such minimalism with a still active modernism. From this perspective Ligeti, like Arvo Pärt, might be felt to tread 'a perilously fine line...between simplicity and vacuity', though without simply ignoring the 'fragmentation and contradictions' which, Clarke argues, remain central, socially and politically, to 'our existing culture'.[27] As a short piece, 'White on White' escapes this problem in a very simple way, by building the ultimate questioning of white by black into the music's fabric, and by identifying closure with the shadowed, quizzical effect of its final chord. That shadowed, open ending, as an ambiguous conclusion to the piece's canonic mirrorings, suggests one of Paul Celan's most telling lines, not set by Harrison Birtwistle in *Pulse Shadows* (see Chapter 9), but arguably emblematic of Birtwistle's entire enterprise: 'Wahr spricht, wer Schatten spricht.' 'Speaks true who speaks shadow.'[28] Musicologists who seek to comprehend and contain the world of twentieth-century music could do worse than use that line as their motto.

3 Rites of renewal and remembrance

Janáček's conventions

Janáček's words about his Second String Quartet (1928) in his letters to Kamila Stösslová provide the musicologist with tantalising clues as to how the music speaks. The quartet is, Janáček declared, 'beautiful, strange, unrestrained, inspired, a composition beyond all the usual conventions'. And he reinforced this sense of something unprecedented in a uniquely vivid way. 'It is my first composition which sprang from directly experienced feeling. Before then I composed only from things remembered', but 'this piece, *Intimate Letters*, was written in fire. Earlier pieces only in hot ash.'[1]

Such language seems to demand an immediate if gentle scholarly put-down. Surely, the cool musicologist remarks, these are the exaggerated musings of an aged romanticiser who had lost any sense of proportion he might once have possessed. For example, how could the composer possibly claim to have gone 'beyond all the usual conventions' when the music of the Second Quartet still acknowledges the long-standing distinctions between consonance and dissonance, and still relies, not only on archetypal generic qualities of song and dance, but also on ways of constructing melody that owe as much to folk traditions as to those of art music?

A cool, musicological alternative to the composer's own account might plunge immediately into detailed matters of structure, observing that the most basic compositional technique on display at the beginning of the first movement is simple repetition – bars 5–8 repeat bars 1–4, with only the slightest differences of dynamics and tempo. But that repetition is immediately followed by an extreme contrast, in tempo, dynamics, tone colour, texture and harmonic orientation: whereas bars 1–8 are loud, rooted on B♭, and with a resonant homophonic thematic statement, bars 9–14 are very quiet – indeed, virtually inaudible in some performances, the solo viola (originally, viola d'amore) playing on the bridge: and the tonal centre – less stable than in bars 1–8 – has shifted from B♭ to C (Ex. 3.1). Taking a slightly broader view, of the kind that study of the printed score facilitates, the analyst of structure might then pause to speculate as to the larger-scale significance of this initial contrast, and also note that, to the extent that the quartet as a whole is 'in' D♭ (as the goal-tonality of the outer movements, with its relative minor and dominant the main keys of the central movements), such an 'off-key' beginning, in a manner which is otherwise the very opposite of preliminary, is

Ex. 3.1 Janáček, String Quartet no. 2, 1st mvt, bars 1–14

a good indication of that capacity to set aside convention which the composer's comments highlight.

It could also be said that even if these bars offer some indications of that debt to 'long-standing distinctions between consonance and dissonance', they have a less evident allegiance to long-standing conventions about the ways in which keys are established and harmony within or between keys progresses. Nevertheless, if the final section of the first movement is cited by way of comparison, it is clear that Janáček uses the opening motive to prepare an unambiguously full close in D♭ major (Ex. 3.2). Even if harmonic means and ends are far from straightforwardly diatonic with respect to chordal structuring – given the frequent addition of tones to basic triads – the effect of decisive tonal closure is undeniable. So, despite the 'directly experienced feeling' of this 'beautiful, unrestrained, inspired' music, it is not divorced from the most fundamental conventions and procedures of tradition. Rather, it uses those conventions and procedures distinctively.

To describe the composer's comments on the Second Quartet as providing 'clues as to how the music speaks' is to suggest that those comments are more hermeneutic than formalist in character, and extended analytical discourse has the

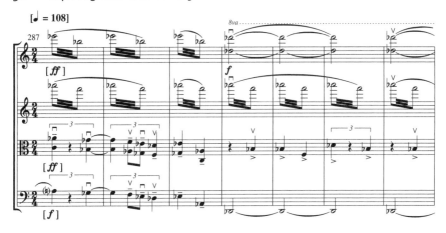

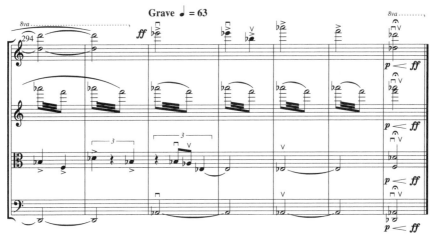

Ex. 3.2   Janáček, String Quartet no. 2, 1st mvt, ending

opportunity to explore the dialogue between these two extremes on the continuum of critical interpretation. This music does not merely display a structure but speaks through it, in a manner which, while personal to Janáček, invites comparison with other, contemporary modes of expression and formation. In this way the work of categorisation begins, and what follows is in large part a response to Roger Scruton's eloquent and provocative interpretation of Janáček.[2] At its heart is a notion of modernity, in the sense of an art created in relatively recent times which itself responds to – interprets – the state of being modern, at least in the early twentieth century. Scruton sets Janáček and Schoenberg in opposition in the way they invite responses from 'modern people', Schoenberg embodying the spirit of 'the modernist avant-garde', Janáček a very different modern spirit: and the difference has to do with an understanding of music's twentieth-century social context:

The appeal of the modernist avant-garde lies surely in the fact that it does not presuppose the spontaneous social order to which Janáček constantly returns us; it is not addressed to a community, but to the individual, who experiences through the music the alienation that reigns in his heart. For such an individual, it is Schoenberg and not Janáček who must be his guide. Hence, in so far as we notice a genuinely modernist audience, emerging in our conditions, it is an audience of sceptical individualists, urban, unattached, and without any real religious convictions.

Set against this is a music – Janáček's – which

> was not derived from the community portrayed in it: it was an attempt to create that community as a musical idea. And that, in part, is why it is so inspiring, and why it still has such authority for modern people. They hear in this music the working out of an ideal – not a metaphysical or mythical ideal, but an ideal of human community. Janáček's authoritative gestures are really gestures of sympathy, towards situations which are idealized by the very act of sympathising. (p. 27)

Scruton is able to hear such 'gestures of sympathy' at the end of Janáček's opera *Kát'a Kabanová*, but not at the end of Schoenberg's *Moses und Aron*. And Scruton believes that what he calls Schoenberg's 'abstract serialism' has failed 'to win an audience' – for the simple reason that this is music which cannot 'win through to the human heart' (p. 26).

I consider the case for the presence of human values in the work of Schoenberg in Chapter 5. Here I will focus on the specifics of Scruton's Janáček-derived technical recipe for a music of truly human modernity, and consider how this fits with Janáček's comments on his Second String Quartet. Scruton wants a music which 'respects the devices that Janáček made such vivid use of: repetition, dance rhythm, diatonic phrases and tonal harmonies'. His other prescriptions are as follows: 'if we venture towards dissonance, then we should follow the examples of Janáček, Bartók and Stravinsky: we should contrast the dissonant chord with the chord that wholly or partially resolves it'. Further,

> composers today need to rediscover the art of creating melodies, for these are the true musical protagonists, the actors on the stage of music... Again, Janáček sets an irreproachable example. His melodies, taken from the rhythm of human speech, and at the same time imbued with a tradition of song and dance, were entirely unsentimental – images of sincere human utterance, as though compelled from the heart rather than put together from a repertoire of formulae. (pp. 28–9)

The extent to which that 'sincerity' speaks of an 'ideal community' more than of intensely personal, emotional concerns is debatable. But it is the technical aspect of Scruton's analysis which is most open to dispute, since it denies any sense of those qualities – subversiveness, instability among them – which the composer deploys to serve his need for self-expression, or even self-dramatisation. After all, *Intimate Letters* is in one sense a diary, not of one who disappears, but of one who offers a close-up portrait of himself as a soul in ecstatic torment, and for whom society – convention – is as likely to be threatening as supportive. It is music having more to do with defiance of, alienation from, community than with idealisations of community. This is not to say that such idealisations – especially as embodied in representations of place – are never found in Janáček: but they coexist, in dialogue with the very different concerns considered below.

The topics of defiance and ambivalence can be traced in both formal and hermeneutic domains: for example, the form of the quartet's first movement might be interpreted as torn between acknowledgement of precedent – the rondo, in particular – and the kind of resistance to precedent that finds fulfilment in an essentially episodic emphasis on the local, the immediate, in preference to the larger-scale and the longer-term. This tendency to fracture 'symphonic' continuity is noticeable in frequent changes of tempo and texture, which go well beyond the typical inflections of a fundamental continuity found in traditional sym-phonism. Yet there is often a degree of association and linkage at the level of pitch organisation and voice-leading, so that even the kind of extreme contrast found near the end of the movement, at Fig. 17, is saved from suggesting a mere juxtaposition of opposites by the motivic connection of descending steps in the viola (Ex. 3.3). The dialogue between connection and disconnection is remarkably intense, even so, with the culminating moment of uncertainty at bars 249 and 250. Exaggerate the break with a slight pause, and this could easily sound like the 'ending' of the first movement and the beginning of a slow movement – if that slow movement were allowed to start with a theme already used in the first movement.

These matters of formal interpretation arise from the character of the music – the kinds of material used in the various sub-sections – rather than from abstract concerns with the possible relation to formal prototypes. The explosive opening – dithyrambic, Dionysian – has generic implications as a wild celebratory hymn of a personal, masculine, pagan – even 'subhuman' – kind, in a composer to whom Apollonian calm and calculation were largely alien.[3] It has the potential to develop as a dance to the same extent as the answering phrase hints at more song-like, feminine gestures of remoteness and mystery – at least as Janáček him-self might have seen it. In the 'B' section of the Rondo, from Fig. 6 (bar 52), the lyric lines above ostinato basses suggest a more equable balance between song and dance. There is even a trace of that most traditional formal device, the transition (bars 87–91), as a cadence is prepared which coincides with the establishment of the principal C♯/D♭ tonality. There has also been a process of motivic evolution,

Ex. 3.3 Janáček, String Quartet no. 2, 1st mvt, bars 245–72

in that the [015] shape in the first violin at bars 100–1 can be derived from the viola theme of bars 9–10.

After the second 'A' section (bars 133–61), in which the D♭ tonality is both reinforced and challenged, the 'C' section of the Rondo (bars 162–265) is predominantly song-like. The episodic quality of this is enhanced by the inclusion of a version of the 'A' section's counter-theme (bars 218ff.), and the song-like character turns again to a more ecstatic, celebratory mode from bar 231 as the tempo increases and the 'false' presto ending is prepared. It is perhaps too easy to 'read' the final stages of the movement as a progression from what Janáček might have perceived as female submissiveness (bars 250–65) to male triumph and an ultimate unity of attitude, represented by the now assertive viola (bars 290–5) and the echoing first violin (bars 296–300). But if the claim in the note with the score (by Otakar Šourek) that the movement 'describes the impression of the first meeting with Mrs S[tösslová]' is taken into account, then a scenario which progresses from separateness to unanimity is not improbable.

Much of the interpretative language used above does not conflict with Scruton's terms. There is indeed admirably unsentimental, dance-like melody, 'taken from the rhythm of human speech'. There is repetition, dance rhythms. But, despite the integrative effect of tonality, those 'diatonic phrases and tonal harmonies' so important to Scruton are thoroughly destabilised, by modal inflections on the smaller scale, and by abruptly juxtaposed shifts and contrasts on the larger scale: and if we question Scruton's technical analysis, his aesthetic interpretation also invites scepticism. Is this music to do with 'an ideal of human community', or is it also, or *rather*, the expression of a distinctly unstable individuality – an exultantly personal, even solipsistic sensuality: might it even relate to what Paul Wingfield has diagnosed as the composer's 'distasteful' tendency to violence in his attitude to women?[4] An unanswerable question: but such questions soon pile in on critical commentaries which range beyond the safe shores of purely technical interpretation. On that technical level, the Second Quartet confirms Thomas Adès's judgement that Janáček's 'single most far-reaching quality' was 'the redefinition of structural tonality through an unprecedented concentration on ambiguous, and particularly enharmonic, key relationships'.[5] And might not Adès's Janáček, whose stylistic qualities are not confined to one late work but range across his entire output, come closer to a modernist practice which is not as diametrically opposed to that of Schoenberg and other composers as Scruton is anxious to suggest?

Janáček in context

In his book on the string quartet, Paul Griffiths noted the relative temporal proximity of Berg's *Lyric Suite* and Janáček's *Intimate Letters*: the *Lyric Suite* was composed in 1925–6, *Intimate Letters* was completed by 8 March 1928. Griffiths even speculated on the possible consequences of geographical proximity: whether the paths of Berg's muse Hanna Fuchs-Robettin, then based in Prague, and Kamila Stösslová might not have crossed around this time.[6] We can choose to underline the common ground of forceful rather than reticent ways of speaking in these two composers, in which case a good comparison would be between the ending of Berg's fifth movement — Presto delirando — and the ending of Janáček's finale, both driven by cumulative repetitions of ostinatos to fiercely abrupt conclusions on fifth-based chords. Yet the essential expressionism of Berg's style becomes increasingly explicit as the work proceeds, and is particularly manifest in the large intervals and flowing rhythms of his finale's main twelve-note melody. Berg's atonality (for all the occasional hints at centred harmonic processes), elaborate polyphony and doom-laden atmosphere embody a quite different style to Janáček's febrile, exuberant blocks of extended-tonal harmony and folk-like melody.

This is not to suggest that Berg's music — its Viennese waltz-like material apart — is devoid of any sense of place. For Berg, folk, or folk-like material could be introduced, as in the Violin Concerto, but more as quotation for poetic purposes than as a generative stylistic or structural source, and the Concerto's modernist discourse has much to do with the opposition between the diatonic triads of the Carinthian folk tune and the triad-based total chromaticism of the pervasive twelve-note row. The result, as Stravinsky caustically noted, commenting on the 'orchestral flagellation' of *Wozzeck*'s D minor Interlude and 'its appeal to "ignorant" audiences',[7] could be alienating in the way it seems to risk bathos in making such calculating, uncontrolled bids for the listener's sympathy. Chapter 4 will consider how Stravinsky himself sought to represent expressiveness — even passion — in ways which risked appearing 'inhuman' in their calculation and detachment. For Janáček, as for Stravinsky, folk or folk-derived materials were altogether more central in significance than they ever were for Berg. But despite his Dionysianism, Janáček cannot be convincingly categorised as an expressionist, partly because he was never as atonal as Berg, or as dedicated to surface fractures. Despite the ambiguities and less than straightforward underlining of positive social values discussed above, the disjunctions which the 'cries of terror' in *Intimate Letters* (or in *The Diary of One Who Disappeared*, 1917–20) create do not inhabit that psychological labyrinth of desperate isolation and pathos-fuelled lamentation where genuine expressionism belongs. Perhaps Šhiškov's long monologue in Act 3 of *From the House of the Dead* (1927–8) comes closest to it, where declamatory forcefulness pushes associations with the folk-like into the background.

It is always difficult to devise a critical vocabulary which links the expressive and the structural, and at least one important twentieth-century composer, Arnold Schoenberg, seemed in no doubt that talk about the 'emotional background' of a composition 'will not furnish enlightenment of the structure'. These remarks occur in the context of the following commentary on the Third String Quartet (1927):

As a little boy I was tormented by a picture of a scene from a fairy-tale, *Das Gespensterschiff* (The Ghostship), whose captain had been nailed through the head to the topmast by his rebellious crew. I am sure that this was not the programme of the first movement of the Third String Quartet. But it might have been, subconsciously, a very gruesome premonition which caused me to write this work, because as often as I thought about this movement, the picture came to my mind. I am afraid a psychologist might use this story as a stepping stone for premature conclusions.[8]

These comments will be more fully considered in the context of the wider discussion of Schoenberg's work in Chapter 5. But one aspect of Schoenberg's technique, his delight in disconcerting his orthodoxy-conditioned listeners by exploitation of the unexpected, especially at the ends of sections and movements, suggests some common ground with Janáček – the quality identified by Paul Griffiths in his comment that 'the arbitrariness of the form [in *Intimate Letters*] is emphasised by endings which are too sudden' (Griffiths, *Quartet*, p. 186).

'Arbitrariness' is perhaps not the right word, since it implies a casual, take-it-or-leave-it attitude rather than a considered, bracing disruption of normal expectations. But both Janáček and Schoenberg go beyond 'the usual conventions' (Janáček's words again) in ways which depend on certain elements of those conventions being retained and, indeed, reinforced. Interestingly, the finale of Schoenberg's Third Quartet ends, like that of *Intimate Letters*, with a process in which thematic motives are fined down or 'liquidated', to use Schoenberg's term,[9] and in which closure is effected through ostinato-like repetition. In spirit, Schoenberg's ending (Ex. 3.4a), like that of the *Lyric Suite*'s finale (Ex. 3.4b), has more of post-tonal dissolution than tonal resolution. The ending of *Intimate Letters* (Ex. 3.4c) may seem abrupt, but Janáček's musical language did not permit the kind of chromatic dissolve so significant for Berg and Schoenberg. In this respect, the composer of quartets in the 1920s to be most closely aligned with Janáček is Bartók.

Certain motives from Bartók's Third and Fourth Quartets are similarly shaped to motives from Janáček's Second, but differences become obvious when matters of harmonic context and formal, textural treatment are brought to bear. During the later 1920s, Bartók's reliance on intricate contrapuntal development, often canonic and inversional, demonstrated his bid to contribute to a generic progress stemming from Beethoven's late quartets, and intersecting – despite Bartók's resistance to atonality – with some aspects of Schoenbergian (and even Webernian) twelve-note technique from the same period. Bartók's work will be considered more fully later in this chapter, where a picture will emerge of a composer who absorbed his sense of place, and people, into a more mainstream form of musical expression and generic modelling, and in which more mainstream notions of the dramatic and the expressive replaced the psychological, erotic specifics so significant for Janáček.

Ex. 3.4   (a) Schoenberg, String Quartet no. 3, 4th mvt, ending

Janáček's greatness in his later works came from the tension between community and independence – a detachment from tradition that is deeply engaged with the constructing of balanced yet potentially unstable musical designs. For Carl Dahlhaus, this stance signalled an 'adherence to the aesthetics of the true' which – in the later operas, at any rate – involved

> the renunciation of forms of stylization which were rooted in the traditional aesthetics of the beautiful. The grammar of the musicodramatic speech had to abandon beautifully balanced periods, perfect syntax and prolixity, and emulate reality in 'prosaic' immediacy of expression. The rhythmic complementarity of bars and phrases, clauses and periods, which was, according to Hanslick, the primary form-building element of classic-romantic music, gave place, in the name of realism, to 'musical prose'.[10]

There may well be more evidence of 'beautifully balanced periods and perfect syntax' in Bartók, Berg or Schoenberg than in Janáček, but this contrast stems as much from the nature of basic material as from predispositions about formal design. The opening of *Intimate Letters* has what I have called a dithyrambic quality:

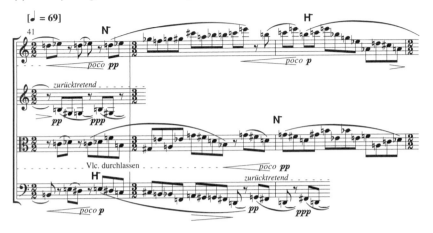

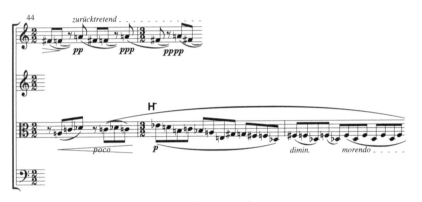

Ex. 3.4   (b) Berg, *Lyric Suite*, 6th mvt, ending

analogous to the wild, vehement character – in the composer's words, 'strange, unrestrained' – believed to belong to ancient Greek hymns to Dionysus. This opens up the possibility of a further comparison, since it was in the late 1920s and early 1930s that Stravinsky contributed to what he himself thought of as dithyrambic expression, in the ballet *Apollo*, and the *Duo concertant* for violin and piano (see Chapter 4).

The interpretative circle continues to turn, and there remain intriguing and attractive associations between what Griffiths designates as 'elements of passionate song and dancing vivacity' (Griffiths, *Quartet*, p. 186) in all the composers considered in this chapter. No generic allusion in *Intimate Letters* is more appealing or haunting than that of what Griffiths terms the third movement's 'sad Slavonic barcarolle'. Here, above all, it is impossible not to sense the composer's acceptance of reality, the ephemerality of human love and life, as Janáček's own comments, refererring to lullaby and an imaginary child, seem to acknowledge. As a whole this movement achieves a delicate balance between stability and instability,

[♩ = 112]

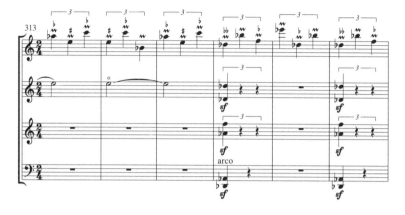

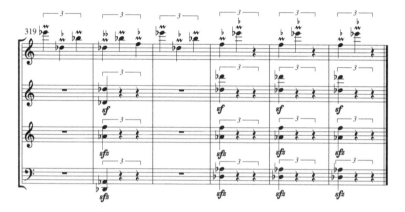

Ex. 3.4   (c) Janáček, String Quartet no. 2, 4th mvt, ending

comforting regularity and abrupt contrast. The Schoenberg comparison is with the Intermezzo from the Third Quartet, where the opening theme shares a delicacy of spirit (and an initial 9/8 metre) with Janáček's. Schoenberg's working-out may be much more systematic, in the Germanic mode, but a comparable feeling of seeking for balance between stable and unstable in a dance-like song is to be heard: and the music offers a resistance to those fracturing propensities of modernism with which neither Janáček nor (I suspect) Schoenberg was greatly in sympathy.

As for Berg's *Lyric Suite*, it is possible to find traces of a sad *Viennese barcarolle* – that is, a barcarolle closer to the waltz than a Slavonic one would be – in the second movement, the Andante amoroso. All these movements – even the Schoenberg – have distinctive alignments between song-like and dance-like music. Yet while Janáček retains connections with these generic archetypes throughout his highly diverse four-movement quartet, Berg and Schoenberg gravitate more towards the symphonic paradigm – as does Bartók: and it is Bartók

Non troppo lento, ♩ = 60

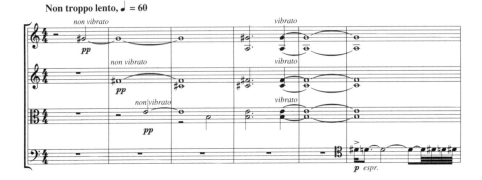

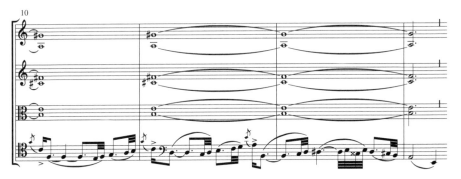

Ex. 3.5   Bartók, String Quartet no. 4, 3rd mvt, beginning

who is found most seriously wanting when a search is instituted for the genre of 'sad barcarolle' – at least in the Third and Fourth Quartets. It might be necessary to move back as far as the opera *Bluebeard's Castle* (1911, last revised in 1918) for evidence of flowing material in compound metre – and even here the material in question runs for a mere four bars (324–7). Judit Frigyesi categorises this as the pastoral theme: however, to the extent that it reflects Judith's repetition of the words 'softly' and 'gently', it surely has as much to do with musical representations of the feminine, and even with the genre of the cradle song or lullaby, as with pastoral.[11]

When it comes to contrasting lyrical material in his instrumental music, Bartók usually opts for dirge-like melodies, often quite intricately ornamental laments lacking the associations with either dance or simple song which tend to be set up by Janáček's lyrical writing. Bartók is at his most personal in such contexts, as the opening of the Fourth Quartet's third movement memorably reveals (Ex. 3.5). For Halsey Stevens, this evokes 'the pastoral melancholy of the *tárogató*, a Hungarian woodwind instrument somewhat like a straight wooden saxophone, originally with a double reed'[12] – the instrument which Mahler famously used as a replacement for the cor anglais in performances of *Tristan*. Generically, such melodies are threnodies, and demonstrate the kind of melodic shaping which Bartók, in his discussion of folk-laments, described as resembling 'the Gregorian recitative'.[13] Frigyesi offers a useful account of the connections between such melodic types and what she calls the 'slow *verbunkos*', or '*Lassú*' (pp. 245–8): and it is possible to trace a generic line from the folk dance she quotes, through the Suite No. 1 of 1905 and the lament melody of *Bluebeard's Castle*, and on to the slow movement theme of the Fourth Quartet. Where Bartók's quartet theme is concerned, connections with the 'hora lunga' rhythms of Romanian poetry have also been proposed.[14]

Bartók and tradition

A firm hermeneutic alliance might be built between Janáček and Bartók, centring on the degree to which, in both lament-like and dance-like music, they use their national accents to reduce if not entirely separate their representations of pathos from associations with Austro-German expressionism. Nevertheless, Bartók moved far closer than Janáček to Austro-German symphonic traditions, and the fact that Bartók was nearly thirty years younger, and still evolving as a composer until his death in 1945, ensured a more complex relation to the whole nexus of political, psychological and technical issues that dominated musical developments between the twentieth century's two world wars.

Bartók has been hailed as 'easily the most outspoken antifascist among modernists':[15] but all discussion of his later music has to acknowledge its apparently abstract emphasis. Whereas both *Bluebeard's Castle* and *The Miraculous Mandarin* (1918–19, orch. 1923–4) lend themselves to interpretation in terms of cultural practice, little after that, apart from *Cantata Profana* (1930) offers the necessary combination of text and music. Rachel Beckles Willson has suggested that one reason why Bartók 'rarely allowed the rough side of peasant music to enter his vocal works' – as distinct from, for example, the 'harsh rumbustiousness of the String Quartet No. 4' – is that he had

> a fundamental inhibition, a reserve about the most powerfully expressive qualities of the human voice. And while harnessing the 'real' nature of the rugged

peasant song was acceptable in a transformed, abstract instrumental work, in a vocal work it would have seemed a mockery of the peasants whose trust Bartók had gained, and whose singing he himself had recorded.[16]

This insight reinforces the challenges which Bartók faced in fulfilling his 'desire' to create a new Hungarian art music through a 'hybridisation' in which elements deriving from both urban gypsy and rural peasant music featured prominently.[17] Bartók's difficulty in reaching a new kind of 'classical' synthesis is acknowledged in the kind of general interpretations of his work which stress the ambiguity of 'a new and integrated musical language which does not in the process hide the fractured character of its elements',[18] and of works like the Concerto for Orchestra (1943; 1945) 'in which difference is celebrated as much as consensus, fragmentation as much as unity',[19] or like the Sonata for Two Pianos and Percussion (1937), whose first movement encourages in the analyst 'a more pluralistic stance, regarding tonality and atonality, syntactic and semantic, internal and external readings as capable of coexisting in the same composition, and even in the same passage of music'.[20]

It might seem that Bartók was increasingly committed to an essential classicism, complaining that in *The Rite of Spring* 'Stravinsky did not escape the danger of yielding to a broken mosaic-like construction', and that the reason Schoenberg's music was found difficult was 'his complete alienation to [*sic*] Nature'.[21] Nevertheless, according to the Marxist philosopher György Lukács, Bartók regarded 'the central question of renewal, of the world, of music' as hingeing

> on the insoluble conflict between the authentic life of the people and the distorting, dehumanizing effects of capitalist pseudo-culture; in his art it is the irreconcilable contradiction between the natural life of the peasant and the alienation of modern man that becomes the point of departure for the solutions to the problems of modern life.[22]

'The alienation of modern man' is the dominant image of Bartók's most expressionistic, Dionysian work, the pantomime/ballet *The Miraculous Mandarin*: for Stephen Downes, this embodies 'the conflict between natural, subjective expression and the mechanical, impersonal production of urban culture which leads to disorientation and dissociation' (p. 50). At the opposite extreme, what Elliott Antokoletz calls 'Bartók's humanistic philosophy of the brotherhood of nations' informs the *Cantata Profana*, a work 'based on highly complex interactions between members of the larger family of nondiatonic folk modes from Eastern Europe and the symmetrical (whole-tone and octatonic) constructions of contemporary art music'.[23] Antokoletz sees the *Cantata*'s 'synthesis' of its materials, which include Bartók's 'revision and combination of the two original folk ballads on a Romanian *colinda*' and 'the opening theme of Bach's *St Matthew Passion*', as pointing 'to a common basis in their symbolistic assumptions' and exemplifying 'the larger trend in Bartók's music towards a new means of musico-dramatic expression and integration of the entire musical fabric' (p. 75). But the *Cantata* could just as well exemplify the persistence of cultural and artistic tensions of the kind that any non-Christian, nationalistic artist might have experienced during the inter-war years. And while Bartók's rejection of religion made him far less susceptible to the seductions of solemn, celebratory rituals than Stravinsky, it also obliged him to compensate in the dramatic character and generic associations of his instrumental works, and to work out in them the kind of concerns that he could not tackle in texted compositions. As Beckles Willson notes, *Cantata Profana* 'stands apart from Bartók's other vocal works', and instrumental composition provided a means of coping with that 'increasing bitterness' which affected his life and thought during and after the 1930s. Just as the *Cantata*'s 'allusions to Baroque oratorio contribute to the sense of ritual which the work evokes' (p. 87), and serve to exorcise that Dionysian tendency on display in *The Miraculous Mandarin*, in particular, so allusions to classical instrumental genres and technical traditions would enhance the power and profundity of the later instrumental works, without leading either to simplistic neoclassical pastiche or to incoherent stylistic juxtapositions.

Bartók in 1939

Having already explored certain comparisons between Bartók and Janáček, using time of composition as the criterion, I will end this chapter by considering Bartók's Sixth and last String Quartet. I said of Janáček's last quartet that the composer's 'greatness in his late works comes from the tension between community and independence – a detachment from tradition that is deeply engaged with the constructing of balanced yet potentially unstable musical designs' (see above, p. 43). This statement was obviously intended to modify Janáček's own singularly unambiguous comments about a strangeness 'beyond all the usual conventions', as well as Scruton's arguments about the 'idealization of community'. By contrast, Bartók's Sixth Quartet has more often been the subject of formal, structural analysis than of the kind of hermeneutic commentary that goes beyond a few straightforward links with known biographical facts – such as the connection between the sad character of the work's motto theme and Bartók's sorrowful departure from his homeland in 1939. The work's position in relation to a tradition stemming from the later quartets of Beethoven has had critical precedence over its more immediate, and more personal qualities: the assumption has been that it shares with most of Bartók's later works the quality of transcending time and place, triumphing over difficult personal circumstances, as well as over the constraints of tradition.

The Sixth Quartet is at the opposite, 'classical' extreme from the turbulence and melodrama of *The Miraculous Mandarin*, and no less well contrasted with the erotic and social (or anti-social) aura of *Intimate Letters*. For Bartók it is no longer a matter of the 'release of the power of eroticism from the repressions of modern life', even if the more specifically musical aspects of this process, the contrast between 'natural, subjective expression' and a music which distorts 'the world of nature', survive. By 1939, life for Bartók was defined less by the conflict between eroticism and conformity, urban and pastoral, than by the struggle between freedom and oppression. The argument that the Sixth Quartet somehow reflects these personal circumstances will therefore conclude that the music's drama involves a distinction between a lament for lost 'nature' (nationality) and the bitter mockery of the oppressively alien: and this fits with the assumption, first explored by Benjamin Suchoff, that the transformation of the work's finale from 'dance movement' to lament was the direct result of the outbreak of the Second World War and the composer's consequent decision to leave Hungary. By the time the quartet was completed, in November 1939, 'the "tempo giusto" of the village dance, conceived in Switzerland, was now replaced by the "parlando rubato" mourning song for the murder of Europe'.[24] In addition, the finale's lament theme had become a motto theme, even though it seems that this decision was not taken during the composition of the finale but 'during the composition of the "Marcia"', the second movement (p. 5). As László Somfai puts it, 'it is indeed the recurrences of the ritornello that so dramatically show the colorful "pictures" or "scenes" (Movs. I, II, III) to be memories of the past in contrast to the overwhelming pessimism of the present, Bartók's view of life in autumn 1939'.[25]

Alternatively, it might be less a matter of the contrast between past and present, memory and actuality, than of the conflict between two presents, that of an idealised, natural, rural Hungary and of oppressive, aggressive forces both within and without. But it is inadequate to force the Sixth Quartet into the role of representing the kind of battle between good and evil represented in Bartók's early tone-poem *Kossuth* (or Shostakovich's Seventh, 'Leningrad' Symphony of 1941). The music's drama arises not from a simple opposition between violence and serenity, but from the troubled interaction between the sorrow of loss and the bitterness at contemplating that loss: and the boundary between these two states, the attempt to preserve a sense of nature and nation as good, and the need to protest, to show hostility to the aggressor, remains blurred simply because the musical means whereby each is represented cannot be kept separate. Even the finale is not so much Suchoff's 'mourning song for the murder of Europe' as an expression of Bartók's own labyrinth of feelings about that 'murder', a complex in which Somfai's 'overwhelming pessimism' is just one aspect.

On this semantic level, the first movement (after the motto-theme introduction) can be read as a dance-like pastoral over which shadows are cast, not only by the more soulful, song-like 'second subject' (from bar 81), but also by developmental processes whose contrapuntal density helps to render the atmosphere more agitated, more aggressive. This movement is already a compelling embodiment of the interaction between 'nature' and 'culture', rural and urban, gentler and more forceful kinds of dance-like motion, and this interaction is most vividly presented in the recapitulation section (from bar 268). At first there is a gently flowing, logically imitative phrase which loses tonal direction: perhaps an 'antecedent' implying a balancing 'consequent' along the lines of the exposition's complementary if open-ended succession (bars 24–30: 31–36). But what follows (at bar 276) is faster, more primitive in its basic opposition of 'white'- and 'black'-note materials – a retrospective allusion to the oppositions which open the Third Quartet (1927). The recapitulation proceeds with a second juxtaposition between the Tempo 1 dance (no longer marked 'dolce' at bar 287, while still graceful in character), and the more reductive, active, primitive 'vivacissimo' (from the end of bar 296), material which aggressively colonises fifth-based triadic writing, but preserves its inherent instability. In the continuing interplay of the movement's later stages, the lyrical material regains the upper hand, first with the restated second subject, then with the tendency of the 'vivacissimo, agitato' (bar 332) to turn homophonic and consonant (D major triads at bars 348 and 352, though the latter in particular is too abrupt to be authentically closural). The rest of the movement nevertheless moves between this tonic, an emphasised subdominant (bars 363–7) and the final quietly decisive tonic major, and even includes the long-rejected first-subject consequent (bars 371–4: Ex. 3.6). The effect is as near to idyllic as this work will manage.

With reference to *Bluebeard's Castle*, Judit Frigyesi has shown how the genre of the 'slow *verbunkos*' can easily infuse the pastoral with a pathetic or even tragic quality, as idyll turns into lament (pp. 267–73). The relationship between the Sixth Quartet's first movement and finale suggests a comparable progression, also countering the sardonic hysteria of the March's middle section and the 'escapist' nostalgia of the Burletta's 'trio', so brutally trampled on in the third movement's final stages. For some, there will always be too much pathos here: devoid of ritual solemnity or processional *gravitas*, the music risks resolving into a desperate plea to be cherished and understood, with stark oppositions between high and low, loud and soft (bars 78–81: Ex. 3.7). Yet the music's genuinely tragic dimension connects not so much with the tearful, self-pitying and self-deluding nostalgia of an urban sophisticate imagining pastoral bliss as with a searing sense of loss, and awareness of a corruption which has permeated country as well as town, the wider world as well as the cherished homeland. Under such circumstances, not even fifth-based harmony can convey much in the way of belief in renewal, and so the appropriate analogy to the composer's deepest feelings is something ambiguously decisive, understatedly ironic in its doubled though not dramatically conflicting treatment of closure.

One way of hearing the Sixth Quartet's final sonority – as F major with added sixth – might appeal to anyone who can recall the most celebrated

Ex. 3.6   Bartók, String Quartet no. 6, 1st mvt, ending

Ex. 3.7   Bartók, String Quartet no. 6, 4th mvt, ending

symphonic use of the added-sixth chord as ending, in Mahler's *Das Lied von der Erde*. But in Mahler's 'Abschied' the chord is unambiguously sustained, in keeping with a resolution from which all bitterness has been purged, as lament yields to contemplation of the transcendent. Mahler's music does not seem to have meant much to Bartók, and yet the march-character of the Sixth Quartet's middle movements — even the Burletta can be aligned with the elephantine galumphing of a very slow march — inevitably suggests connections with Mahler's regard for that genre's emblematic cultural status, at once celebratory and oppressive. Bartók risks accusations of simplistic gesturing in his recourse to the kind of sneering glissandos and static ostinatos that contrast with the second movement's more intense imitative writing (bars 58ff. and 174ff.), and which make the central episode (bars 80–114) seem miscalculated as a parody of mindless, tasteless folk improvisation rather than a passionately 'natural' countering of jackbooted violence. In this respect the Burletta is the more controlled and convincing in its representation of a soulless urban-fascist world.

As noted earlier, Bartók's representations of pathos can be ascribed to his Germanic, art-music inheritance: and while it is simplistic to suggest that his later music is utterly devoid of a Dionysian dimension – see, for example, the finales of the Fifth Quartet and the Concerto for Orchestra – he did not turn this in the direction of the kind of emphasis on dithyrambic celebration with which Janáček embraced, without idealising, nature and community. The 'humanistic philosophy' of *Cantata Profana* was transmitted through music in which tension matters as much as, if not more than, synthesis: and it was this feeling for drama in which human action could never free itself from anxiety and self-doubt that determined the scope and significance of Bartók's musical achievements. What makes the Sixth Quartet so memorable and disturbing an experience is the possibility that both the atmosphere and structure of the music owe as much to the composer's doubts about his own character and capacities – his inability to be at peace with himself – as they do to any intention to portray a world in which nations were unable to live together without violence.

The Sixth Quartet is exceptional among Bartók's later works in not providing decisive resolutions and upbeat endings. It would be difficult to demonstrate that the quartet was somehow a greater achievement than, say, the *Music for Strings, Percussion and Celesta* (1936) or the Second Violin Concerto (1937–8), on the grounds that it dealt more openly and honestly with the composer's 'real' feelings and experiences of the world. But, in a direct comparison, those upbeat endings can seem rather forced, rather unnaturally exuberant, alongside the terse and unambiguous melancholy of the Sixth Quartet's last bars. Here, the feelings involved are no less 'directly experienced' than those in Janáček's *Intimate Letters*. They are not 'unrestrained', still less 'beyond all the usual conventions'. But Bartók's lack of fully-fledged Apollonian serenity did not prevent him from effectively balancing the centrifugal fracture of modernist disruption against aspirations to the kind of multi-level integration of structure which is, ultimately, classical in spirit.[26]

4 Transcending the secular

From classical to neoclassical

Some of the most vivid verbal portraits of Bartók have been left by his publishers. Hans Heinsheimer described the composer as 'living in an unsmiling, hushed world where there was little room for our human frailties and no pardon for our sins',[1] while Ernst Roth sketched a 'small, thin, taciturn man' behind whose 'unapproachable façade lay an extreme intolerance in both artistic and human matters', and whose 'reticence and intolerance were no deliberate protection from a world which would not understand him. They were his very nature and only in his music could he escape from it.' Roth concluded that 'Bartók was not an unhappy man in the usual sense, but neither was he a happy one who enjoyed himself and his music. In artistic and political matters alike he was an idealist, without practical objectives' (p. 127). Another acquaintance referred to his incomparable 'moral rectitude, purity and unassailable puritanism' (p. 36). Yet he could also appear 'disappointed' and 'disillusioned' (p. 61) – even 'a pathetic little man – but an intensely proud one' (p. 84).

Attempts to map these images directly onto Bartók's compositions might also prove pathetic: but Roth's suggestion that his music was as much an escape from a hostile world as a portrait of that world merits further examination. As argued in Chapter 3, the Sixth Quartet is exceptional not for its occasionally overt pathos, but for the immediacy of the connection between this mood and the composer's personal circumstances in 1939 – the death of his mother, his decision to leave Hungary and Europe. Allowing such factors to affect the composition meant a modification of the equilibrium and integrity of musical design which had become Bartók's favoured mode of procedure during the 1930s. Even when due allowance is made for those fracturing, pluralistic aspects noted in Chapter 3, such major works as the Fifth String Quartet, the Sonata for Two Pianos and Percussion and the Second Violin Concerto embody a 'modern classic' orientation rather than something more purely modernist – an orientation captured in Paul Wilson's observations about 'a multi-level integration of structure'.[2] And even if, as with Sibelius, sketch materials for these apparently abstract symphonic works were uncovered with annotations indicating a personal, autobiographical 'agenda' to do with people and places close to the composer's heart, this would not radically affect the claims about his music's concern with balance and integration, its capacity for admitting contrast, fracture, diversity — but not allowing these features to predominate.

Nevertheless, Bartók was no slave to emotional neutrality, or to the purely architectural delights of formal manipulation and construction: variety of expression, the playing off of the dynamic against the lyrical, was essential if those large-scale works were not to seem arid and formulaic. Bartók's music quite lacked the 'detachment' sketched by his verbal portraitists, and (as noted in Chapter 3) the absence of the kind of religious faith that gives value to ritual and ceremonial might have helped to deprive his music of Apollonian serenity, as well as of that 'cold', tragic aura so important to Stravinsky. Even when Bartók's subject-matter impinges on Stravinsky's, as in *Village Scenes* (1926), there is no Bartókian equivalent to the hieratic poise with which *Svadebka* (*Les Noces*) ends. Bartók could always accommodate the kind of Dionysian abandon encapsulated in his relatively early *Allegro barbaro* for piano (1911) within his classically inspired designs, and even an element of Apollonian constructivism. But Apollonian calm was another matter. Even the quiet expressiveness of chorale-like passages, as in the Third Piano Concerto (1945), tends not to evolve into sustained processional solemnity. Bartók's classicism is rooted in the world, and in humanity. His music is the apotheosis of the secular, and less a matter of 'escape from the world' than of showing the world what human truth could be like.

One reason for interpreting Bartók in this way is to underline a contrast with Stravinsky, in whom the interaction between Russian and other national contexts was paralleled by a need to explore the interaction between sacred and secular subjects and modes of expression. Stravinsky's abiding but adaptable Russian-ness has been seen as all-too-perfectly consistent with right-wing political and social sympathies — pro-fascist, anti-Semitic:[3] by contrast, Bartók appears an innocent victim of political developments, and remained a victim until his death. This contrast of character and temperament can also be extended to a distinction between the confident iconoclasm of Stravinsky's neoclassicism, which preserves and even enhances the formal discontinuities of modernism — even if it also rejects the expressionistic manner with which modernism before 1920 was primarily associated — and the concern to validate and yet transform traditions characteristic of Bartók's modern classicism, in which stylistic allusions to Bach or Beethoven are, on the whole, less direct.

There is another consequence of this distinction between neoclassicism and modern classicism: to the extent that neoclassicism depends on sudden shifts, conflicts and disorientating textural and stylistic effects, it is as much an outgrowth of late romanticism as of earlier, genuine classicism. Yet the music by Stravinsky generally categorised as neoclassical is not the result of an attempt to be 'inexpressive': rather, it concerns the possibilities for expression which arise when the concept of 'expressiveness' is no longer tied to the aura of a late romantic style.

Stravinsky's most extreme formulation of this aesthetic position – courtesy of Robert Craft – comes from the years after 1950, the time of his twelve-note miniatures, and focuses on the intensity of feeling available to those Timurid miniaturists who were not allowed to depict facial expression. When Stravinsky/Craft declare of one of these miniatures that 'two lovers confront each other with stony looks, but the man unconsciously touches his finger to his lips, and this packs the picture with, for me, as much passion as the *crescendo molto* of *Wozzeck*' the implication is as unambiguous as their fastidious distaste at the 'orchestral flagellation' of *Wozzeck*'s 'D minor' Interlude.[4] If understatement, or its equivalent, is employed, then the limits of the expressive effect are determined only by the imagination of the observer: but it is the observer whose interpretation is crucial, complementing the restrained depiction of the artist rather than merely observing a vehemence of expression which can scarcely be overstated.

A Stravinskian musical equivalent of two lovers confronting each other in an atmosphere of heightened restraint is found in the final stages of *Svadebka* (1914–17), when the Dionysian celebration is over and the husband salutes his wife in a simple modal melody to the even simpler accompaniment of chiming bells and pianos (Ex. 4.1). This is music of supremely eloquent gravity: but in context it is also highly charged, and redolent of human sensuality. Presumably Stravinsky did not regard it as opening up a tragic dimension, similar to that identified in his comments on *Apollo* (1927–8): 'if a truly tragic note is sounded anywhere in my music, that note is in *Apollo*. Apollo's birth is tragic, I think, and the Apotheosis is every bit as tragic as Phèdre's line when she learns of the love of Hippolyte and Aricie – "Tous les jours se levaient clairs et sereins pour eux"' (p. 34). What Stravinsky must mean by 'tragic' here is a particular kind of expression that aspires to utter serenity. His comments conclude with the tongue-in-cheek comparison with Racine – 'Racine and myself were both absolutely heartless people, and cold, cold' – whose implication is that only the apparently heartless have the sympathetic detachment and artistic judgement to do justice to the tragic circumstances of humans who seem sublimely unaware of their vulnerability and mortality. Only the apparently heartless can be true artists, because true artists need to separate themselves from humanity, rather like gods.

Tabulating the similarities and differences between himself and Schoenberg, Stravinsky cited their 'common belief in Divine Authority' (p. 108). Such a belief might give an artist a special sensitivity to human fallibility, and to ways of representing this in non-liturgical works of art. Stephen Walsh's description of the final stages of *Oedipus rex* (1926–7) – 'the atmosphere is one of terror and theatrically real catastrophe, not the commemorative or prophylactic disaster of the Stations of the Cross or the Burial Service'[5] – makes this point brilliantly. It also confirms that the neoclassical Stravinsky could create an atmosphere in which the absence of cool Apollonian serenity is as marked as the absence of a Bergian *crescendo molto*:

Ex. 4.1   Stravinsky, *Svadebka/Les Noces*. From Fig. 133. French text only

a truly tragic dramatic crux, with the terror and sense of catastrophe subject to the laws of lucid ordering. This is in obedience to Apollo's demand, as would be formulated in the *Poetics of Music* lectures (1939–40), that 'for the lucid ordering of the work...all the Dionysian elements which set the imagination of the artist in motion...must be properly subjugated before they intoxicate us, and must finally be made to submit to the law',[6] one element of that law being that 'variety is valid only as a means of attaining similarity' (p. 34). This would appear to rule out modernist multiplicity, and yet Stravinsky's neoclassical compositions indicate very clearly that 'similarity' need not mean stability, in the sense of traditionally classical unity and resolution. Just as polarities remain fundamental to the music, so pathos – the presentation of characters in such a way that we may perceive them as vulnerable and deserving of human sympathy – is never wholly absent.

If Apollo's ascent to Parnassus can inspire feelings similar to those which arise from contemplation of the doomed love of Hippolyte and Aricie or the tragedy of Phèdre, it may not be so eccentric to react to the climax of *The Rake's Progress* (1947–51) with twin sympathies – not only for the anti-heroic Tom Rakewell as he is struck mad and sings a piercingly simple song of innocence and ignorance, but also for the defeated demon Nick Shadow, whose raging yet implacable despair is depicted in music of stark and irresistible power (Ex. 4.2). Who, in an effective performance of this scene, can resist all sense of a hero's unwelcome defeat at this point? But the ambiguity is immense: at his most aggressive and heartless, the devil himself seems to become vulnerable, the stabbing rhythms and dissonant tonal clashes representing authoritativeness and despair with almost Wotan-like intensity, but with very un-Wagnerian brevity.

Such effects are not entirely beyond the world of sacred music, where unrestrained lamentation and exuberant praise can be as valid as gently wor-shipful contemplation of divine beneficence. It is nevertheless this latter quality which most efficiently corresponds to religious ideas of transcendence: a state where nothing of the irreligiously pagan survives. This is the basic distinction that informs Richard Taruskin's reading of *Svadebka*, which 'makes an impression quite unlike the terrifying *Rite*. Whereas the earlier "pagan" ballet was orgias-tic and biological, *Svadebka* is a work of dignity and reserve, finally of religious exaltation (specifically Orthodox, Stravinsky insisted).'[7] No less confidently gen-eralised are Taruskin's declarations that 'what *The Rite* and *Svadebka* have fun-damentally in common is Stravinsky's lifelong antihumanism – his rejection of all "psychology"', and that there is a 'dark side to this celebration of the unques-tioned subjection of human personality to an implacably demanding – and, by Enlightened standards, an unjust – social order' (p. 391). Evidently, what is re-garded as truly 'dark' is not just Stravinsky's complicity in the oppressively unjust social conventions of his chosen subject-matter, but the fact that he regarded the contemporary equivalents of such conventions with approval.

Ex. 4.2   Stravinsky, *The Rake's Progress*, Act 3 Scene 2 from Fig. 201

The critical modulation in this judgement is no less familiar from a certain strand of writing about Wagner, which is concerned to map the composer's attitudes and verbal pronouncements onto his compositions.[8] Stravinsky had fascist sympathies, therefore his compositions reflect his fascist sympathies, and anyone who fails to perceive or accept this is 'reading' those compositions falsely. Yet Taruskin's analysis of *Svadebka* contains the seeds of its own critique, since – despite its aura of thoroughness – it is slanted, concerning itself only with matters which confirm the already-asserted conclusions. Thus, 'the most striking feature of *Svadebka* as a musical composition is its unprecedented reliance on anhemitony, the musical idiom that ... ideally reflected Turanian[9] mentality in its "relative poverty and plainness", its "complete submission to simple schematic rules", and its "schematic clarity and lucidity"' ('Stravinsky and the

Subhuman', p. 425): and Taruskin's analysis is designed to prepare the conclusion
that

> the hidden octatonic background that harmonizes and controls the audible
> diatonic surface is a perfect metaphor for the constraints of immemorial cus-
> tom that invisibly rule the day-to-day subjectively free-flowing currents of life
> in Stravinsky's imagined folk world, harmonizing the thoughts and actions
> of individuals with the transcendent organic community of the composer's
> dreams, just as the long-sought and triumphantly successful final scoring for
> four keyboards and punctuating percussion captures to perfection the nature of
> symphonic society, as something 'perfectly impersonal, perfectly homogeneous,
> and perfectly mechanical'. Together, these symbols of ideally harmonized exis-
> tence lend *Svadebka* both its incomparably compelling aesthetic integrity and
> its ominously compelling political allure. (p. 448)

It is worth questioning the status of that 'allure', since it is difficult to imagine listeners to *Svadebka* being inevitably attracted, *en masse*, by the social circumstances depicted. A more typical (Western) reaction is likely to be a recognition
that this 'society' is stylised, remote, fascinating, primitive. In addition, the tech-
nically minded listener could well find as much of tension on the musical surface
(between competing tonal and harmonic elements, if not between a 'hidden' background and an actual foreground) as the kind of 'complete submission to schematic
rules' that it suits Taruskin to emphasise. Such polarities might appeal more to listeners who find greater tension between the 'orgiastic' and aspects of 'dignity
and reserve' in *Svadebka* than Taruskin does: and as a result those listeners might
doubt whether even a composer who was a 'lifelong antihumanist' was content
with depicting 'the unquestioned subjection of human personality', or whether he
might not have found himself acknowledging, at least to a degree, the poignancy
and uncertainty of the consequences when social constraints and customs impose
themselves on human personalities. Just as the fact that the 'community' as represented on stage accepts the 'ceremonial murder' of the victim in *The Rite of
Spring* 'without remorse' does not mean that everyone hearing or watching the
ballet becomes anxious to restore a social order based on such 'customs', so the
impact of the forces of convention affecting the bride and groom in *Svadebka* is
as likely to prompt doubts and sympathies in audiences as any longing for an
idealised past. For good or ill, present-day listeners to both works will probably
sense the distance between these powerful social rites and the forces governing
their own lives. What is shown as 'perfectly homogeneous' in *Svadebka* is not
a metaphor for an ideal society but an image of spiritual transcendence – an
'eternal truth'. The 'dignity and reserve' embodied in the music suggest a personal
spiritual fulfilment as well as the disciplined functioning of a ritual-dominated
society.

Dithyramb

From as early as the triumphant ending of *The Firebird* (1909–10) – music which in the orchestral suite is called 'Final Hymn' – Stravinsky had associated celebratory apotheosis with repetitive, resolving simplification. Such humanly ful-filling happy endings lose their high romantic bombast when they are transformed into numinous benedictions, solemn and serene, as in *Svadebka*, *Symphonies of Wind Instruments* (1918–20) and *Symphony of Psalms* (1930). As suggested earlier, these apotheoses tend to be the most purely Apollonian moments in Stravinsky. Yet more often than not there is a less than absolute distinction between such sober hymns and the wilder dithyrambic music by means of which, even in such neo-classical works as *Symphony in Three Movements* (1942–5) and *Orpheus* (1947), Dionysus will be invoked.

In her discussion of 'performed inflections', Naomi Cumming argues that

> they must necessarily display singularity – at least to some degree. They are not fully determined by the score... [and] as a result, the problems which attend descriptions of 'nuance' in sound quality remain at issue when a grouping of notes, whether an ornament or other melodic figure, are inflected to become 'gestural'. Even when the pattern being considered is a common one ('appoggiatura', 'changing note', 'emotion-laden turn'), its performance as an inflected 'gesture' cannot be characterized fully by labelling the figural type.[10]

In a footnote, Cumming admits to deriving the label 'emotion-laden turn' from Peter Dennison's lectures on Wagner and Mahler, although the example she herself quotes (without discussing the turn itself in detail) is the opening of the slow movement from Tchaikovsky's Violin Concerto (Ex. 4.3a).

Clearly, composers can influence the nature of descriptive interpretation by specifying a genre with which the figural type itself may be connected. Tchaikovsky does not call his Andante 'song of regret for lost happiness'. Mahler, who uses an 'emotion-laden turn' at the very beginning of the finale of *Das Lied von der Erde* (Ex. 4.3b), has a text to which he gives the overall title 'Der Abschied'. Nevertheless, the turn-figure is not confined to the movement's funeral-march topos, appearing at the start of the contrasting 'song of transcendence' as well (Ex. 4.3c), and serving to reinforce the contextual multivalence of the figure's expressive connotations.

Such melodic patterns can be identified in music of all periods, in all styles, although their relation to a particular harmonic context will vary ac-cording to voice-leading conventions. For example, when Stravinsky begins the finale, called 'Dithyrambe', of his *Duo concertant* for violin and piano (1932) with the turn, the assumption that the second and fourth pitches are dissonant upper and lower neighbours to the principal tone is called into question by the sus-taining of the lower note, D, in the piano chord (Ex. 4.4a, p. 65). This is Stravinskian extended tonality in action, with notions of convergence and divergence, and of an

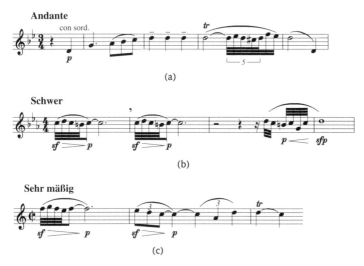

Ex. 4.3 (a) Tchaikovsky, Violin Concerto, Andante
(b) Mahler, *Das Lied von der Erde*, 'Der Abschied', beginning
(c) Mahler, *Das Lied von der Erde*, 'Der Abschied', 2 bars after Fig.7

'emancipated' dissonance in which 'higher consonances' are the norm, replacing the time-honoured principles of diatonic voice-leading (Stravinsky, *Poetics of Music*, pp. 36–8).

The centre around which the contrapuntal lines converge and diverge is C, and there are associations with several of Stravinsky's earlier neoclassical slow movements. The turn figure is prominent in the first phrase of the Wind Octet's 'Tema con Variazioni' (1923), where it has a 'baroque' formality worlds away from the initially restrained pathos of Tchaikovsky or Mahler. But the opening of 'Aria II' from the Violin Concerto (1930) is a more obvious textural and expressive precedent, and it is likely that the concerto's appropriation of 'classical' (baroque) generic prototypes – toccata, aria, capriccio – prompted the *Duo concertant*'s succession of 'Cantilène', 'Eglogue' (I and II, like the concerto's pair of arias), Gigue, and 'Dithyrambe'. Here, however, the 'classical' evocations are divided between the musical (cantilena, gigue) and the poetic, the latter explicitly ancient Greek. An eclogue is a short pastoral poem, and, in obvious contrast, as noted in Chapter 3, a dithyramb is 'an ancient Greek choric hymn, vehement and wild in character'.

Given this definition, a Stravinskian dithyramb might be expected to embody the very apotheosis of the Dionysian, perhaps after the manner of *The Rite of Spring*'s 'Danse sacrale', which is certainly 'vehement and wild in character'. Even there, however, the prominence given to repeated patterning can be felt to act as a constraint on total Dionysian abandonment, and such constraint is more prominent still in the later depiction of violence in the 'Pas d'action' from *Orpheus*, where, according to the score, 'the Bacchantes attack Orpheus, seize him and tear him to pieces'. At the height of his neoclassical phase, Stravinsky seemed to attach more importance to the dithyramb's generic role as a hymn, and a path can be traced from the 'Hymne' which begins the *Serenade in A* (1926) and the choral 'imploration' at the start of *Oedipus rex* to the *Duo*'s finale. Thus, although the *Duo*'s 'Dithyrambe' does not reproduce the opera-oratorio's initial 'gesture of panic and despair',[11] a quality of chant-like supplication is preserved.

No less pertinent here is Walsh's diagnosis of Stravinskian intent: 'Clearly Stravinsky wanted us to understand his characters partly as refugees from the Verdian stage, whose masks conceal, not the cold immobile beauty of Greek statues, but grimaces which we, when we go to the opera, accept as the outward sign of an emotion too great to be borne in silence. In other words, it is the simple directness and sheer force of operatic feeling which Stravinsky wanted to suggest as attributes of these statuesque victims of the most horrendous moral torments yet devised by speculative man' (p. 49). Balancing the statuesque and the tormented, by means of 'formalised barbarity' (p. 65): the achievement of *Oedipus* is evidently not reproduced in the *Duo*'s 'Dithyrambe'. But it is evoked, and the connection between allusion to a Verdian 'Lacrimosa' and an ancient Greek 'imploration', suggested by Walsh, helps to define the gestural context of the movement's celebration of the 'emotion-laden turn' as the focus for instability in emotional as well as structural terms: and, once conceived in this way, this music is difficult to dissociate from those 'self-regarding' arabesques (p. 41) which – initially, at least – embody the voice of Oedipus himself.

The hymn-like form of the 'Dithyrambe' in the *Duo concertant* is suggested by its strophic basis – four sections whose parallel durations are best described in terms of semiquaver beats: A has 23, A^1 62, A^2 32, A^3 33 (plus final pause). This schema immediately highlights the exceptionally extended second strophe, the most developmental section, in which the violin gradually ascends to an exultant high C, and the harmonic context is predominantly major mode. Stravinsky's notation of this strophe as a single bar, after the initial overlapping connection with Strophe 1, underlines the character of lyrical freedom, intensified rather than offset by the co-ordinated contrapuntal intricacy of the violin and piano in combination. A subtle, multivalent periodicity results from the way in which the violin's returns to E and C, with C eventually transferred into higher registers, interact with a bass line whose reversions to C are especially decisive, even though both E and G are also emphasised. But the sense of expressive liberation in this strophe is only possible because it both develops and reacts against the material and character of Strophe 1. Here – simple in outline – there is a decorated, stepwise descent in the violin from Eb to A (this last note displaced to a lower octave). Combined with this are two contrapuntal lines in the piano, filled out with some doubling, mainly in thirds: the right hand's octave descent, G to G, and the left hand's arch shape – C, D, Eb, D, C (also with some octave displacement). Despite the emancipated dissonance, the material is diatonic to C (minor),

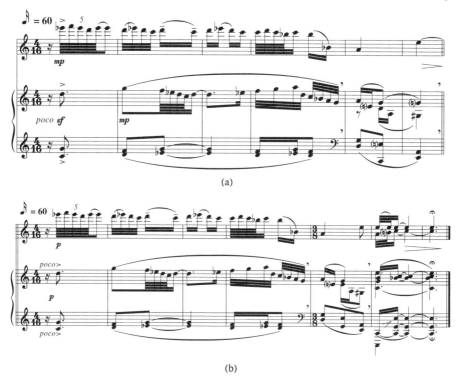

Ex. 4.4   Stravinsky, *Duo concertant*, 'Dithyrambe'
          (a) bars 1–6
          (b) bars 17–23

at least until the cadence in bars 5 and 6 counters tendencies to convergence by a modal shift (E♭ to E♮) and a strongly dissonant clash (G♯/G♮) (Ex. 4.4a). When this intensification recurs in Strophe 4, it is resolved onto the relatively stable chord of C major with added minor seventh (Ex. 4.4b), a sonority that recalls the finale of the *Symphony of Psalms* – though there it is too unstable to serve as the last word, and is displaced by the pure C/E consonance.

Here and now, there and then

> The main obstacle to appreciation on my part is a barrier of taste created by what seems to me like a mixture of gamelans, Lehár, and some quite superior film music…Nor is it easy to imagine music more inane than the 'Joie du Sang des Etoiles', or more vapid than the melody, in 'Chant d'Amour II', for Ondes Martenot, which instrument provides the musical equivalent of a colonic irrigation.[12]

Stravinsky's comments on Messiaen's *Turangalîla-symphonie* (1946–8) show little fellow feeling for a composer whose belief in 'Divine Authority' was no less profound, but whose way of representing that belief in music differed radically.

Paul Griffiths has described Messiaen as 'a musician apart', and 'alone...among major twentieth century composers in his joyously held Catholic faith, which was unswerving, however much he came to value non-European cultures'.[13] What marked Messiaen out as special was not so much that 'joyously held' faith, but his commitment to 'a theology of glory' (p. 495). As Griffiths also points out, Messiaen shunned the kind of depictions of Christ's passion and crucifixion which so many modern religious composers have used as a means of linking the spiritual to the human. Yet Messiaen was no more interested in stressing the human aspect of Christ than he was in contributing music for the enactments of the liturgy, for which he regarded plainsong as 'the only proper music'.

Something of a paradox ensues, since Messaien managed to remain faithful to the concern of the 'Jeune France' group, to which he belonged as a young musician, 'to reemphasize passion and sensuality in music' (p. 492), and to do this by way of generic associations rooted in song and dance which normally sought out varieties of ecstasy and only very rarely engaged with the favoured twentieth-century genre of lament, or with any compensating Apollonian serenity. Even when expressing 'warm, sweet stillness' (p. 498), as in 'Le baiser de l'Enfant Jésus' (from *20 Regards sur l'Enfant Jésus*, 1944), Messiaen is too fervent to be truly serene, and, as Griffiths comments, moments of bleakness and menace are rare – he instances the representation of the owl in 'La chouette hulotte' (*Catalogue d'oiseaux*, No. 5, 1956–8) and Scene 7 ('The Stigmata') of the opera *Saint François d'Assise* (1975–83) (p. 492). The fervour is vital, as the best way of ensuring a sense of humanity in music so obsessed with the divine and the beyond, and with timeless ritual rather than evolving narrative. Yet Griffiths's claim that 'instead of affirming the orderly flow of everyday existence, this is music which acknowledges only two essences: the instantaneous and the eternal' (p. 496) risks losing the interaction of those other essences, the sensuous and the spiritual, a polarity which helps to give Messiaen's music its paradoxical character – modernist in structure but singularly antimodernist in atmosphere.

This paradox is reinforced by another polarity, between those works from the composer's earlier and later periods which preserve the consonance–dissonance distinction, and those from the late 1940s to mid-1960s which avoid traditional triadic harmony. This polarity is far from absolute: for example, in *Quatuor pour la fin du Temps* (1940–1) the music's harmonic character ranges from the suspended tonality of the opening 'Liturgie de cristal' to the chromatic but unambiguous major tonality of the finale, 'Louange à l'Immortalité de Jésus', which derives from an organ work composed ten years before.[14] Both types of music are vintage Messiaen in their singular focus on images associated with the score's dedication to 'the angel of the apocalypse, who raises a hand towards the heavens, saying "there shall be no more time"'. What this suggests, in practical musical terms, is the use of time – and sound – as a means of invoking a transcendent state of devotion, or spiritual rapture, and Messiaen's means of achieving this in these two movements are complementary: while 'Liturgie de cristal' shuns strongly accented, regular rhythmic patterns, 'Louange á l'Immortalité de Jésus' involves a contrast between the unchanging rhythmic tolling of the piano part and the more flexible though far from 'free' rhythmic patterns of the violin.

The *Quatuor*'s first movement might seem a classic case of modernist superimposition, the four instrumental voices exploring their different materials in rapt oblivion of the effects of combination. The composer's commentary invokes a time 'between 3 and 4 in the morning: a solo blackbird or nightingale improvises, surrounded by a shimmer of sound [poussières sonores], by a halo of trills lost very high in the trees. Transpose this onto a religious plane and you have the harmonious silence of heaven.' Leaving aside the theological mystery of how silence can be harmonious, it is clear that Messiaen's vision involves perception of the natural world as a sounding manifestation of the (silent, timeless) supranatural. With the avoidance of regular rhythmic patterns (replaced by 'rhythmic pedals' – fixed cycles of durations – in cello and piano) comes the parallel avoidance of traditional harmonic gravitation: in Schoenbergian terms the B♭ major tonality indicated by the key signature is suspended by the rejection of functional diatonic progressions or contrapuntal combinations, although a degree of orientation is provided by the tonic triad initially outlined by the clarinet, whose fifth then becomes the lowest note for the first twelve piano chords. Even on their own, the piano chords are evidently too dense (clouded, shimmering) to enable their triadic, tonal components to become prominent, or to convey any sense of a polarity between bass line and melody. The larger-scale linear motions away from and back to F in the lowest voice have enough consistently stepwise movement to suggest a degree of directional logic, relative to a highly inflected dominant chord: but this very consistency highlights the independence of the other textural strata, while the periodic returns of clarinet and violin to birdsong motives, giving some emphasis to B♭ major elements, hint at the kind of conjunctions which would be available if the structure of the movement were not designed to minimise their significance.

By not ending the *Quatuor* with music matching the first movement's atmosphere and technique, Messiaen confirmed his concern to represent the work's apocalyptic imagery with more insistently regular rhythms and less potentially atonal textures: to give the music a human voice. The 'hommage' of the last movement's title can only be that of humanity, and Messiaen describes the music's 'slow ascent towards the extreme high register' as 'the ascent of man towards his God' as well as 'of the Child of God towards his Father, of the deified Being towards Paradise'. The piano part begins, as in 'Liturgie de cristal', with a chord on the dominant note of the movement's tonality. This time the E major tonality is extended rather than suspended: and although there is no literal, root-position tonic chord

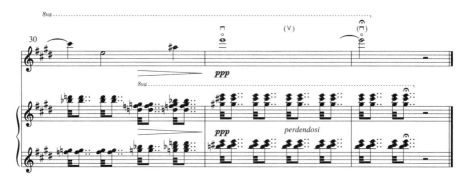

Ex. 4.5   Messiaen, *Quatuor pour la fin du Temps*, 'Louange à l'Immortalité de Jésus', ending

in E major, or a conventionally voiced cadential progression in that key, degrees of distinction between consonance and dissonance are maintained. The overridingly 'tender, ecstatic' atmosphere is seriously threatened only in bar 12, near the end of the first of the movement's two sections, where the harmony is most distant from the tonic, and the violin–piano relation is most dissonant. The equivalent point in the second, concluding section (bar 28) is therefore the moment of climactic, consonant, tonic-chord resolution, after which the music extends and enriches that resolution with a further ascent and an inexorable dying away (Ex. 4.5).

Anthony Pople finds Messiaen's 'obsession with the eternal' to be 'profoundly subversive in the context of the Western humanist tradition'.[15] Yet the associations his music sets up with other less theologically minded representatives of that tradition provide a rich source of ambiguity. Wilfrid Mellers homes in on a fundamental paradox in writing of the last movement of the *Quatuor* as effecting 'a miracle, in that the music, moving in time as all music must, seems to obliterate it'. Yet at the same time there is a distinctly corporeal quality to an ending in which the added sixth chord is prominent: 'that this (Debussian) chord became a cliché of cocktail lounge jazz may hint at how eroticism may, at several levels, be a gateway to paradise!'[16] Most writers who avoid associating themselves directly with Stravinsky's withering critique of *Turangalîla* will argue that Messiaen transcends the mundane, the corporeal, the 'kitschy', through his intense, if naive, sincerity: and at least one commentator, Richard Steinitz, has proposed an association with 'those nature-worshipping German Romantics' of the early nineteenth century 'who strove for a new synthesis of art, religion and the whole of creation'.[17] Steinitz nevertheless makes a distinction between the romantic apprehension of nature as sublime, which enhances the sense of human inadequacy and isolation, and the kind of 'escape from the "self" to espouse the whole of creation', which, in his view, deprives the expansive sonic canvases of *Des canyons aux étoiles* (1970–4) of any human presence: 'a narrative of human drama would have interfered distractingly in this theocentric song of praise' (p. 483), and any hope that

> the wandering, nineteenth-century American pioneers, the Mormons... had been assigned parts in *Des canyons* as care-laden pilgrims, who could have trudged through the pages of the score like Childe Harold through Berlioz's Italian landscape, or crossed over the river of death, like Mr Valiant-for-Truth, to be greeted by a hard-won A major as 'all the trumpets sounded for him on the other side', are doomed to disappointment. (p. 483)

Steinitz therefore prefers the 'Cedar Breaks' movement, where Messiaen 'comes closest to discovering in nature a wild anarchy, an Ivesian unity in diversity' (p. 479), to the rather too 'orderly and inevitable' effects which obtain elsewhere (p. 474).

One could argue against Steinitz that there is as strong a sense of the 'drama' of human feelings about nature in *Des canyons aux étoiles* as there is in Strauss's *Eine Alpensinfonie*: in both, what is heard is the result of the human observation of, and presence in, a particular landscape. In Messiaen's case, unlike Strauss's, that human presence is not 'acting', as part of any sequence of events more elaborate or narratable than standing still in awe-struck astonishment. But it will not do to propose an extreme absence of human presence in Messiaen, or to claim that *Saint François d'Assise* is devoid of all dramatic, human characterisation. That characterisation may be limited, restricted to demonstrating that all, saints and sinners alike, are immediately or ultimately possessed by a Messiaen-like faith: but restriction rather than absence is the issue.

Messiaen's middle-period works favour the density and aperiodicity of the *Quatuor*'s first movement over the ecstatic lyricism and relatively traditional phrase structuring of its finale: generically, they favour the mosaic over the narrative. With *Couleurs de la Cité Céleste* (1963) there is also a concentration on more abrasive, less 'shimmering' tone colours, so that the vision of the apocalypse is more dazzling, and arguably truer to the composer's synaesthetic aspirations for music, than before. As befits the music's more radical technical qualities, associations between its sections and generic archetypes evoking song and dance are far less apparent than in the *Quatuor*, even though some of the faster passages based on the regular durational successions of chant do suggest a celebratory, dance-like measure. Spiritual ecstasy is still symbolised through a polyphonic superimposition of natural spontaneity (birdsong) and human devotion (plainchant), but the mosaic modernity of Messiaen's thinking at this time leads to an ending in which these distinct representations of praise are starkly juxtaposed, the birdsong in a piano cadenza and the plainsong in a short hymn-like strophe for brass and percussion whose chordal construction recalls the densely non-functional sonorities of 'Liturgie de cristal'. In *Couleurs*, however, there is granitic rhythmic regularity, the object being to capture a sonic resonance emanating from the chant phrases ('Alleluia du Saint-Sacrement') placed at the top of the texture. But the main effect of this dazzling, multi-chromatic resonance is to neutralise the modal centredness of the chant, the clash between modality and dissonant, atonal harmony suggesting an irresolvable tension between the composer's human awareness of the contemporary nature of his musical language and his continued desire to deal with theological verities in appropriate musical fashion.

In his respect for national traditions culminating in Debussy, his interests in the Orient, and his rejection of much that was most fundamental in Austro-German music, Messiaen is nothing if not French. Yet that is not to say that the sense of place — in particular, of the Paris where he lived and worked for so long, or the various other locations to which his music can be linked — is ever more than a means to a rather different end, the focus on a very different 'place'. As Paul Griffiths says of the last large-scale orchestral work, *Eclairs sur l'Au-Delà...* (1988–92), the music

> arrives at its destination in heaven — though this is not properly an arrival when heaven has already been glimpsed so much along the way, and when the music's time has always been the eternal time of repetition, reversal and endless protraction rather than the earthly time of progress, pulse and development.[18]

It is this virtual elimination of an earthly perspective on the vision of heaven which makes Messiaen in his time so unusual. The sacred music of the minimalists aside, the spirit of the later twentieth century seems more appropriately represented in a range of compositions which bring sacred and secular, temporal and eternal, into confrontation, and in which the representation of the spiritual might well aim to point up the problems of earthly intolerance, and the other inadequacies which can be identified in the way religions respond to earthly life. In Britten's *War Requiem* (1961) and Penderecki's opera *The Devils of Loudon* (1968–9) the limitations of religions and their rituals are given particular point. It may be less clear whether the value of religion, spirituality, belief in the the existence of God and Heaven, are themselves being called into question in such works. But there remains a fundamental difference between composers whose scepticism and doubt do much to shape their creative works and those whose certainty and confident beliefs carry all before them.

Among composers affirming the fundamental significance of spirituality in music, none since 1950 has been more ambitious and dedicated than Karlheinz Stockhausen, whose seven-opera cycle *Licht*, begun in 1977 and finished in 2002, is 'a cosmic drama, a sacred ritual that speaks of the destinies of mankind, the earth and the universe'. As Robert Worby has pointed out,

> the operas that constitute *Light* are not so much vehicles for the musical settings of text, where a libretto unfolds to tell a story, but rather they are a mechanism for integrating the elements of opera – music, text, set, costume, lighting, props, dance, acting, etc. – in new ways. Each opera does tell a story with characters interacting dramatically and musically, and the operas fit together to form a chronicle of Biblical magnitude, but music, rather than textual narrative, is the primary structural force.[19]

This is evidently a radical enterprise, and performances of single operas, or extracts from them, have evoked mixed reactions. There have been doubts about the quality of the music as well as about a dramatic concept in which the general and the particular seem to confront each other so awkwardly. Given the scale of the enterprise, it is perhaps not surprising that Stockhausen should have composed these works for a team of principal performers who are family members and acolytes, or that his own contribution, as the supreme controller of sound projection, should have been as crucial in actual performance as in creation. Are performances of *Licht* without the composer and his close family conceivable? Only with time will it become clear whether *Licht* can establish itself with other performers, and with reasonably regular presentations. But even if it does, it will remain a work very personal to Stockhausen, a work which draws on Stockhausen's own life story as well as on transcendental texts, including the Bible and the Urantia book. Its sheer size and comprehensiveness mean that *Licht* is likely to remain an extreme example of a late modernist attempt to transcend the worldly, the earthly. But, as with Messiaen's visions, and the no less intensely spiritual works of composers as different as Alfred Schnittke, Jonathan Harvey and James MacMillan, musical perceptions of the beyond and the eternal can only be placed in the world by earthly means, using human performers and humanly controlled technology. Whether these earthly aspects are indeed transcended, or remain the most appealing feature of the artistic experience, is something for the individual listener to decide.

5   Overlapping opposites: Schoenberg observed

Character

> Because of the many attempts to connect the past with the future one might be inclined to call this an Apollonian period. But the fury with which addicts of various schools fight for their theories presents rather a Dionysian aspect.[1]

Whether or not Schoenberg's allusion to one of this book's *Leitmotive* reveals a calculated avoidance of the Nietzschean aspects so openly taken up by Stravinsky, he normally steers clear of imputing these attractively elusive qualities to specific compositions. Rather, he adopts the apparent detachment of a cultural observer, an exile alienated as much by the tensions within his own creative personality as by the upheavals which world events have imposed on him.

Adorno provides a useful encapsulation of those tensions, claiming that 'while inflicting the most deadly blows on authority through his work, he seeks to defend the work as though before a hidden authority, and ultimately to make it itself the authority'.[2] Musicological commentators on Schoenberg seeking to demonstrate their own authority have often invoked another usefully ubiquitous continuum − tradition/innovation: and this context has also been cited by Schoenberg's composer-pupils. Thus, for Roberto Gerhard, 'Schoenberg's sense of belonging to a tradition and of working in the main stream of that tradition is alive in every phase of his evolution, even at his most boldly innovating.'[3] Gerhard did not conceal his awareness of the challenge Schoenberg the man presented even to those close to him: 'as a personality there was something truly formidable, almost unapproachable about Schoenberg. ...Even in repose, the burning eyes in that ascetic face and the faint expression of disdain in the peculiar shape of his mouth had an extraordinary power of intimidation.' Gerhard was, we now know, even more outspoken about Schoenberg, as both man and composer, in other jottings,[4] and several of the commentators discussed below connect that 'extraordinary power of intimidation' with a more far-reaching authoritarianism. But the point about Schoenberg's relationship to 'tradition', deriving from his own comment (1931) that 'I venture to credit myself with having written truly new music which, being based on tradition, is destined to become tradition',[5] has always been a gift to writers eager to balance talk of the music's difficulty with emollient claims about its comprehensibility. An essay I wrote to mark the centenary of the composer's birth in 1974 had the resounding title 'Schoenberg and the "True Tradition": Theme and

Form in the String Trio',[6] the quoted phrase coming from Stravinsky's encomium for those

> perfect works, the *Five Pieces for Orchestra*, *Herzgewächse*, *Pierrot*, the *Serenade*, the *Variations* for orchestra, and, for its orchestra, the *Seraphita* song from op. 22. By these works Schoenberg is among the great composers. Musicians will take their bearings from them for a great while to come. They constitute together with a few works of not so many other composers, the true tradition.[7]

Thus spake Stravinsky, the convert to twelve-note atonality who evidently preferred Schoenberg's 'freely' atonal compositions to his twelve-note ones. But by the 1970s it was becoming clear that the bearings taken by contemporary composers were altogether more complex and diverse than allowed for in Stravinsky's predictions for the future (other aspects of which are considered in Chapter 4 above). Hans Keller, who had declared at the time of Schoenberg's death in 1951 that 'he was born too early. It was really his premature birth which the newspaper obituaries, unintentionally, mourned',[8] used the platform of a centenary concert series programme-book, twenty-two years later, to elaborate this theme, and to proclaim a pessimistic conclusion: 'Schoenberg couldn't have chosen a worse moment for coming too soon: the break-up of the general musical language would have caused chaos in any case, but since it came too soon, it caused something worse than chaos, i.e. pseudo-communication': and Keller lambasted a contemporary situation in which music,

> from being an act of precise communication...descended to the level of mere stimulation...Schoenberg thus emerges as musical history's most tragic figure – its most uncompromising clarifier and its leading confuser at the same time...The current crisis of communication is not merely, not even chiefly, produced by one musical language having split into several. The one language has also, over a considerable part of the contemporary scene, evaporated into none.[9]

By present-day musicological standards, Keller appears far more concerned with the technical than the cultural interpretation of the situation he defines. Yet he also lacked the tools for considering the kind of relations between voice-leading concepts and Schoenberg's post-tonal counterpoint which later theorists have employed as a means of balancing out aspects of 'old' and 'new' in Schoenberg's music after 1908. As Milton Babbitt shrewdly perceived, in a characteristically convoluted sentence, Keller's

> coupling of Réti and Schenker in his writings strengthened the sense of one-sidedness, for – at most – the Schenker he appeared to know and value was the Schenker of 'diminutions' at foreground level or of context-free communalities rather than the richer Schenker which Hans should have savoured as often

revealing the more embracing, singular bases of structured musical individu-
ation through parallelism of processes at a subsuming succession of temporal
and structural levels.[10]

Keller's analytical practice, concerned with the unity of contrasting themes rather
than with the composing-out of fundamental harmonic-contrapuntal structures,
nevertheless provided some indications of how this kind of 'premature' music could
communicate, if not in the same way as tonal music, then in a manner which made
the symbiosis of difference and similarity between the genres and procedures of
post-tonal and tonal composition aurally explicit. So, despite the fact that most
more recent commentators on Schoenberg have avoided engaging directly with
Keller's fierce and seemingly implacable rhetoric, and have explored a variety
of historical and philosophical frameworks, they have found themselves working
within the framework of the kind of old/new dialectics to which even Keller was
ultimately beholden.[11]

Models

Schoenberg's String Trio Op. 45 (1946) is among the works cited in Keller's
guidelines for symphonic composition:[12] 'inspired composers' are commended to
explore

> the symphonic implications emerging from the use of two home keys, not by
> way of progressive tonality, but within a concentric tonal framework: there is
> no end to the variety in which structural functions can be split and made to
> interpenetrate each other, so long as they remain well defined. Outside tonality,
> the Fourth Quartet and the String Trio are Schoenberg's supreme achievements
> in this dimension. (p. 190)

This passage refers by implication to Keller's earlier discussion of Schoenberg's
invention of 'the most violent harmonic contrast imaginable for symphonic purposes — that between atonality and tonality' in the Second Quartet. Keller also
detected 'shades' of this in the Fourth Quartet

> with its suppressed D minor — and if a mere observer may, for once, allow
> himself a positive forecast, however tentative, there are symphonic possibili-
> ties here which have hardly yet been exploited, though a clear indication of
> Schoenberg's awareness of them is given by the String Trio's repeated A minor
> [*sic*] passage, sufficiently stressed to include the dominant leading note, and by
> its harmonic context. (p. 186)

What Keller meant by this is clarified in an earlier article, 'Principles of
Composition' (1960),[13] where he wrote of the Trio's

> recapitulated A major passage, a tonal eruption which is all the more decisive
> for Schoenberg's use of a note (D♯) that isn't tonal to the key. He would not

be Schoenberg if he did not imply extensive functional harmony within this compressed space. The D♮ assumes the significance of a leading-note to the dominant and thus confirms the tonic *qua* tonic, placing the passage (as Tovey would have said) not merely 'on' the key, but 'in' it. Why, then, don't the *avant-couriers* who praise the piece as one of Schoenberg's greatest…take note of this outbreak of tonality…? Is it possible that they don't hear the key, just because it is not driven home by way of a cadence *à la Ode to Napoleon*? Or are they vicariously ashamed of it? Or is it simply that they feel how profoundly the tonal passage fits into the atonal context, but cannot see why?

Keller then admits (disarmingly, for him) that he can't see why it fits either. What he can say is 'not merely that the phrase could only be Schoenberg but – at the risk of seeming to beg the question – that it is characteristic of this particular work. Further we cannot go for the time being, for the serial "sense" of the passage is a symptom of its fitness, not a cause' (Keller, 'Principles', pp. 216–17).

This passage, bars 233–7, is included in Ex. 5.1, and will be discussed in context shortly. As for going further, several later commentators on Schoenberg have moved beyond Keller's tonal/serial, opposition/integration structuralism to consider the music hermeneutically, and to explore matters of modelling. This transforms Keller's background/foreground trope (according to Christopher Wintle, Keller believed that 'Schoenberg's twelve-tone foregrounds were composed against…a background of well-defined, well-implied, but violently suppressed…tonal expectations'[14]) from its context of the engagement between form and perception into wider regions of meaning and expression. Among the contributors to this transformation process considered here are Martha Hyde, Joseph Auner and Michael Cherlin.

During an account of Schoenberg's Third String Quartet, Keller describes the opening ostinato as starting 'before the beginning, with an accompaniment to nothing', and notes that other composers to have done this included Haydn 'in his "Bird" Quartet, Mozart in "the" G minor Symphony, Beethoven in the Ninth, Schubert in his A minor Quartet, Mendelssohn in his Violin Concerto – and, of course, Bruckner in all his symphonies' (Keller, 'Schoenberg', p. 187). Martha Hyde sees the Schubert connection as all-embracing: 'so integral to Op. 30 that to dismiss it as an ornament for initiates is to ignore an intense and far from comfortable dialogue with the past that accounts for much of the later work's structure and should deepen anyone's appreciation of its achievement'. Hyde generalises this 'intense and far from comfortable dialogue with the past' into a concept of 'dialectical imitation', a 'kind of critical exchange' creating 'a contest that is neither free of ambiguity nor easily resolved'.[15]

Hyde's analysis, like Keller's, is more structural than hermeneutic, dealing with such aspects as the way in which the 'seven-note tonal segment of Schoenberg's principal row [the last seven notes comprise an A harmonic-minor

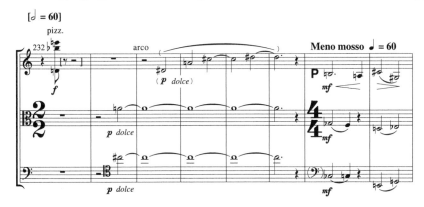

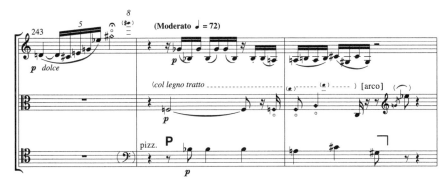

Ex. 5.1   Schoenberg, String Trio, bars 232–45

scale] is ordered so as to allude *simultaneously* to all three of Schubert's themes [in the first movement]' (p. 227). For Hyde, these imitative strategies are dialectical because 'Schoenberg's twelve-tone method both challenges and is challenged by Schubert's tonality' (p. 230). The result is an 'uneasy or aggressive relationship' between the two works, and Hyde argues further that 'Schoenberg's anxiety was to connect his own ample creative space to the German classical tradition', for by replacing Schubertian tonal symmetry with twelve-tone inversional symmetry he 'misreads and marginalises the features that generated Schubert's form' (p. 232).

One need not entirely go along with this contextual aspect of Hyde's interpretation to find the specifics of her analysis persuasive – and they might have been even more so had she discussed all four movements of Op. 30, not just the first. Especially skilful is the way she explains Schoenberg's departure from Schubertian modelling in the movement's coda, so that

> the new piece invokes the old and conjures it to speak of the coming into being and the affiliations of the new. Out of this dialectical imitation, this not wholly fictive dialogue, Schoenberg's twelve-tone sonata locates itself in the German tradition, which is made to anticipate and authorize his development of that tradition. The coda makes clear how enabling the dialogue has been. Schoenberg's imitation of Schubert does not lead backward into deepening engagement with a past classic. It leads forward into a new territory and asks its audience to follow. (p. 235)

Just how many members of that audience will actually be able to appreciate the Schubert/Schoenberg dialogue on the level Hyde describes it must be open to question. But there are other works from this period which confront tonal materials more directly: I will comment on two, the last of the Op. 35 pieces for male chorus, 'Verbundenheit' (April 1929), and the Concerto for String Quartet and Orchestra, after Handel's Op. 6 No. 7 (March–April 1933). Both are discussed in important studies by Joseph Auner.[16]

Schoenberg's references to matters Apollonian were noted briefly at the beginning of this chapter, and despite his cryptic reference to the Suite Op. 29, it is evident that 'cold' Apollonian serenity, of the kind found in Stravinsky's ballet *Apollo* (1928), was not something to which he had easy access. Yet there is another aspect of the term, which Bryan Simms relies on when arguing that 'the presence of extensive sketches' for *Die glückliche Hand* (1910–13) 'suggests a decidedly Apollonian approach to creativity – methodical, reflective, and filled with second thoughts': and although the greater degree of discipline required by adherence to twelve-note technique promoted this 'new Apollonian conception of music', the complementary, disruptive spirit of Dionysus – that 'fury' of which Schoenberg wrote in this chapter's epigraph – was never very far away.[17]

Schoenberg's concern with the social function of art and the possibility of achieving a workable synthesis between tonal and post-tonal elements was strong during his Berlin years, something apparent in 'Verbundenheit', one of the most reflective and restrained of all his works. As Auner comments,

> the use of tonality in the context of this set of pieces, as well as the particular form it takes in this movement, can be explained in terms of Schoenberg

reaffirming a bond between his music and the tonal tradition, while at the same time using familiar means to educate performers and listeners about the essentials of his compositional language. As with the textual clichés that are made newly meaningful, 'Verbundenheit' demonstrates how the familiar materials of tonal music can be rethought and renewed through contact with his serial technique.   (Auner, 'Op. 35', pp. 112–13)

Auner shows how these contacts are achieved by way of analogies with twelve-note procedures, even though 'Verbundenheit' does not literally fuse the tonal and the twelve-note. When it comes to the 'Handel Concerto', however, Auner sees the relationship between past and present, old and new, as more problematic. His argument is that this work 'ends with something like an admission that despite Schoenberg's best efforts to forge "an entirely new structure", only the ruins of the past remain' (Auner, 'Concerto', p. 313). As a result of Schoenberg's failure to remake Handel 'in his own image, the String Quartet Concerto offers evidence of how problematic and contested Schoenberg's own identity had become' (p. 296): and Auner reinforces this bleak conclusion by citing Adorno's judgement that Schoenberg's later works 'begin to acquire the character of the fragment', giving 'a fragmentary impression, not merely in their brevity but in their shrivelled diction'.[18]

Schoenberg's thinking about the role his own identity might play in a purely instrumental work returns us to the Third Quartet, and an aspect of its interpretation – mentioned in Chapter 3 above – which Martha Hyde does not consider. Schoenberg probably introduced the reference to the 'fairy-tale, *Das Gespensterschiff* (*The Ghostship*), whose captain had been nailed through the head to the topmast by his rebellious crew' in his note on the quartet to highlight his declaration that 'being only an illustration of the emotional background of this movement, it will not furnish enlightenment of the structure'.[19] But, as Michael Cherlin perceives, this strategy of underlining non-conformity between 'emotional background' and 'structure' reflects the characteristic, and contra-Apollonian, Schoenbergian attitude that 'conflict is central to the creative process itself. "Systems" that replace the conflict between expectation and surprise with "method" undercut the very source of wonder that they attempt to capture.'[20]

In deeming Schoenberg 'a latter day Heraclitan', whose 'post-tonal language brings unresolved opposition or conflict to the forefront of the musical language', Cherlin prepares the conclusion that 'if we are to hear the work of Schoenberg, or any significant composer for that matter, in terms of a tradition – and how else shall we hear him well? – then we need to recognize the positive role played by opposition'. Cherlin's analysis of the String Trio[21] certainly goes some way to identifying not simply how things fit together (Keller's prime concern), but how contrasts persist: and, although Cherlin cites Keller's discussion of the 'A major' fragment (bars 233–7), his own account of the music's 'evocations of tonality' is more inclined to elaborate Silvina Milstein's study of 'the tonal implications of a number of passages where G and D initiate or terminate tonal motions'.[22] The purpose of these evocations of tonality, Cherlin argues, is to 'imply and then deny closure', and 'Schoenberg uses phrase structures towards similar rhetorical ends' (Cherlin, 'Trio', p. 589). In broad terms, Cherlin regards the Trio's use of 'extreme contrasts and even apparent non sequiturs' as evidence that 'the work seems alternately to remember and then abandon the musical languages of its antecedents; these "memorial" aspects include form, phrase design, evocations of tonality, associations with the music of Beethoven, and the centrality of an emergent "waltz strand"' (p. 602). This acknowledgement of background, or context, as plural, and perceptibly so, helps to advance our understanding of Schoenberg's relation to modernist aesthetics and modernist compositional techniques. But Cherlin's own analytical practice is equivocal in seeking closure at the expense of 'unresolved opposition', not least when he writes of the 'evocations of waltz figuration' as something which 'cuts across the boundaries of the principal sections, binding them together as a unified whole' (p. 591). There is certainly more to be said about the 'plural coherence' of the Trio, especially in the context of other late works whose religious content requires that memory, and history (both Austro-German and Jewish), be confronted in a rather more worldly way.

Meanings

In his actual practice Schoenberg never committed himself fully to the idea of the totality of relationships, of panthematic composition. From his Opus 10 on his entire production oscillated between the extremes of the totally thematic and the athematic... [T]he String Trio leans... towards the athematic, at least in its rhythmic articulation: coherent or even comprehensible themes are scarcely attempted. Schoenberg's conception of a fully constructed totality overlaps with the opposing impulse. He rebels against the principle which he himself established, perhaps just because it is established, and he longs simply to let himself go.[23]

One way in which to rationalise the musical experience of the Trio's developmental recapitulation (Part 3) is as motion within a continuum ranging from extreme turbulence to relative tranquillity. This is not a process generated from an unbroken 'background': apart from reinforcing those textural disruptions characteristic of the work's earlier stages, it presents a dialogue between opposing tendencies which gradually shifts its emphasis from one extreme (turbulence) to the other (relative tranquillity). This dialogue has several different aesthetic and generic aspects: for example, while the more turbulent material is unambiguously

Ex. 5.2 Schoenberg, String Trio
(a) bars 248–50
(b) bars 263–6

instrumental in character, the more tranquil material has certain vocal qualities. And while both types of material display dance-like associations (see especially the contrast between a relatively energetic phrase (bars 248–50) and a more gentle one (bars 263–6), Ex. 5.2), I would complement Cherlin's 'emergent "waltz" strand' with a wider range of generic allusions and associations. Basically, I would

Part 3

(a)

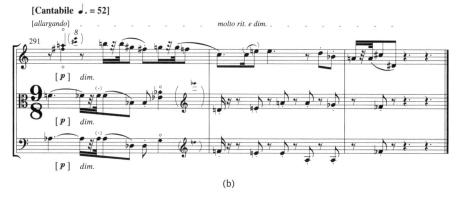

(b)

Ex. 5.3   Schoenberg, String Trio
          (a) bars 208–9
          (b) bars 291–3

trace a dialogue between the ghostly march style of the turbulent material at the outset of Part 3 (as of Part 1) — material which has the quality of 'threatening danger' specified for the opening of Schoenberg's *Accompaniment to a Film Scene* (1930) (Ex. 5.3a) — and the lilting evocation of barcarolle and berceuse that gains strength in the most sustained presentation of cantabile material with which the work ends (Ex. 5.3b). To constrain Part 3's progression to a 'death–rebirth' scenario would be crude in the extreme, yet the fact that the music stems from, and also represents, Schoenberg's being brought back from the brink after a cardiac arrest, gives extra intensity to the point at which the two types of material are first 'confused'. Bars 238–41 have the quality of a brief lament which could develop into a fully-fledged funeral march; bars 244–5 adumbrate the more flowing, gentle quality of a lullaby for the reborn, the revived (see again Ex. 5.1, p. 77).

The degree to which this music moves from an emphasis on discontinuity to an embrace of continuity is underlined by the differences between bars 232–7

(Ex. 5.1) and bars 292–3 (Ex. 5.3). In the first extract, the common factor of the two 'whole tone' trichords (E, D, B♭; D♯, C♯, A) is repressed by the extreme textural contrast (earlier, Schoenberg had split the two trichordal statements between the end of Part 1 and the beginning of Episode 1, bars 51–6). At the end, the same six pitch-classes provide the concluding hexachord of the tranquil violin melody. Here Schoenberg reveals one of the work's fundamental serial elements, an eighteen-note row, as a melodic statement in a way which can be read as offering an element of revelation, resolution, where so much previously had been incomplete, ambiguous, disrupted. But this shift of emphasis reinforces the sense in which the work as a whole has involved tension, confrontation between connection and disconnection, and the ending sounds not so much like the absorption of instability into stability as like the establishment of a distinctive but precarious balance between opposing forces. As Christopher Hasty summarises the nature of the Trio and the *Violin Phantasy*, 'both of these works quite magically unite the shock of discontinuity with glimpses of a wholeness in which the most diverse characters can succeed one another without confusion'.[24] Cherlin talks in somewhat similar terms when he suggests that, at the end of the Trio, 'one need not be aware of the twelve-tone logic to hear the musical idea drifting from voice to voice, unable or unwilling to find closure' (p. 590), and that ultimately 'we find not closure but a drowsy drifting off that is most emphatically not death' (p. 593). Yet – ironically, perhaps – Cherlin's narrative concerning Part 3 of the Trio is too selective and discontinuous to do justice to the ambiguous multivalence of the approach to and effect of this 'non-ending'.

Although the last outburst of turbulent music was back in bars 276–9 (with a muffled after-shock in bars 280–1), the break-up (after bar 288) of the flowing rhythm which presents berceuse in its purest form suggests that dissolution might be a more decisive factor here than resolution. If the dominant image is one of rebirth, it is a rebirth which uncertainly confronts the unknown, even the unknowable, a new situation in which the confidence of faith is inaccessible. Having once described the effect of this ending as 'compounded of diffidence and tenderness',[25] I have no wish to argue that these qualities are on opposite sides of a binary divide. But the diffidence and tenderness are responses to a violence and assertiveness which have been set aside rather than definitively eliminated, and Cherlin's up-beat reading of the Trio's conclusion risks taking decisiveness to extremes in the way it implies a shift from the Dionysian to the Apollonian: 'the dance is now a source of release from the anxiety that has pervaded much of the work...Death, stripped of its macabre mask, has become peace' (p. 593). Such certainty becomes even more questionable when the music of the Trio is put back into the wider, worldly context of Schoenberg's attitudes and ambitions – social as well as technical, religious as well as aesthetic.

Music, religion, politics

In 1946, the year of the String Trio, Schoenberg wrote an essay, 'Criteria for the Evaluation of Music', in which he affirmed that 'music conveys a prophetic message revealing a higher form of life towards which mankind evolves'.[26] For Steven Cahn, this vision of the modern prophetic artist first appears in the fourth of the Op. 22 songs, a setting of Rilke's 'Vorgefühl' (Premonition) (1916), whose governing image is that of a storm, and which 'stands as a first attempt at grappling with the roles of priest and prophet as a problem of synthesis'. Cahn concludes that 'both Rilke's verse and Schoenberg's music announce not words of salvation and comfort, but the storm in all urgency. At the same time, Rilke and Schoenberg announce the absolute necessity to live it through. For the sake of this uncompromising message, the artist aspires to the true role of the prophet.'[27] Given such ambitions, the task of educating performers and listeners involved much more than the promotion of social harmony: it was a matter of spiritual fulfilment.

These considerations also indicate why Schoenberg could not leave the tentative, yielding statement which ends the Trio — banishing the post-Mahlerian marching assertiveness of its Dionysian stratum — to stand as his most characteristic tone of voice. This ending seems to embody a retreat from a defiantly prophetic persona to one that can resist neither a degree of comfort (in faith, survival) or an element of resignation: the stoical serenity of honest doubt seems, if only briefly, to challenge emphatic certainties. The assertive voice of prophecy and religious persuasion soon returns, however, and least ambiguously in *A Survivor from Warsaw* (1947), which, for Reinhold Brinkmann, bears a 'decidedly messianic' message: 'it carries the positive image of the artist as leader into the future through all the political and spiritual breakdowns and, as such, articulates an old-fashioned, individualistic nineteenth-century optimism'.[28] But Schoenberg could hardly embrace optimism unalloyed, not just because it was, as Brinkmann admits, 'old-fashioned', but because, as a Jew, he 'was irrevocably convinced that the historical experiment of assimilation was doomed to failure and that the socio-cultural dissonance it had generated was likely to remain forever unresolved'.[29] This is why defiance rather than optimism, assertion rather than gentleness, becomes the dominant tone, and it is the emphasis on tenderness, submission, which makes the ending of the Trio so unusual.

Commenting on Brinkmann's article in 1997, I urged the characterisation of Schoenberg as an artist 'articulating as much of 20th-century pessimism as 19th-century optimism', in light of that 'balance in late Schoenberg between divergent tendencies which resist rather than implement synthesis, and a mood of defiance in face of death' in which 'the roles of "victim" and "victor"' cannot be 'as easily distinguished as may initially seem to be the case'.[30] Support for the persistence of a pessimistic dimension might also be derived from Bluma Goldstein's argument, in her study of *Moses und Aron*, that Schoenberg turned away from biblical orthodoxy in his apparent belief that the Jewish nation 'could seemingly best survive not in an integrative cultural situation where it would have to contend with other peoples and cultures, but rather in a metaphysical state of being in which all worldly connections were severed or renounced'. Goldstein reiterates the charge of Schoenberg's 'troubling…antidemocratic and authoritarian predilections and solutions, blatantly apparent in Moses's autocratic rule over the Israelites at the conclusion of *Moses und Aron*, [and] in the authoritarian organizational structure planned for the Jewish Unity Party'. Her conclusion, more charitably expressed than Richard Taruskin's, but the more telling as a result, is that 'one can only hope that his pronouncements and solutions were merely a gauge of the despair and helplessness experienced in response to a world that seemed to be reeling out of control'.[31]

No less weighty, in a quite different way, is Camille Crittenden's suggestion that by 1947 'Schoenberg's Judaism was less important to him than some scholars have hoped and implied', and that even *A Survivor from Warsaw*, while not simply an opportunistic cashing in on a topic of current concern, owed its existence as much to 'immediate external circumstances' as to 'an intrinsic imperative to create such a piece'.[32] Crittenden claims that 'even as the piece attests to Schoenberg's tremendous creative powers, its compositional history also reflects the bitterness and disappointment that characterized many moments of his final years': and it seems equally true that (in another commentator's view) *A Survivor* 'draws meaning from processes of disjuncture and disruption, establishing frames of narrative, language, and musical style only to shatter them by the intrusion of radically dissimilar elements that refuse assimilation'.[33] In making this analysis, David Isadore Lieberman does not confront the associated technical topic of the challenges to comprehensibility which Schoenberg pioneered, and which William Benjamin outlines in his contribution to the same volume.[34] Rather, Lieberman underlines the sense of Schoenberg's alienation and anger with an interpretation of *A Survivor from Warsaw* as a work in which the composer withdraws from German music 'the right to inherit that which he considered his most enduring legacy, and which he had developed specifically for the benefit of German music: the method of composing with twelve tones related only to one another' (p. 212).

It is difficult to imagine more strongly opposed perspectives on Schoenberg's possible feelings about German traditions, and ways of using them both positively and contemporaneously, than those provided in Cherlin's analysis of the Trio, and in Lieberman's commentary on *A Survivor from Warsaw*. But such disparate conclusions about such different works are typical of recent Schoenberg scholarship, and reflect — to put it positively — the protean diversity as well as the psychological complexity of the man, no less than the technical and aesthetic complexity of his work. Schoenberg's twin roles as 'aesthetic theologian' and 'pure' musician are similarly difficult to disentangle, and it is as unsatisfactory to impute nothing but extra-musical significance to the gently dissolving endings of the String Trio, or the Third and Fourth Quartets – at the opposite extreme from the tumultuous affirmations of *A Survivor from Warsaw* or the *Violin Phantasy* – as it is to claim that both types of ending are nothing more than demonstrations of formal rightness. Even if an ending like the Trio's is felt to confirm an aesthetic aspect of the work as embodied in an overall motion from the Dionysian to the Apollonian, the sense of 'unresolved opposition' that is equally persistent can perhaps be linked to the higher or deeper continuum between the exigencies of Apollo and Dionysus (or Heraclitus) on the one hand and those of the Jewish God on the other. Whether the music is turbulent or serene, and even if it aspires to be absolutely non-referential in shunning texts and relishing the solution of formal and technical problems that are only meaningful in the context of 'the language of music', Schoenberg's beliefs, in which the possible social, religious role of art coexists with the mundane concerns of a human being under constant financial pressure, seem to find vivid expression in his music's special and sustained tensions.

It is evidently unwise to adopt an exclusively secular critical frame for Schoenberg, reading all the 'prophetic' aspects of his work as foretelling the survival of expressionistic modernism. Despite such a brief moment of calm as 'Verbundenheit' (a vision of 'the consolation of mutual obligations in human society')[35] and, much later, 'Dreimal tausend Jahre' (to do with his 'aspirations for the newly recreated Israel'),[36] Schoenberg had constantly to confront the probability that such moments were provisional and unstable, and likely to be further destabilised when projected on a larger scale, as in the tonality-alluding twelve-note *Ode to Napoleon* (1942). Auner's characterisation of the String Quartet Concerto as offering 'evidence of how problematic and contested Schoenberg's own identity had become' (Auner, 'Concerto', p. 296), and the composer's general tendency thereafter to reflect rather than transcend the fractured, fragmented condition of musical modernity rings true. Nevertheless, Adorno (as so often) went too far in writing of Schoenberg's last works as splintered, offering a 'fragmentary impression', and it could be significant that much recent critical discussion, like Bluma Goldstein's of *Moses und Aron*, is more interested in, and more persuasive about, the words than the music. Adorno's more useful idea of a circumstance in which the 'conception of a fully constructed totality overlaps with the opposing impulse' is reflected – obliquely, of course – in William Benjamin's outline of an approach to a music 'that achieves its univocality through the fusion of contradictory elements' (p. 32). Indeed, Benjamin's initial description of Schoenberg's overall development, both religious and musical, fits well with those paradoxical contradictions and conflicts on which Adorno invariably focused:

> the development of Arnold Schoenberg's religious thought, in the direction of an uncompromising ethical monotheism, is paralleled by gradual changes in

his approach to composition, in the direction of conscious, rational control of the creative process...[A]s his music became, in a sense, more knowable and intersubjectively describable, Schoenberg came to understand God as absolutely unknowable and indescribable, as the God of Moses as interpreted by Jewish philosophers since Maimonides. (p. 1)

Benjamin even argues that

> as he struggled towards the twelve-tone method in the years 1920–24, Schoenberg realized that Judaism provided a historical model for what he was attempting as an artist. He came to see that the Jewish concept of law – as mediation between an unknowable God and the task of constructing a meaningful social existence – offered a parallel, on a grand scale, for his efforts to devise a method of pitch organization that could mediate between the ideal of a piece...and the listener's need to follow a musical argument over time. (p. 33)

What should be stressed in response is that with Schoenberg there could be no simple mapping of 'world' onto 'work', no simple progression in his musical thinking from intuitive spontaneity to overriding rational control, any more than there was from anarchism to authoritarianism in his thinking about society and religion. Rather, those aspects of the twelve-note method which were – indeed – methodical, and even systematic, functioned primarily to provide the stimulus for composing 'as before', with as much freedom and flexibility as the conjunction of spontaneity (instinct) and constraint (technique) allowed. Even if, when writing words about that proposed 'Jewish Unity Party', Schoenberg talked of 'the idea of the chosen people, militant, aggressive, opposed to any pacifism, to any internationalism' (Goldstein, '*Moses*', p. 188), the music he found for Moses at the end of Act 2 of *Moses und Aron* is not primarily militant or aggressive but compassionate, despairing, and ultimately – perhaps – resigned. One is as likely to hear a sense of militancy undermined, of vulnerable humanity, in this music as of authoritarianism straining to assert itself against all the odds. Further, it seems more than probable that it was Schoenberg's acceptance of the way in which his musical 'voice' functioned and flowered that not only kept him composing but also made it conceivable for him to create works on religious, ethical, political subjects – even if, as Crittenden contends, Judaism was 'less important' to him (at least by the later 1940s) than most scholars have assumed (p. 246).

Whatever the truth of that, and of the associated possibility that exploring connections between past and future (from the post-Nietzschean perspective of dialogues between Dionysus and Apollo) was a more satisfying artistic calling than attempting – failing – to represent the unrepresentable divinity, critical and technical interpretation of Schoenberg in the new century must surely have as much recourse to the sacred/secular continuum of topics as to the classical/modernist continuum: and in acknowledging both dimensions there will be a better chance of doing justice to music which remains as resistant to easy comprehension half a century after his death as it did in 1951, or at the centenary of his birth. Peter Franklin was right to call for greater boldness in the study of 'this linking of musical idealism, intolerant political authoritarianism and the mystical doctrines of ancient faith in a far from holy alliance whose rich problematic is precisely that of Schoenberg's rich and problematic music'.[37] Keller's definition of Schoenberg as both 'clarifier' and 'confuser', as far as the music which has come after him is concerned, remains pertinent. But this complexity can enhance the aesthetic impact, for those musical (not just musicological) listeners willing to give time to Schoenberg's works. After all, even with *A Survivor from Warsaw*, analysts like Crittenden who focus on the age-old role of descending semitones in musical laments should not forget the no less plausible allusion to the descending semitone with which Wagner sets two statements of the word 'Wahn!' at the beginning of Hans Sachs's monologue in Act 3 of *Die Meistersinger*. Even in late Schoenberg, depiction of savage inhumanity is inseparable from memories of the power of music to represent much finer feelings. This composer spoke authoritatively about the human condition in all its aspects, and not simply as a dogmatic authoritarian alienated from joy or sorrow.

6 The subject of Britten

Finding one's place in society as a composer is not a straightforward job.[1]

Fulfilment, frustration

In July 1964 Benjamin Britten won the first Aspen Award, given to honour 'the individual anywhere in the world judged to have made the greatest contribution to the advancement of the humanities'. In his acceptance speech, Britten came up with some appropriately humanistic declarations. 'I certainly write music for human beings...I also take note of the *human* circumstances of music, of its environment and conventions' (pp. 10, 11). It was, he declared, 'the composer's duty, as a member of society, to speak to or for his fellow human beings' (p. 12). Refusing to condemn Johann Strauss or George Gershwin for 'aiming at providing people – the people – with the best dance music and songs which they were capable of making', he claimed that 'it is quite a good thing to please people, even if only for today. That is what we should aim at – pleasing people today as seriously as we can, and letting the future look after itself' (p. 17).

In a later interview, Britten outlined a similar theme: 'I believe in the artist serving society. It is better to be a bad composer writing for society than to be a bad composer writing against it. At least your work can be of *some* use.'[2] But what does 'writing for society' involve, and how is 'use' to be defined? The implications of this involve the kind of accessibility and 'serious' appeal which go beyond the instantly gratifying qualities of popular entertainment, and which see the artist as rooted, with positive feelings about 'home' as well as about humanity. Britten's fervent hymn to belonging in his Aspen speech – 'I belong at home – there – in Aldeburgh. I have tried to bring music *to* it in the shape of our local Festival; and all the music I write comes *from* it. I believe in roots, in associations, in backgrounds, in personal relationships. I want my music to be of use to people, to please them, to "enhance their lives" (to use Berenson's phrase)' (pp. 21–2) – understandably says nothing about the nature of the personal relationship that mattered most to him, and still less about the feelings of alienation and guilt which seem to have coexisted with those ideals of belonging and social responsibility. Predictably, therefore, the tendency of later commentators on Britten to emphasise not just that 'heavily repressed sadism' which Hans Keller had diagnosed around 1950,[3] but also the consequences of the composer's pacifism, homosexuality and misanthropy, has promoted a view of his musical development as governed more by pessimism and retreat than by openness and optimism. Looking back from the early 1990s, Paul Griffiths detected an 'overwhelming sadness' coming from his sense of 'a sharp, eager mind withdrawing itself'.[4] Around 1940, Griffiths suggests, there 'came a change not only in manner but in the whole musical outlook…Britten goes, with no transition, from boyhood into middle age.' A similar point was made by Robin Holloway when he described *The Prince of the Pagodas* as 'the only work of Britten's maturity (apart from the *Spring Symphony*) that realizes fully the gaiety and brio with which the Young Apollo's voice had disconcerted the melancholy water-meadows and coronation rhetoric of this country's musical norms in the interwar years'.[5]

Griffiths's diagnosis of Britten's relation to society suggests a reality very different from that constructed by the composer's Aspen rhetoric. For Griffiths, 'the secrecy, the constant cautiousness about what was being revealed, left the music lamed', and 'it is hard not to regret the lost possibility of a father-figure who could have revolutionized British music in the 1940s and 1950s'. Seen in this way, Britten's usefulness to British society appears limited indeed. Nevertheless, few other commentators have agreed that Britten's music was actually 'lamed', and Philip Brett is more representative in his view that 'covert treatment of the issues of sexuality may have offered itself as a personally effective remedy. The result was an engagement in his work, first with the social issues of his experience of homosexuality, later with the metaphysical ones, that trod various fine lines between disclosure and secrecy, allegory and realism, public and private.'[6] Far from finding the musical result dull or limited, Brett suggests that 'part of the attraction of Britten's art is the knife-edge it walks between the genuine and the sentimental, between honesty about life's difficulties and a longing for resolution and comfort'. For Brett, Britten's usefulness to society comes not from demonstrations of rootedness, or the depiction of a satisfying social environment, but rather from warnings about the dangers of both personal and collective violence and intolerance, as well as about the inevitability, for some, of loneliness and frustration. Artists may aspire to work for society, and to find fulfilling relationships within society, but, as Britten himself acknowledged in his Aspen speech, they must never expect the establishment of a place in society to be 'a straightforward job'.

One of the many ambiguities that can be traced through Britten's work results from his concern to counter melancholia with subjects that promote not just resolutions but happy endings: to represent, if not a transcendent serenity, then a calm and resigned acceptance. For example, the three *Parables for Church Performance*, from the 1960s, are obliged by their religious content to end positively. Yet those endings also represent a kind of release in which humanity is humbled, and such humbling by divine grace is matched in the secular operas by the fulfilment of release which comes when human protagonists accept their own flawed natures. In this sense, the endings of *Billy Budd* (1950–1, rev. 1960) and *Death in Venice* (1971–3) are not depictions of Captain Vere and Gustav von Aschenbach as tragic failures but expressions of sympathy, eloquently understated, with their failure and frustration. If this is 'writing for' rather than 'against' society, it can only be for a society rather different from that represented by a naval vessel in time of war, or the disease-ridden city within which *Death in Venice* unfolds. HMS Indomitable and Venice both share some of the qualities of 'The Borough' in *Peter Grimes* (1944–5), as 'homes' in which the protagonist's rather solitary sense of belonging is offset by collective hostility and incomprehension. Britten did not aim to preach simplistic sermons about the benefits of social cohesion, but to explore, and to some extent relieve, his feelings about society's inherent and probably incurable failings.

The trend away from uninhibited 'gaiety and brio' in Britten's later works is therefore much more than an involuntary move into a lamed, self-pitying sadness. Commentators who have no sense of the composer's modern classicism, his impulse to integrate and synthesise, even if this is 'countered, offset and even, on occasion, frustrated, by strong and irreducible ambiguities',[7] can sometimes reveal unrealistic expectations about what his expressive range might plausibly encompass. It is, for instance, pointless to expect a sudden lurch into a full-blown post-Bergian expressionism when the feverish rites of Dionysus are depicted in *Death in Venice*. But to conclude that Britten's music is, above all, Apollonian is equally misleading, since (as already suggested) it cannot be other than equivocal about wholehearted calm and serenity, or about the poise and elevated sense of transcending the everyday that marks out Apollo's realm. Even in *Young Apollo* (1939), in which the god is explicitly evoked, it was physical beauty rather than the kind of sublimely chaste transcendence suggested in the final stages of Stravinsky's *Apollo* that Britten had in mind. He told the young Wulff Scherchen, who inspired the piece, that 'it was "founded on the last lines of Keats's *Hyperion*", which describe the young Apollo's "golden tresses" and "limbs / Celestial" '.[8]

Relatively unambiguous serenity can occasionally be found, and it is possible to hear clear links between the B♭ major 'Romance' from the *Variations on a Theme of Frank Bridge* (1937), intended to represent Bridge's 'charm' (Ex. 6.1), and the B♭ major movement, 'Antique' from *Les Illuminations* (1939), inscribed to Edward Sackville-West (Ex. 6.2). Both enrich their basic tonalities without darkening the dance-like mood of poised elegance which, in *Les Illuminations*, matches Rimbaud's portrait of the physical beauty of the 'gracieux fils de Pan'. As soon as the atmosphere becomes more intense, however, serenity is occluded, and the music moves towards that world of post-Mahlerian lament which was an especially important element in the larger-scale works of Britten's earlier years – the *Frank Bridge Variations*, the Violin Concerto (1939) and the *Sinfonia da Requiem* (1940).

Ex. 6.1   Britten, *Variations on a Theme of Frank Bridge*, 'Romance', beginning

One of the most powerful features of the last of the *Seven Sonnets of Michelangelo* (1940) is the way in which the serene poise of the opening is restored after the more overtly passionate central phase, which switches from major to minor, and has heightened dissonance: with the return, longing yields to fulfilment. As with Rimbaud's 'Antique', however, the 'well-born nobility' hymned here is more a matter of human physical perfection than of transcendent spirituality. By contrast the Francis Quarles text, which Britten used for his *Canticle I* (1947), inspired a beatific conclusion which seems genuinely Apollonian in its subtle integration of spiritual and sensuous (Ex. 6.3, p. 94). This expression of ideal, stable unanimity, subtly sketched

Ex. 6.2   Britten, *Les Illuminations*, 'Antique', beginning

in the brief canon within the final cadence, is the very antithesis of the dramas of loss, separation, incompatibility and failed relationships with which Britten more commonly dealt. Later examples of a comparable tone are rare, although the poised, 'antique' 'Socrates und Alcibiades', the third of the *Sechs Hölderlin-Fragmente* (1958), is a possible instance.

Such Apollonianism was most obviously precluded when, as I have argued elsewhere, 'Britten the uncertain Christian' walked 'the knife-edge separating aesthetic self-confidence from social self-doubt', and 'directed his generic allusions

Ex. 6.3   Britten, Canticle 1, ending

towards those moments of purely human self-understanding and illumination that have their own transcendent expressive force'. This is why I believe that the final stages of *Death in Venice* do not fail to live up to the expressive and dramatic demands of the subject-matter. 'It is, after all, the great tragic irony at the heart of the triumphantly integrated music drama that is *Death in Venice* that Aschenbach's profession of faith in his "Hymn to Apollo" leads him not to the fulfilment of love, but to a lonely death, with no hint of Christian consolation.'[9]

It is not difficult to regard the pilgrimage to disaster which Aschenbach undertakes as the ultimate expression of those features which were first noted in Hans Keller's 1950 article, 'Resistances to Britten's Music: Their Psychology':[10] and in a study of Britten's musical character written at much the same time, Keller stated that 'Britten is a pacifist. It is an established fact that strong and heavily repressed sadism underlies pacifistic attitudes.'[11] Keller was well aware that Britten felt no compulsion to suppress turbulent, even violent moods in his music, but he nevertheless believed that Britten was 'a musical pacifist too', in the sense that 'the vital aggressive element' in the music is complemented by a 'violent repressive counterforce against his sadism'. Keller could see the dangers of this kind of critical vocabulary, and observed that while, in real life, pacifism was 'an illusion', in art it is 'realism *par excellence*, producing as it can the quickest possible communicability of new discoveries'. Nevertheless, 'the only guarantee...that pacification will not degenerate into compromise is genius'. In Keller's formulation, therefore, Britten's genius lay in his ability to communicate his new musical discoveries by means of a violently repressive countering of that 'vital aggressive element'.

We might wish to debate the precise technical features of those constraints which Keller would have identified as 'musical pacifism': and we have only to compare events like Grimes's striking of Ellen and rough handling of the apprentice with Wozzeck's murder of Marie, or the treatment of the rape in *The Rape of Lucretia* (1946–7) with the depictions of sexual aggressiveness in *Lulu* or *Lady Macbeth of the Mtsensk District*, to sense that there is a degree of restraint, and even of repression, in Britten's musical representations of violence. But these differences do not require the conclusion that the Britten examples lack dramatic power, any more than Stravinsky's stylisations of violence and horror in *Oedipus rex* lack impact. In the later stages of *Billy Budd*, for example, the effects and degradations of life in time of war are realised with the greatest vividness. But the hanging of Billy, the mutinous rumblings of the ship's crew, and the climactic torment of the endless battle in Captain Vere's mind between guilt and absolution, are depicted in music which might seem to be seeking a metaphor for repression in the priority it accords to discipline and economy: and it is a very moot point whether this creates a sense of distance from the sordid reality of the real world, or – uncompromisingly – embodies the essence of that world. The same issue is raised by the *War Requiem* (1961–2), which might be expected to offer Britten's most considered thoughts on the binary opposition between peace and violence. Yet neither Wilfred Owen's poetry nor Britten's music represents the waging of war purely as the expression of sadistic impulses: there is bitterness, stoicism, irony, heroism, but no pleasure in the infliction of pain, and the ritualised generic progression in the *War Requiem*'s final movement from march to lullaby provides a strong infusion of classicising calm to counter the earlier representation of panic-stricken aggressiveness.

That progression from march to lullaby is also relevant to the dramatic epiphanies of Owen Wingrave and Gustav von Aschenbach in Britten's last pair of operas. In *Death in Venice* the parallel between the pacifist, or repressed sadist, as outsider and the acknowledgement of sexualities alternative to heterosexuality is at last overt. As suggested above, *Death in Venice* might indeed be the major work of Britten's which best fulfils Keller's idea of a 'musical pacifism' in which vital aggressive elements are forcefully countered, if not actively repressed. But it is not Britten's most radical opera in technical terms: his approach to the genre was more innovative, and musically even richer, in *The Turn of the Screw* (1954).

Masking Dionysus

The radical status of *The Turn of the Screw* stems to no small extent from the decision to use youthful voices at the heart of the action. The generic consequences of this decision, with respect to the social or aesthetic sources of the opera's materials, will be considered in some detail shortly. Yet it was a further consequence of choosing Henry James's novella that the immoderate behaviour of Peter Quint and Miss Jessel had to be portrayed, not simply as threatening, but as attractive to innocent, corruptible children, as well as meaningful to more knowing adults. As later with *Death in Venice*, neither uninhibited sexuality nor explicitly brutal violence was dramatically salient, and the seductive subversiveness of his presence, shown by Quint's initial, cadenza-like melismas (Ex. 6.4), suggests an implacable refinement which is even more sinister than his more conventionally threatening physical and psychological attributes.

Of all Britten's operas, *The Turn of the Screw* is the most confined in its social perspectives, focusing on the claustrophobia-inducing domestic environment and excluding the wider world which is so crucial to *Peter Grimes*, *Albert Herring* (1946–7) and *Gloriana* (1952–3). In *The Rape of Lucretia*, too, the pressures of social, even political conditions on one particular household are central to the drama, while in *Billy Budd* it is the world of war, and the constraints under which those who wage war are obliged to act, that determine events. What happens in *The Turn of the Screw* is inconceivable without the existence of a set of (Victorian?) social conventions: and although the precise constraints which oblige a wealthy guardian to leave his wards in the care of servants and hired help are not explained by James, the effect is little different from present-day parents consigning their children to boarding school for long periods. But the tensions which govern Britten's operatic narrative are not really to do with an opposition between a local environment and the wider world of politics and society. They are much more involved with the infiltration, and ultimate destruction, of domestic stability by an otherness which exists as a ghastly parody of domestic bliss. Here, the notion of a subversive domesticity at war with traditional values provides a compelling metaphor for Britten's sadistic-pacifistic musical instincts as defined by Keller. In musico-dramatic terms, *The Turn of the Screw* follows a path of generic allusion which exploits subversion and parody alongside equally persuasive attempts to assert control and stability: to create a climate of domestic normality

Ex. 6.4 Britten, *The Turn of the Screw*, from Act 1 Scene 8

and decency. The 'war' here is not between an individual, an outsider, and the wider society of insiders, who determine what is right and proper for insiders and outsiders alike. The 'war' is limited to the private, domestic domain: and what is meant to be a haven of security and comfort is turned upside down and inside out. Given what was characterised in Chapter 1 (with reference to Sibelius) as the propensity of modern-classic symphonic music to project the personal, the domestic, into the public arena, it is relevant to recall Britten's well-documented liking for quite conventional kinds of domestic stability, as well as his special sensitivity to the tension between such stability and the social, public factors which constantly threaten it.

In *The Turn of the Screw* the gulf between Bly and the wider world can only be bridged with extreme difficulty. But what does impinge all too easily on this constricted location is the 'other' world of the ghosts – the sense in which the ghosts bring their threatening, anti-transcendent otherworldly environment to bear on the genteel, civilised world of the living. Much has been written about Britten's embrace of musical 'otherness', his use of elements from foreign, and especially Far Eastern, traditions to represent the strange and the danger-ous – thereby giving modern-classic voice to that Dionysian dimension which, in the twentieth century, is more frequently found in modernist works. Allusion to 'pseudo-gamelan sonorities born of an orientalism which functions as a mecha-nism for projecting taboo desires on to "the Other" self'[12] is rather less pronounced in *The Turn of the Screw* than in later works, not least *Death in Venice*. But in any case, the specifics of the 'orientalism/Other' allusions only account for part of the range of dialogues and interactions which constitute Britten's musical language. With Britten, the mobility between personal and social, domestic and public, home and abroad, English and foreign, Western and Eastern, had special connotations to do with stability and instability, and with the whole topic of relationships with tradition which can be characterised in terms of tensions between subversion and affirmation, or betrayal and fulfilment. These multifarious relationships function with particular power and richness in *The Turn of the Screw*, and it is no surprise that the opera has attracted a wide range of musicological commentary, even from writers who have little to say about Britten's other works.

The music theorist Edward T. Cone has even written about James's story without mentioning Britten's opera. Cone discusses the James in the context of ambiguity in late Brahms, and sets out a version of what we might term a 'classic' aesthetic. 'To be artistically effective', ambiguity

> must be bounded. Not all instances of ambiguity admit of resolution, but the
> most successful are delimited by a context of relative directness and clarity.
> That is why Henry James stressed the importance of a 'lucid reflector' in the
> telling of his stories, and that is perhaps why [James's] *The Turn of the Screw*,
> for all its fascination, remains for many of us something less than a first-rate
> work of art. Unbounded ambiguity results in what we call vagueness: ambiguity
> resolved or successfully delimited is described as subtle.[13]

From this it seems quite possible that Cone would regard Britten's opera as 'subtle', whereas James's story is merely 'vague'. Gary Tomlinson, by contrast, is exercised by what he regards as Britten's all-too-unsubtle failure to grasp the opportunity offered by James to underline the anti-materialistic unreality of otherwordly presences.

Tomlinson's thesis is 'that opera, throughout its history, has been a chief staging ground in elite Western culture for a belief in the existence of two worlds, one accessible to the senses, the other not'.[14] This is 'alternative history' with a vengeance, and while it is no more or no less reductive than other comparable projects, Tomlinson's elaborate hermeneutic agenda serves to render him impervious to the paradoxes and irreducible oppositions of modernism – at least in the two twentieth-century operas he discusses, *Moses und Aron* and *The Turn of the Screw*.

Tomlinson's reading of *The Turn of the Screw* is particularly radical and challenging, depending as it does on regarding Britten, not as some kind of conservative, or modern classicist, but as a contributor to what Tomlinson terms 'the mainstream of operatic modernism'. The immediate context for this remark about modernism is an Adornoesque form of hermeneutics that turns Britten's opera into 'an unintended exemplary tale of the implausibility, in the modern age, of ghosts made too solid'. As Tomlinson elaborates the point, 'Britten's singing ghosts place his work in the mainstream of operatic modernism reaching back to *Parsifal*. Just as the overweening solidity of Wagner's objects [spear, grail]…made claptrap of their claims to divine powers, so the uncanniness of Britten's ghosts does not survive their vocal assertion of subjective autonomy.'

This gives a good flavour of Tomlinson's confrontational style and capacity for contentious generalisation. But even if we go along with his conviction that opera's nineteenth-century move into modernity involved a corresponding shift of emphasis from the numinous to the material, it seems supremely rough justice to declare that such a shift is capable of depriving *Parsifal, Moses und Aron* and *The Turn of the Screw* of all ambiguity and aesthetic value. I would argue, to the contrary, that opera, as a genre supremely able to give body to human concerns, has fulfilled itself during the modern era: and even if Tomlinson is right to question whether the modern voice can sustain a metaphysics, I believe that the material, the non-metaphysical, is a sufficient source of expressive intensity, and of emotional authenticity, to validate the modernist project – not that Britten was really a modernist, of course.

Tomlinson is not the first commentator on *The Turn of the Screw* to note the difference between a source and a derivation. The source – a prose text which by definition need not commit itself on the question of what exactly is visible to whom: and the derivation – an opera in which, whatever ambiguities remain about which of the operatic characters actually see and hear the ghosts, those ghosts are eminently visible, and audible, to the audience. Tomlinson's complaint is that the modernist Britten 'could not sustain' the 'systematic ambiguity' with respect to the ghosts which is crucial to the effect of James's story – still less preserve their essential 'uncanniness': and the logical conclusion of his argument is that giving Peter Quint and Miss Jessel both visible and audible presence ensures that there is nothing essential to distinguish them from living seducers and menacers. But Tomlinson makes no allowance for the fact that once Britten had composed Mrs Grose's narrative of the deaths of Quint and Miss Jessel (in Act 1 Scene 5), it would take a listener of extraordinary inattentiveness to confuse the 'solidity' of their

Ex. 6.5   Britten, *The Turn of the Screw*, from Act 1 Scene 5

presences with that of the other characters. The housekeeper's narration freezes on
a dissonant dominant which is chilling in the extreme (Ex. 6.5), because the deaths
she describes are no matter for lament and sorrow, but the cause of immediate
and intense anxiety. We could even say that the music at this point encapsulates
the psychic if not physical violence that comes to be associated with Quint and

Jessel later in the opera: and there is no hint, here, of that complementary if eerie tenderness and sense of fantasy which Quint reveals when he begins to sing, and which enthralls Miles at least as much as it frightens him.[15]

Tomlinson suggests that 'an ambiguity-preserving operatic *Turn of the Screw* presented as the governess's internal monologue, in the fashion of Schoenberg's *Erwartung*' might be a more authentically Jamesian alternative to Britten's multi-vocal version. But a demonstrably and persistently deluded Governess would surely be even less of a focus for ambiguity than the one Britten provided, since there would have been no basis for the conflict between normality and strangeness, between the domestic and uncontrollable otherness, which served to make this story so attractive to the composer in the first place. Moreover, the operatic materiality of the ghosts might help to strengthen the doubts audiences have about the Governess's feelings for the children, and Miles in particular – an important aspect of the composer's interest in this tale.

In pursuing his theme of problematic materiality, Tomlinson homes in on the musical details of the way in which Peter Quint is characterised: 'As Quint is by far the more prominent of the ghosts, so his vocalized body is the more solid.' In his 'seductive cantilena to Miles in Act 1 Scene 8' his

> frequent circling back to the...high E♭ lodges this pitch in our ears as the sonic body, so to speak, of the ghost. Thereafter Britten does his utmost to solidify this body. He makes E♭ the center of Quint's singing throughout the remainder of Act 1 Scene 8 and in all his subsequent appearances.

Allegedly, Britten 'dwells on this pitch to the point of obsession. Indeed, so prominent is the pitch that its final shift up a half step to E♮ [in Act 2 Scene 8], marking the governess's triumph and Quint's farewell to Miles in the final scene, carries no power to efface it.'

This is a breathtakingly reductive reading, dedicated with blinkered single-mindedness to the purpose of underpinning Tomlinson's contention that 'Quint's voice...militates against the uncanniness his portrayal must aim for'. But for this reading to hold true, Tomlinson must move quickly away from the notion of the 'seductive cantilena' – that is, the generic and expressive nature of Quint's material in the final stages of Act 1 – to an exclusive concern with the pitch of E♭ that allegedly grounds that material and prevents a proper 'uncanniness' from coming across. And his parallel claim, that 'Britten's insistence that the ghosts should sing undermined the signal mystery of James's story', is no less reductive in its failure to explore the ways in which opera can transmute mystery into menace, and a special, genuinely operatic kind of ambiguity.

A closer reading of the opera's ending soon indicates that there is no actual, literal 'shift' from E♭ to E during Quint's farewell, which can also be heard as more regretful than vengeful. What happens next is that the Governess realises that Miles

Ex. 6.6   Britten, *The Turn of the Screw*, from Act 2 Scene 8

is dead, and that she has not 'triumphed' at all. Her despairing recall of Miles's Latin song embodies a musical tension between directedness and instability: directedness towards the final A major triads, and the unstable chromaticism in which the last G♯ is left unresolved, and the final D♯s, in the voice, all resolve onto E, leaving the Governess's last G♮ as the final index of persistent horror or 'otherness'. As for those final A major chords, has a resolution ever sounded less positive in its mixture of implacable conclusiveness and fastidious distaste (Ex. 6.6)?

At the end of the opera, Quint has indeed dematerialised, but the consequences of his presence and of his character remain, to counteract the Governess's 'triumph'. Here, at least, normality is restored. There is nothing visible, tangible, 'out there': but human beings remain as much the victims as the beneficiaries of their own mixed motives. Quint's 'seductive cantilena', when added to the other aspects of musical characterisation which Tomlinson fails to mention, adds up to a physiognomy of that particular 'otherness' which it is now commonplace in Britten studies to interpret as a representation of homosexual or pederastic guilt.

From a wider perspective, however, there is a sense in which the 'other', whether transcendent or malevolent, is not a source of comfort to those who inhabit the modern world — unless, that is, they are committed to a religious way of life. Britten's aesthetic entails, pre-eminently, a poetics of loss, and its defining genre is the lament.[16] Even in twentieth-century art, however, loss could be complemented by consolation, or by an inconclusive struggle between fear and hope: and in Britten's operas ideas about complementation are brought into the generic, musical fabric to supremely powerful effect, especially where the distinct but interacting worlds of children and adults (alive and dead) are involved.

The constraints of genre

The genres which Britten employs for the children's music in *The Turn of the Screw* are dictated as much as anything by the need not to make excessive physical demands on their voices. Arias, or large-scale, symphonically structured ensembles, are less likely to work in practice than songs, chants, a variety of miniature forms. Such genres introduce a further layer of ambivalence, to do with the interaction between music which is 'really' sung as part of the action (the so-called 'diegetic' dimension) and passages — especially dialogues and narratives — which are set to music not because the characters are 'really' singing but because this is opera. Even richer ambivalence, requiring even more detailed and sensitive analysis, can be accessed when the way in which the orchestra moves between engaged semantic commentary and relatively neutral 'accompaniment' is considered. But I will focus here on the topic of the children's music, and the restrictions which this imposed on Britten.

By far the most showy music for a child in the opera is purely instrumental — Miles's surreal piano solo in Act 2, which 'modulates' from quasi-Mozart to pseudo Rachmaninov or Gershwin: and the contrast between this exuberant display and the more constrained vocal writing for Miles is pointed in the extreme. These constraints do not prevent the children being used in scenes whose generic complexes are more extended and elaborate — Miles's participation in the final passacaglia is an obvious instance. But the connotations of the treble sound are inevitably intimate, limiting the scope of a chamber opera whose setting (as I have already emphasised) is more private, domestic, than social in the sense of involving a public arena.

From this perspective it would fit well if the ghosts' music were more conventionally operatic, pushing against the generic boundaries of the small-scale, intimate framework — seeking, in a word, to subvert that framework. It would also suit this interpretation if the music for the adults (the governess and the housekeeper) mediated between children and ghosts, yet with a stronger commitment to stable domesticity, shunning the flamboyant and that whole, other musical world of the seductively operatic. It is in this connection that the image of a sublimely disciplined Apollo subduing the devious Dionysus could become salient. But in *The Turn of the Screw*, as in *Death in Venice*, subduing or masking Dionysus is difficult to separate, in its consequences, from yielding to Dionysus, and saving Miles from Quint turns out to be little different from losing Miles to Quint. Dionysus subverts Apollo just as much as Apollo subverts Dionysus, and although operatic display may dissolve into anti-operatic intimacy – Quint's final melisma into the Governess's appropriation of Miles's 'Malo' song – this progression is not paralleled by a progression from despair to contentment.

For Lawrence Kramer, in a typically contentious essay entitled 'Revenants: Masculine Thresholds in Schubert, James, and Freud', there is ambiguity in the role Quint performs as

> the man who ends Miles's boyhood, or what the governess defines as Miles's innocence. The sign of this ending may be both beautiful and sinister, as Benjamin Britten suggests... by doing what James would not: reproducing it. Britten allows Quint to call Miles's name in a long melisma, haloed by echoes on the celesta, that is exquisite in all senses of the word: lyrical, overwrought, delicate, oriental, fey. Perhaps James suggests something of the same ambivalence in the image of Miles on the lawn in the moonlight, 'motionless and as if fascinated, looking up' toward the tower – or his own window. The ambivalence collapses, in both the opera and novella, when the end of boyhood comes all too literally and thereby collapses the narrative. Miles dies when the governess demands that he sees Quint at the window, and the boy, 'after a second in which his head made the move of a baffled dog's on a scent', sees nothing. His death suggests that the withdrawal of the sign, whether because of the governess's neurotic possessiveness or of Quint's malignity, is lethal.[17]

What Kramer appears to be saying is that, although Miles unambiguously dies, his death cannot, or need not, be ascribed to a single, unambiguous cause. Such a reading has the advantage, where the opera is concerned, of suggesting a second aspect of the ending, where the governess's unfeigned grief is allied to a refusal to admit exclusive, personal responsibility for Miles's death. Rather, the librettist's line, 'what have we done between us?', signals a defensive assertion of collective responsibility, embracing guardian and housekeeper, as well as Quint, Jessel and the governess herself. And, as noted earlier, Britten's response to the line, if this is not too simplistic a parallel, is with music which is definite and indefinite, resolving and dissolving at the same time (see again Ex. 6.6, p. 102).

Like Lawrence Kramer, Philip Brett is fascinated by the narrow yet complex social topography of *The Turn of the Screw*. But his discussions could almost be read as a riposte to Tomlinson, suggesting that an obsession with the apparent materiality of the ghosts masks more important matters. Brett moves critical interpretation of the opera closer to Britten's own life and character:

> just as Britten, who had never suffered real persecution for his homosexuality, came to terms – in the terrifying manhunts of *Peter Grimes* – with the paranoid fears common to most homosexuals, so in *The Turn of the Screw* the composer, who seems never to have forced himself onto his young friends,

explored (or exorcised) through the agency of Henry James the possibility of a dominant man–boy relationship implicitly sexualized. Bringing the ghosts alive and giving them words meant that the Quint–Miles connection had an effect quite different from the suggestive, ambiguous horror of the story (which depends for much of its effect on the reader's own vulnerability). Britten's Quint sings songs of allure and delight to which Miles fully responds. The ambiguity in the opera does not depend on whether or not the ghosts exist but springs from a musical question as to how different in kind are the relationships, and which is worse for the poor boy: that with the predatory ghost, or that with the smothering governess.[18]

There are several problematic and tendentious aspects to this analysis: but on the crucial point that the central ambiguity focuses on 'a musical question' – the ways in which the music represents the relationships between Miles on the one hand and Quint and the Governess on the other – Brett is correct. On the topics of genre in general, and music for children in particular, Philip Rupprecht also has useful things to say. By way of implicit reproof to Tomlinson, Rupprecht argues that 'the irreducible ambiguities' of *The Turn of the Screw* 'recreate, in distinctly operatic terms, the inbuilt ambiguities of James's literary form'. For Rupprecht,

> the function of the children's songs...is to keep the question of their morality ([as] angels or devils) irreducibly open. If the audience is convinced one way or the other – that the children are corrupt, or that the Governess is deluded – the tale loses its bite...In the book, our knowledge of the children is from the Governess's point of view; in the opera, our knowledge of the children is above all musical, and it is here that the possibility of retaining the Jamesian literary ambiguity resides.[19]

Whatever we think of the specifics of Rupprecht's analysis, he is right to argue that there is far more to be said about an interactive ambiguity involving the children in both James and Britten than Tomlinson allows for. It is even possible, perhaps, to regard the children as more knowing, less innocent, than the Governess, and the final tableau of the opera as tragic because the Governess's truly child-like immaturity is so nakedly exposed.

At the other extreme, it is also possible to sense some kind of complicity between the Governess and Quint. This has been noted by Brett, in connection with what he calls

> a deeper ambiguity, surrounding the very nature of Quint's 'threat' to Miles. The seductive theme in which he utters Miles's name...is first vocalized by the Governess in Scene 1 and is again heard on her lips in Scene 5, after the disclosure by Mrs Grose of the facts of Quint's death...Are we to understand musically that Quint's relations with Miles are projections of her fears and desires?[20]

Brett might simply be identifying a certain casualness on the part of a composer working, as ever, at speed, and using his material without sufficient care for the precision of its symbolic associations: either that, or the conscious connection of the 'seductive theme' with both Quint and the Governess signifies for Britten their common destiny in losing a loved child. But the musical idea is certainly striking, giving the Governess access to the kind of melismatic vocal writing which signifies the alien territory of the ghosts. She is as much the victim of malevolence as the children, and, as her more 'adult' music suggests, she is no less susceptible than the children (or the ghosts) to the possibility of functioning malignly. To reiterate, one way of reading the opera's ending emphasises the governess's apparent refusal to accept sole, or even prime responsibility for Miles's death – a death which can be seen as the direct result of her misjudgement of the situation in which Miles finds himself.

One final aspect of this opera's need to cultivate the small-scale and intimate lies in the brevity of the twelve-note 'screw' theme, and of the instrumental variations that for the most part divide and link the vocal scenes. It would make little musical sense to follow the precedent of *Grimes* and detach this orchestral material from the opera for separate, concert performance. It is not that this particular theme and variations only make sense in a context of purely domestic music-making, or even that the music evokes only those genres and instrumental combinations which are domestically viable. For Britten, writing an opera did indeed seem to require the subsequent quasi-domestic exorcism of a chamber work. Humphrey Carpenter regards *Canticle III: Still falls the rain* (1954) as 'an epilogue' to *The Turn of the Screw*. Similarly, *The Holy Sonnets of John Donne* (1945) are 'an epilogue' to *Peter Grimes* (Carpenter, *Britten*, p. 227), and *Canticle II: Abraham and Isaac* (1952) is 'an epilogue' to *Billy Budd* (p. 304). In each of these cases, Carpenter can point to similarities and differences of character and technique which do not render the idea of 'epilogue' utterly implausible. Yet it is really only with *Death in Venice* and the Third String Quartet (1975) that we can speak of a chamber-scale epilogue which refers explicitly to the opera it follows. The quartet distils the relatively private out of the relatively public, in a concert work whose 'Venice' is Britten's own construction, as much as the place evoked by Thomas Mann in his novella: a familiar location where Britten could be foreign yet feel at home, a place subversive of conventional notions of what constitutes a city: and, not least, a place which had been reasonably kind to *The Turn of the Screw*, whose first performance was given there.

As noted in Chapter 2, Craig Ayrey has used his view of Debussy as a 'deconstructive composer' to argue for an analytical method 'that offers systematic procedures but is predicated on ambiguity'.[21] In Britten's case, analysis as discourse, involving the recognition that 'opposition itself is a relation, a mode of connection between disparate units', seems a possible way of building on the foundations laid by the more elaborate studies of the interaction of structure and semantics — like Roy Travis's analysis of *Death in Venice*,[22] or the recent work of Philip Rupprecht, with its heady conjunction between various modes of graphic representation and reduction, and post-Bakhtinian dialogue theory. If we add in another topic, of how younger British-born composers, from Judith Weir to Thomas Adès, have reacted to and reflected Britten's example, if not his style, it is surely beyond dispute that there remains ample scope for further study of the reception of Britten's music, and of the ways in which that music relates to the composer's life, as well as to the society in which he lived.

7 Engagement or alienation?

Between politics and art

Characterising a composer's work in terms of a philosophy, political ideology or some other system of beliefs is common-place. The reverse is much more rare, and it is a special feature of Hitler's national socialism that a historian can plausibly describe it as a 'politics of faith, purveyed by a mock-messiah…whose imaginative world was some loathsome travesty of the mythic world of Wagner, divested of the latter's syncretist religiosity and dedication to art, and devoted instead to permanent racial struggle'.[1] In the same context, Michael Burleigh wisely observes, 'the fact that the Nazis went to great lengths to appropriate Wagner should put one on one's guard in making too literal a connection' (p. 98): and this admonition should be remembered whenever the heady exercise of characterising composers in terms of such factors as political engagement or social alienation is undertaken.

John Cage, according to James Pritchett, was a composer whose politics were 'an extension of his art'[2] – and the reverse is also true. Living in post-Second World War America, Cage was free to espouse the belief 'in individualist anarchy as the "best form of government"', and to declare without fear of oppression that 'the best arrangement of people and sounds was to have them free to be themselves, "unimpeded and interpenetrating"'. In 1974, Cage wrote that 'by making musical situations which are analogies to desirable social circumstances which we do not yet have, we make music suggestive and relevant to the serious questions which face Mankind'. Alienated but engaged, he offered an unambiguous cultural idealism, fuelled by scepticism, with respect to what 'musical situations' and 'social circumstances' had so far been able to achieve. Cage could point to 'many musical examples of the practicality of anarchy', but not to any evidence that those examples had had any significant practical effect outside or beyond the aesthetic sphere: and although his *Lecture on the Weather* (1975) demonstrates his freedom to express 'his disgust with the institutions of American government', requiring the (very un-indeterminate) reading at every performance of a preface which 'makes the meaning even more explicit', the cause of anarchism as an alternative to existing political and social institutions has not, so far, been greatly advanced by his work.

Cage, of all composers, resists confinement within a single aesthetic category, and although James Pritchett claims that 'Cage thought that many, if not all, of his post-1957 works were musical analogies to anarchy in one form or another', Pritchett immediately cites the case of *Etcetera* (1973), which breaks these bonds to the extent of containing 'both freedom and control, anarchy and government'. This proliferation was characteristic of a composer motivated by deep-seated dissatisfaction with current artistic and political norms, and the two dissatisfactions come together in Cage's very purposeful, very iconoclastic attempts to transform life into work. In the case of *0'00" (4'33" No. 2), solo for any player* (1962), which involves 'a very personal action, one that is ephemeral, not to be repeated', the score consists of the following instruction: 'in a situation provided with maximum amplification (no feedback) perform a disciplined action'. Four 'qualifications' to this instruction were soon added, but 'because there is no mention of sound, and no means for describing or measuring the sorts of sounds that the piece will entail, *0'00"* does not exist as a compositional object − a series of sounds − but only as a process, an action by the performer' (p. 146). Nevertheless, that action will tend to be less anarchic than if the score/instruction had given the performer the choice of an *un*disciplined action: and the effect of Cage's subversive scepticism with respect to more conventional concepts of the musical work seems to be the result of an interaction between 'object' − the initial instructions, and 'action' − the unrepeatable event itself. That any event deemed 'artistic' is unlikely to display the purest kind of anarchism is reinforced by Cage's 'music circus' concept, in which 'a musical anarchy was produced, wherein the performers and listeners were no longer told what to do, and Cage retreated to such a distance that his role as organizer and designer, *while crucial*, was practically invisible' (p. 158, italics added).

When artistic analogies for political beliefs are sought in the modernist era, ambiguities involving what is crucial and what is inessential are sure to result. Nor is it to be wondered at that the representation of overtly political objectives in Cage's works should have won no more obvious political or social impact for those works than it has for those of a less overtly political composer like Pierre Boulez. It is difficult − probably impossible − to connect the political, cultural manoeuvres which brought Boulez's IRCAM and the work he has done there into being to any philosophical or social content in the works themselves. Cage's *Lecture on the Weather* is far more openly ideological than Boulez's *Sur Incises* (1995−8), and that remains true even if *Sur Incises* (to be discussed in Chapter 11), along with its major predecessors *Répons* (1980−4) and '...*explosante/fixe*...' (1991−3), is held to display techniques analogous to the harmonious interaction of disparate, even conflicting personalities at IRCAM.[3] Nevertheless, the works of Cage and Boulez alike belong in the world of Western democracies which tolerate high art, if only through indifference to it. Very different circumstances arise when undemocratic societies are so lacking in indifference that they seek to control art, and suppress that which fails to fulfil a politically designated social function.

Richard Taruskin has written as follows about Shostakovich's Third String Quartet (1946):

> the horrors broached in the Third Quartet... and the tight-lipped reticence with which it ends, can all be linked with the events and moods of the just-concluded Patriotic War, and that may have been their immediate motivation. But they can be read in many other contexts as well. Some are personal. Some are political. But how do we distinguish them?[4]

No doubt, some technical aspects of the quartet can be usefully discussed without exclusive reference to political or personal matters. Thus the great moment of climax and crisis in the Third Quartet's finale (Ex. 7.1) may reflect both the sufferings and horrors of war, and of political persecution, while providing a no less vivid evocation of the romantic tradition of lamentation extending from Schubert's String Quintet to Schoenberg's First Quartet. The power of the music comes from all these associations, particular and general, and it is not necessary to distinguish between them to acknowledge their interactive potency. Nor do these associations interfere in any way with the immediate and substantial impact of the actual material and the actual context for that material in the finale of Shostakovich's Third Quartet.

When Taruskin writes of linking musical atmosphere and external events he takes it for granted that composers – like Cage – have detectable attitudes to external events which flow across into their musical 'attitudes', or style. In the case of Bartók's Sixth Quartet (discussed in Chapter 3), it might well be concluded that 'the tight-lipped reticence with which it ends can... be linked with the events and moods' of the impending war, as these affected Bartók's thinking about his life in Europe. (Something similar could be said of Stravinsky's *Symphony in C* of 1938–40, even though this is often cited as a exemplary instance of a musical work detached in tone and mood from the composer's fraught personal circumstances at the time: indeed, that it offers an 'escape' from such circumstances.[5]) In Bartók's case, his 'thinking', and also his own fraught circumstances, could have involved the need to secure his continuing career as a composer – to sustain a working environment in which he could create musical links with external events, embodying his attitudes to experiences which were threatening to creativity. Bartók's Sixth Quartet, like Shostakovich's Third, does not just present an expressive gamut between representation of the 'horrors' of war at one extreme and the 'tight-lipped reticence' of one who seeks to offer art as a civilising corrective to horror and violence at the other. It reflects deep scepticism about a world and its institutions in which such anti-artistic circumstances can come about: a world which could best be redeemed by rethinking certain traditional modes of expression and formation rather than by wholeheartedly rejecting them.

Ex. 7.1   Shostakovich, String Quartet no. 3, fifth movement, from Fig. 107

Ex. 7.2   Shostakovich, String Quartet no. 3, first movement, beginning

A work from the postwar years that is unambiguously scornful of warfare, Britten's *War Requiem*, is also reticent, if not exactly tight-lipped, in many decisive respects, and seems to reflect the composer's awareness of general scepticism about the justification for pacifism by offering an analogy with Britten's own scepticism about the ability of the Latin liturgy, on its own (and especially in combination with traditional tonal structures) to do justice to the horrors of twentieth-century violence and loss. All these features, along with the most popular concert *Requiem* not to involve such scepticism, Verdi's, are evoked by Britten in the interests of making his own distance from, yet dependence on, these features the more usefully distinct. Yet for Britten, like Cage, the principal frustration was not fear of governmental reprisal but the likelihood of social indifference, even to work which proclaimed a specific social message. Shostakovich's position was very different.

As my earlier comments on Boulez indicate, no composition, however apparently 'abstract' in character and intent, can be totally closed off from formal as well as expressive analogies with relevant institutions, social or political. For example, to state that the opening of the first movement of Shostakovich's Third Quartet (Ex. 7.2) involves a tension between gentle, consonant dance-like patterns and chromatic inflections which soon destabilise the diatonicism of the first four bars – provoking the music to oscillate between blithe confidence and bleaker uncertainty (around Figures 9 and 10) – makes political contextualisation plausible, while at the same time confirming procedural ploys characteristic of Shostakovich's music in all genres and from all periods. If it is pointless, as Taruskin implies, to attempt to separate 'personal' from 'political' in such interpretation, perhaps it is no less pointless to try to distinguish the sceptical (or detached) from the idealistic (or conformist) within the personal sphere. The personal is itself multivalent: yet the predominance of destabilising procedures and sorrow-laden moods in Shostakovich's music makes it hard to exclude all possibility of political critique.

A work like Cage's *Lecture on the Weather*, which conveys a detectable political or philosophical attitude, is both a 'work' – with aesthetic qualities subject to reception and critique – and an expressed attitude to something outside music. Yet other ways of expressing a commitment to anarchism, like participation in anti-capitalist riots during heads of government summits, are likely to be more effective in promoting the anarchist cause than performances of *Lecture on the Weather*, even if the latter's status as a work of art is not seriously compromised by its double function. By contrast, Cage's *0'00"* is primarily a 'work', with any expressed attitude closer to an aesthetic than a political position, and in any case more implicit, not spelt out verbally in a performed preface. It is therefore closer to Shostakovich's Third Quartet, which can be regarded as the result of socio-political circumstances in which the composer was prevented from expressing subversive political attitudes directly in his music. Shostakovich nevertheless consistently and naturally wrote music suggesting the kind of manic-melancholic expressive continuum of personal emotional states (stemming from the persistence of the romantic tradition) that hint at analogies with hostile social and political views, and the acute anxieties which afflicted him at the height of his career could have been the consequence of fears that his 'purely musical' instincts could so easily be misconstrued by the paranoid *apparatchiks* of the Soviet cultural establishment.

Marxism and after: Kagel

Of the many twentieth-century composers attracted by Marxist ideology before 1960, two – Michael Tippett and Mauricio Kagel – will be considered here. The contrasts between the conservative democracy of 1930s Britain and the Peronist regime of 1950s Argentina are obvious, but in any case the very different artistic evolutions of these composers probably owe more to the different alternatives to Marxism which they espoused. With Tippett, a questing, psychologically orientated humanism, in which the otherness of active homosexuality was central, was compatible with mainstream instrumental and vocal genres, even though (during the 1950s) he became increasingly sceptical about the ability of these – and of his own musical style – to do justice to the mythic and emotional themes proper to serious art: art which should aspire, as Tippett put it, with a misleading hint of religious purpose quite irrelevant to this non-believer, 'to try to transfigure the everyday by a touch of the everlasting'.[6] Nevertheless, Tippett did not choose exile, and was able to indulge his passionate cosmopolitanism, especially after 1960, with frequent travel to America and Asia. Kagel left Argentina in his mid-twenties, and it was in Germany that his predilection for the surreal and the subversive achieved its fullest expression. Although, as Paul Attinello writes, Kagel's earliest work in Argentina already cultivated a surreal modernism, opposing 'the neoclassical style dictated by Juan Perón's government',[7] he was not threatened with incarceration in a Gulag for his failure to adopt a more populist idiom. Nor was his 'political and artistic' sympathy with anarchists rather than communists seen as sufficiently subversive to warrant a bullet in the back of the neck. During the 1960s the leading Argentinian composer Alberto Ginastera moved from neoclassicism to atonal serialism without losing status as an establishment figure in Buenos Aires, and Kagel was far from isolated in his radical interests even if, before 1960, it was clear that to cultivate such interests was to work against the grain.

While it cannot be said for sure that Germany provided more fertile ground for Kagel's development than Argentina might have done, direct contact with European culture, both ancient and modern, was a huge stimulus to the deployment of the kind of anarchism that saw conformity as a threat, and used established generic and stylistic reference as the basis for that most paradoxical of modern phenomena, the anti-institutional work of art. Kagel's *Staatstheater* (1967–70) is quite as subversive of opera's serious, even sacred mission to bring sublimity into Western culture as Cage's *Europeras* (1987, 1991), while remaining close to the kind of expressionism and post-expressionism which has determined much of moment in twentieth-century opera after Berg (Zimmermann, Reimann, Birtwistle, Maxwell Davies, Rihm). In later years, however, Kagel developed more subtle ways of exploiting the difference between freedom and discipline, with a technique described by one commentator as 'collage masquerading as conventionally structured music'.[8]

In Björn Heile's words, 'this dialogics of collage technique and compositional controls is observable in all of Kagel's works since the early '70s', and the effect is that 'even when quoting "foreign" material, he will not let it "speak for itself"…but make it "his own" by integrating it with his newly composed music and conception of the piece as a whole' (p. 295). By treating tonal material serially (Heile instances the *Variationen ohne Fuge über 'Variationen und Fuge' über ein Thema von Händel für Klavier op. 24 von Johannes Brahms (1861/62)* of 1973) Kagel's music 'fuses – or rather forces together – the incompatible: it is sytematically impure and intentionally unorganic. It denies both the functionality of tonal chords and the systematic and unifying role of the series. The combination of historical tonal material with recent serial manipulation effectively de-historicizes the music' (p. 292).

Appropriately, critical opinion is divided as to the degree to which Kagel either displays reverence for tradition, or, by contrast, ridicules it. The Kagelian paradox, as Attinello describes it, is that the Western European musical canon merits the respect of being deconstructed, not simply reproduced so faithfully that the reproduction is either indistinguishable from the original, or manifestly inferior to the original; and this thinking is of a piece with Kagel's increasing interest 'in relating to rather than rebelling against history and culture' (p. 311). It was, after all, the attitude found in Schoenberg when he moved away from late romantic tonality after 1907. Kagel's use of the surreal or the ironic is always directed to an elite able to appreciate the subtleties, the in-jokes and cross-references, as, supremely, in his *Sankt Bach Passion* (1981—5). Here the anarchic edge appears to survive only in the understated banality which replaces authentic Bachian solemnity and sublimity: and yet that very understatement might be felt to be more profoundly subversive – and therefore destructive of tradition – than an explicitly expressionistic collage of old and new, purloined and personal, could ever be. Refreshingly different such music certainly is, and also refreshingly ambivalent in leaving open the question of whether it is more concerned to please or to provoke.

Kagel's note on his five-and-a-half-minute 'Impromptu for piano', *A deux mains* (1995), homes in on his scepticism about one hallowed aspect of tradition, the concept of improvisation: 'Perhaps it was my innate doubt as to whether the notion of musical improvisation can ever be realised in such a way that one could really speak of improvised music that was one of the reasons for my composing this piece.' The potential paradox is then reinforced: 'it seems as though it is my lack of intellectual rapport with the pure doctrine of improvisation – if indeed this ever existed – that has often led me to get involved with forms that find their perfect consummation in giving shape to impromptu musicality'.[9] This implies that the creative stimulus for *A deux mains* lay in exploiting a confrontation between elements which appear spontaneous (even anarchic) and controlling factors which give those elements a shape – 'shape' involving not just the local contour of a musical idea but also the creation of a musical form for the piece as a whole. *A deux mains* embodies a shape comparable to those of other shaped – structured – compositions, even approximating to an overall binary form, despite the piece's various abrupt shifts of tempo and texture. The sense of paradox extends into the style of performance: Kagel wishes the pianist to play 'just as precisely yet capriciously, extravagantly yet glassily, as if this music were flowing through their fingers for the first time, unsuspected and absolutely of the present – impromptu': and these complementary qualities are reflected in the interaction between predictable and unpredictable in the piece's material and structure, as well as in its Satie-like blend of lightness and gravity.

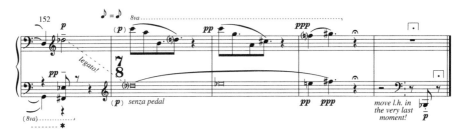

Ex. 7.3   Kagel, A deux mains, Impromptu for piano, ending

A deux mains is a very modest demonstration of the kind of sceptical take on traditional musical genres, styles and institutions which Kagel has explored much more ambitiously in *Staatstheater* and the *Sankt Bach Passion*. Its effect depends not so much on the ability of audiences to tell the difference between 'genuine' improvisation – which, as Kagel implies, might well be extremely rule-bound in practice – and highly crafted composition, as on knowledge of what the title 'impromptu' implies historically. Listeners unaware that the genre has a history – involving Schubert and Chopin, in particular – might therefore miss something of Kagel's characteristic blend of allusiveness and irony. But very few listeners are likely to be left unaware that there is nothing transcendently sonata-like about the music, and that its economy, and the way its strong changes of mood and texture are achieved without opening out the music into regions of large-scale virtuosic writing, confirm its association with smaller-scale, miniature salon pieces of the kind that are performed in hundreds of recital programmes every year. Kagel instructs the performer to play the final, cadential B♭ with a last-minute move of the left hand that is obviously intended as a wry allusion to the sort of spontaneous bright idea that is supposed to inform genuine improvisation from beginning to end (Ex. 7.3). The effect supports the view of *A deux mains* as an affectionate, even nostalgic celebration of how traditions – in the character of concerts, as well as in the genres of composition – can be indefinitely continued, rather than an anarchic manifesto urging the replacement of such traditions with something absolutely new. In this reading, the piece celebrates the freedom of the composer to be underwhelming, to conceive of the impromptu as something consistently unanarchic, and to be political only by implication, in keeping with the attitude that led Kagel to abandon Peronist Argentina in the first place. At the same time, however, the suspicion persists of a masquerade whose very gentleness is provocative, and of a music more subtly subversive than overtly revolutionary and disruptive structures could ever be.

Beethoven and after: Tippett and Shostakovich

If Kagel's poker-faced quasi-traditionalism risks evoking the kind of academicism that, deprived of any surrealist associations, might have been acceptable to Stalinist aestheticians, Tippett's engagement with populism was usually contingent on a humanism that regarded art as Beethovenianly aspiring and provocative. The ironic, frustrating crux of Tippett's career as a composer, and perhaps the moment when he came closest to an 'agony of spirit' comparable to Shostakovich's (*Tippett on Music*, p. 85), was therefore to find his parent culture, after 1960, becoming more philistine as it grew more libertarian: and this despite his own exemplary exploration of a heterogeneous modernism as dependent on adaptations of popular genres like the blues as on grapplings with the cultural legacy of the Holocaust.

In 1980 Tippett wrote a short review of Shostakovich's recently published *Testimony* which was less concerned with the usual questions of textual authenticity than with Tippett's views about the kind of 'truth' which Shostakovich's music reveals:

> To give a personal example: I first heard Shostakovich's Eleventh Symphony only about four or five years ago. This symphony is supposed to be concerned with the events of the 1905 revolution. I was quite sure when I heard it that the use of 1905 was a kind of political alibi, since this was a matter of known revolutionary history. The music to me was self-evidently about Shostakovich's own experiences in the continual catastrophe of his life. This he confirms: 'I wanted to show this recurrence in the Eleventh Symphony. I wrote it in 1957 and it deals with contemporary themes even though it's called 1905. It's about the people, who have stopped believing because the cup of evil has run over.'

What is new to me is his categoric statement that he knew this to be entirely understood by his public. The music must remain his only true memorial, and this is because it is a music which, carrying the message of humanity under stress, has crossed all frontiers to speak to the world, though experienced by a composer of dedicated patriotism. (pp. 81–2)

Tippett saw Shostakovich as a tragic figure, embodying a 'deep agony of spirit between his love of Russia and her great history and his experience of its present corruption'. Tippett's own circumstances in the postwar years could hardly have been more different, and his ideals, which he frequently discussed in print, can be glimpsed in comments he made in 1969 about Charles Ives, whose aim was 'to accept the local, the contemporary, the immediate, and so transform it, or contrast against it, [so] that we obtain glimpses of a visionary, even transcendental reality' (p. 85). Like his near-contemporary Elliott Carter, Tippett felt that Ives's experiments 'can become uncouth, his philosophical transcendentalism can overwhelm his art'. Unlike Carter, however, Tippett was still willing to follow Ives in bringing historical icons of transcendence (Beethoven), and contemporary instances of the vernacular (for Tippett, primarily the blues) into confrontation with the more purely personal aspects of his own musical voice – and not shying away from risking the 'uncouth' in the pursuit of relevance and profundity.

In contrast to Cage's representations of an ideal anarchy which renders parliamentary democracy as irrelevant as enlightened despotism, or Kagel's quasi-surrealistic countering of culture's pretensions to the superhuman, Tippett explored those 'representations of chaos' that he saw as helping to define the cultural ethos of the Western humanist-democratic world. The result, especially in the works coming after his third opera *The Knot Garden* (1966–9), is an art whose range of cultural reference and allusion reinforces its restricted appeal the more determinedly it aspires to the making of emblematic statements about the current state of the world and the role of the serious artist within it. The example of Beethoven, seen as aspiring to visions of social and spiritual perfection rather than documentary representations of actual 'corruption', is seminal, even though Beethoven's later compositions engaged far less immediately with the real world of then-contemporary ideas and institutions than Tippett's. The difference, it appears, is in Tippett's desire to counter his own earlier certainties with a passionately concerned scepticism.

Beethoven stood for an attitude to art defined by Tippett in 1953:

when music as an independent art flowered at the end of the eighteenth century, the European climate of opinion was already deeply involved in the swift and shattering process by which value was going over from the world of imagination to the world of technics. And the artistic consequences of the depreciation of value given to the imaginative world, meant that the effort of imaginative creation began to assume, already in Beethoven's time, that superhuman quality, that desperate struggle to restore the spiritual order by increasingly transcendent and extraordinary works of art. (p. 193)[10]

Tippett accepted the need to restore the balance between imagination and 'technics', and defined his own task as being to 'find some way to speak through the space suit of the technological man to the imaginative man within'. Yet his awareness of the horrors of modern civilisation prompted the exclamation 'what price Beethoven now?'[11] In the modern world, the role of the artist is less 'to restore the spiritual order' than to represent that 'polarity of knowledge obtained through intellectual processes (the knowledge of scientists) and that obtained from deep inner sensibilities (the knowledge of creative artists)' (*Tippett on Music*, p. 246).

This particular polarity can be contrasted with the kind of musical polarities which do not so much represent the opposition between scientific and artistic knowledge as mediate between different artistic visions of humanity. Tippett said of the conception of his Third Symphony (1970–2) that

> what steered me eventually towards a vocal finale was the chance hearing of a BBC radio programme comparing different interpretations of Mahler's *Das Lied von der Erde*. I realized that when he came to plan his settings of Chinese poems translated into German, Mahler wanted to articulate the songs as a specific shape. The result was a symphony – first movement, slow movement, a scherzo comprising three songs, and then a finale. I began thus to plan and organize lyrics that would have a shape – of human beings moving from innocence to experience. (p. 96)

In defining that psychological, social progression, Tippett could also have had a more fundamental symphonic polarity in mind, between the sublimely renunciatory vision, projected by a solo voice, at the end of the Mahler, and the exuberant, collective celebration of social harmony at the end of Beethoven's Choral Symphony. The Beethoven references in the finale of Tippett's Third Symphony cast that composer in the role of supreme anti-sceptic, a passionate but naive idealist whose straightforward demonstration of a progression from chaos to order was a dream which had long since disintegrated. Tippett's use of Beethoven supports Nicholas Cook's claim that the Choral Symphony has become 'profoundly ambivalent' for a late twentieth-century culture (or musicology, at any rate) so acutely attuned to multiplicity and fragmentation.[12] Whereas in Beethoven's finale all is resolution, Tippett's own symphonic conclusion is determined by his desire 'to preserve the underlying polarities' (*Tippett on Music*, p. 100), and these are not merely the harmonic alternatives of centring the music on A or C (alluding, perhaps, to the tonal span of Mahler's *Das Lied*) but also the generic alternatives (which interact the better to reveal their essential differences) between Tippett's versions of the blues, and of the grand, quasi-operatic scena. The ultimate continuum is therefore bounded by song-like lyricism at one extreme and musico-dramatic declamation at the other.

Tippett's allusions to Beethoven continued after the Third Symphony, affecting scores as different in character as *The Mask of Time* (1980–2) and the String Quartet No. 5 (1990–1). These allusions suggest that for Tippett, as for Ives, Beethoven was not just the 'naive idealist' of the Ninth Symphony, but also a principled liberator, legitimising the taking of artistic steps into the visionary unknown. For Kagel, too, in his more ironic way, Beethoven was important as 'the man who freed music' – freed it to mock his own memory, thereby demonstrating that that memory was indelible and inescapable.

For Shostakovich, whose musical language was in substance closer to Beethoven's, the issues were different, the cultural stakes higher. Richard Taruskin believes that one of the reasons the Third String Quartet is so significant is that it shows Shostakovich turning 'irrevocably to late Beethoven as his model. The third movement is a violent scherzo like the one in the Ninth Symphony', while 'the fourth begins with a unison passage marked espressivo that summons up the Beethovenian recitative mode for the first time (of many) in Shostakovich's quartet career'.[13] The associative nexus of that 'unison passage' extends a good deal wider than Beethoven alone – to Schubert, Bruckner, Mahler and Schoenberg: but the music certainly engages with the whole fraught topic of the kind of modelling that can evoke Beethoven. Laurel Fay has noted that, in connection with the Third Symphony (1929), which Shostakovich submitted as part of his graduation portfolio, 'the composer emphasized the optimistic spirit of the work, acknowledging the influence of Beethoven's Ninth Symphony on his choral finale, a paean to the annual observance of workers' solidarity'.[14] One of the most bitterly sarcastic passages in *Testimony* pours scorn on the idea that Stalin loved Beethoven's music, and asked for the Choral Symphony to be performed, on the grounds that 'he loves everything exalted, like the mountains. Beethoven is exalted, that's why he loves him too.'[15] But Soviet aesthetic commissars were always willing to admire artworks produced (allegedly against the grain) within capitalist, decadent societies, and hold these up as models to Soviet artists. For a composer as dependent on the Western classical and romantic tradition as Shostakovich, it was therefore possible for evocations of the spirit of such art to be seen as a sinking of personal identity in a collective tradition that sang songs of hope and resilience in anticipation of the Brave New World of Soviet Marxism. There was nevertheless a fine line to be drawn between nineteenth-century models, from late Beethoven to Mahler, which appeared to express the kind of serenity and sense of fulfilment judged suitable for Soviet audiences, and that spirit of decadence which merely reflected prevailing, non-Soviet social and philosophical values. Allusions to such a spirit could only be justified in the mid-twentieth-century Soviet Union, when a musical composition was concerned to show how it was possible to progress from despair to joy, from decadence and the horrors of war to the healthy wholeness and positive vision of life in Stalin's world. After Stalin's death in 1954 the kind of unhappy endings which are rife in Shostakovich's later works were easier to justify.

Judging Schnittke

Ivan Moody's *New Grove* article on Alfred Schnittke ends with the following, heavily qualified judgement: 'If the criticism might be made that Schnittke's expressionistic all-inclusiveness could lead to the near-suppression of purely musical argument, this was perhaps inevitable in a composer who was concerned in his music to depict the moral and spiritual struggles of contemporary man in such depth and detail.'[16] Stripped of equivocation, this subscribes to the view that connecting musical compositions in 'depth and detail' to the real, contemporary world of 'moral and spiritual struggles' can result in work which, in purely musical terms, is unsatisfactory. But in failing to distinguish between the personal and the political – Schnittke's own character and state of health, as distinct from the Stalinist and post-Stalinist cultural contexts – the *Grove* judgement seems as unrefined as one of Schnittke's early collage-style works.

Writing in the early 1990s of the earlier Schnittke, Richard Taruskin declared that 'however harsh or aggressive or even harrowing, the music never bewilders': it

> seems ever engaged with the grandest, most urgent, most timeless – hence (potentially) most banal – questions of existence, framed the simplest way possible, as primitive oppositions (though the dialectics are no longer unremittingly negative). With a bluntness and an immodesty practically unseen since the days of Mahler, Schnittke tackles life-against-death, good-against-evil, freedom-against tyranny, and (especially in the concertos) I-against-the-world.[17]

Taruskin also makes the inevitable comparison with Shostakovich: both composers manage 'to skirt the pitfall and bring off the catharsis – a catharsis a mere hairsbreadth from blatancy and all the more powerful for having braved the risk'. Further, 'Schnittke's best scores, like those of Shostakovich, are reminders that the tawdry and the exalted can be near-twins at the opposite extreme from the safe and the sane' (p. 102). Like Shostakovich – 'like Solzhenitsyn, for that matter' – Schnittke 'has earned the right to preach to us. The appeal of his music often lies less in our response to its sound patterns than in our sense of the composer's moral and political plight (and the fragility of his life, if we know about his recent strokes and heart attacks)' (p. 104).

Taruskin makes clear-cut connections between Schnittke's health (fragile), culture (morality and politics), and what *Grove* calls 'purely musical argument' (sound patterns). Evidently, the 'personal' and the 'political' are no more neatly independent of one another for Schnittke than they are for Shostakovich. Even though he might never have been at risk from the worst consequences of Stalinist repression at its most brutal, his 'freedom' during the 1960s and 1970s to be as anarchic and pessimistic as he liked, while not leading to his ostracism by the official composers' union, led to frequent attacks in official publications and a ban on foreign travel. This ban remained in force until the Gorbachev transition years, from 1985, by which time Schnittke's health problems imposed a choice between staying put and going into exile.

All these factors might seem to support a version of the *Grove* judgement: Schnittke was never sufficiently detached from, or sceptical enough about, the contemporary world, and his own place or role in it, to write unambiguously great music. Given the expressive extremes established by the depiction of religious ecstasy in the *Choral Concerto* (1984–5) and of existential despair in the Viola Concerto (1985), it is the latter quality towards which the final compositions gravitate with numbing self-absorption, uttering unambiguously heartfelt cries of despair which have little or no wider social, political relevance. To characterise, *Grove*-style, the Symphony No. 8 (1994) as concerned with 'the moral and spiritual struggles of contemporary man' is to impose an unreasonable burden on music which speaks of much narrower and more personal concerns, and even though 'purely musical argument' is attenuated in the extreme, the sense of struggling with personal despair, and of progressing to a final, uncertain affirmation, is moving in its very simplicity. With no strength left to explore Cageian anarchism, Kagelian irony, or Tippett-like secular transcendence, Schnittke was left with the remnants of his own earlier, abundant scepticism about musical traditions, technical and generic, a scepticism which, as with many earlier twentieth-century progressives, required the composer to engage in serious dialogue with those traditions rather than blithely to assert an absolute alienation from them.

Not that it is easy to detect how serious, or how sceptical Schnittke's response to tradition might be. The String Trio (1985) is one of his most memorable works in the haunting economy of its thematic material and the strongly delineated profiles of its harmonic and formal procedures. The fact that it was commissioned by the Alban Berg Foundation to mark the centenary of Berg's birth has encouraged commentators to consider what Schnittke shared with Berg. Schnittke's Germanic connections, by birth and language, and his particular love for Vienna are well attested.[18] Yet Alexander Ivashkin wisely problematises the German connection: 'he keeps the symphonic tradition alive and one may certainly detect the influence of German culture, German forms and German logic; but at the same time Schnittke virtually destroys the symphonic tradition by showing its erosion' (p. 165). For Ivashkin, 'Schnittke really lies between two traditions, with German rationalism on one hand and Russian irrationalism on the other', and it is the latter tradition that does most to fuel 'Schnittke's scepticism towards structural guarantees and the symphonic "framework"' (pp. 165, 166). It is unlikely that Schnittke was consciously relying on this scepticism to make his String Trio as different as

Ex. 7.4   Schnittke, String Trio, beginning

possible from the modern Germanic precedent created by Berg's teacher Arnold
Schoenberg. As noted in Chapter 5, Schoenberg composed what Michael Cherlin
defined as a work which 'seems alternately to remember and then abandon the
musical languages of its antecedents': and there is a 'dialogue between opposing
tendencies'[19] whose complex and multiple generic attributes move subtly and un-
predictably between the polar opposites of remembering and forgetting – tonal
nostalgia and twelve-note expressionism, tenderness and aggressiveness.
Schnittke's focus on much simpler, more obviously traditional thematic material
actually makes his Trio less 'irrational' than Schoenberg's. Its generic allusions –
slow waltz, chorale, 'improvisatory' expressionistic outburst – are more overt, the
kind of opposition between diatonic motive and dissonant harmony – set out unambiguously at the very beginning – more sustained (Ex. 7.4). This music seems

Ex. 7.5   Schnittke, String Trio, ending

to move beyond scepticism about the value of traditional modes of expression into the resigned acknowledgement of the inescapable appeal of simple traditions, and the role of the modern composer in preserving those traditions through distortion rather than through imitation or transformation. In the final stages of Schnittke's Trio, the simple tune returns, in a relatively stable context confirming its G minor tonality, but the work ends as the stability dissolves around a chord that underpins the G tonic and dominant with their semitonal shadows, C♯ and A♭ (Ex. 7.5). As with Schoenberg's ending, 'dissolution might be a more decisive factor here than resolution',[20] yet there is rather less sense of any resistance to the poetics of loss, or of any alternative to the language of lament.

Affirmation, irony

Whether or not we agree with *Grove* that the hyper-austere, texturally attenuated state of Schnittke's final works amounts to 'near- suppression of purely musical argument', it is difficult to deny the difference in character between Schnittke's Eighth Symphony and Cage's *Lecture on the Weather*, where the suppression of musical argument is not only consciously intended but adopted for positive aesthetic reasons. By contrast, the final works of Shostakovich, while unremittingly anti-transcendent in their abundant allusions to the composer's despair at the prospect of personal extinction (with nothing comparable to the resigned sublimity of the ending of Mahler's *Das Lied von der Erde*), retain more 'well-made' musical substance, as indicated by the extent to which they still relate to traditional genres and processes: indeed, far from appearing to suppress such relations, they are intensified in the last three string quartets and the Viola Sonata. A very different fusion of 'anti-transcendence' with well-made musical content is provided by Kagel, whose favoured referential mode is, if not the literal opposite of lament, potently ironic in its allusions to the substance of traditions and precedents.

With Tippett the persistence of substance is allied to the persistence of a concern to balance or even counter scepticism with the quest for non-religious transcendence. Tippett, especially in his later works, is probably less involved with the kind of musical 'argument' that reflects a Beethovenian sense of purpose than with the evocation or revelation of magical, sublime states. Yet although the distance of these works from their parent genres and traditional compositional procedures suggests a continued scepticism about – rather than wholehearted rejection of – those traditions, the musical effect is never merely sardonic or wry. Even the (often rather laboured) ironies and witticisms of *The Mask of Time* and the last opera *New Year* (1986–8) aspire to be visionary, not debunking, in keeping with Tippett's abiding ambition 'to try to transfigure the everyday by a touch of the everlasting'. His wish to match the achievement of Gustav Holst, who 'transcended his time, his location, his roots, showing himself a true visionary' (*Tippett on Music*, p. 75), is nevertheless evidence of abiding scepticism about the extent to which art should involve itself exclusively in the world as mundane, everyday. Tippett's problem was to square his secular spiritual fervour – his belief that 'we are morally and emotionally enfeebled if we live our lives without artistic nourishment' (p. 15) – with his lack of the kind of sympathies with religious ceremony and convention that inspired Schnittke's *Choral Concerto*. As Tippett observed in connection with his Third Symphony, 'affirmation had to be balanced by irony' (p. 96): and in his best work, that balance, between acknowledging contemporary social and political realities and the urge to transcend those realities with finer feelings and more elevated imagery, is struck with remarkable technical resourcefulness and emotional conviction.[21]

How could a serious twentieth-century composer not regularly feel alienated from the social, political world, even in times of peace and prosperity? To be a serious composer – even if successful – is to be a member of a minority within a minority: the practitioners and supporters of 'classical' music, and the best-adjusted composers during the later twentieth century were probably those, like Ligeti and Xenakis, whose wartime experiences encouraged them to relish the post-war freedom to be themselves. They sought no social role, beyond being available to occasional disciples (students, musicologists). By contrast, the efforts of serious composers from Britten to Henze and Maxwell Davies to be 'useful', and engage directly with cultural practice, have tended to underline the disparity between the scope and consequence of such initiatives and the very different developments within the world of commercial entertainment. If new serious music might have been expected to increase its appeal during an era in which education, leisure and wealth also increased, then the twentieth century can be deemed a missed opportunity. With the fragmentation of serious artistic expression came an inevitable creative self-consciousness in which scepticism about tradition consorted awkwardly with the kind of idealism that saw radical change as a realistic as well as a necessary development. Yet the most radical change of all, a flexiblity and tolerance that enabled some serious musicians to value Mahler as much as Boulez, made it certain that the more traditional of those composers (in company with still more traditional composers from the more distant past) would take the largest slice of the market represented by live concerts, broadcasts and recordings. Whether or not the slice available for more radical, progressive spirits is sufficient to ensure that the quality of such work is adequately appreciated, it is certainly smaller, and likely to remain so.

8   Rites of transformation

Words about harmony

The New Grove article 'Requiem Mass' ends its final section, 'After 1900', with a paragraph describing 'works that exist on the fringe of the genre'. Just three are mentioned, by John Tavener (*Celtic Requiem*, 1969), Charles Koechlin (*Requiem des pauvres bougres*, 1937 – unfinished) and Hans Werner Henze (*Requiem*, 1990–2). Of the three, the Henze is the only one which 'dispenses completely with voices', and this nine-movement, seventy-minute score is admirably summarised in a single sentence: 'Though its message is humanist and political rather than religious (the "Dies Irae" and "Rex tremendae" movements were provoked by events of the 1991 Gulf War) it shares with liturgical settings a preoccupation with, as Henze puts it, "the human fears and needs of our time, with illness and death, love and loneliness".'[1]

Henze has said a good deal more about *Requiem*, especially in his autobiography, and some of these comments will appear below. Their main concern – as is often the case when composers comment on their own works – seems to be to balance the music's personal character against its debts to the past. With *Requiem*, that past has something to do with 'our shared but solitary experience of Wagner's chromatic language', as well as with 'harmonic (and melodic) gestures from German Romanticism':[2] and there are resonances not only with other works of Henze's, like *Tristan: Preludes for Piano, Tape and Orchestra* (1973), but also with other German Requiems, including Bernd Alois Zimmermann's *Requiem for a Young Poet* (written between 1967 and 1969, but conceived back in the 1950s) which quotes Wagner's *Tristan* as well as many other things.

Zimmermann's music tends to arouse strong feelings – and he is not even mentioned in *Bohemian Fifths*. Yet the two composers are comparable in some respects, not least in seeking for alternatives to 'year zero', avant-garde thinking in the 1950s. There is nevertheless a great difference between Zimmermann's no-holds-barred pluralism, with its often highly mannered confrontations between quoted fragments of real pieces (reviving, it now seems, a then-unfamiliar Ivesian ideal), and a technique which Henze describes as evolving out of a regard for Fuxian counterpoint. This, he says,

> contains an essential idea that is of profound significance today, more especially against the background of free tonality. I am thinking here of the degrees

of tension that arise when two or more lines converge, a tension that can be increased or decreased by means of part-writing...I continue to write polyphonically, following the ancient rules, even when I violate them for artistic reasons. (p. 33)

From the inchoate context of these remarks it can be deduced that Henze is uneasy about such relatively technical self-analysis. Well he might be, for he touches here on a fundamental aspect of his work, the way it aspires to an integration and consistency which can only be deemed 'classical'. Yet is it not an archetypally modernist, anti-classical strategy to pinpoint the supreme tension of 'following the ancient rules, even when I violate them'? Though not content with Zimmermann-style collage (nor, perhaps, was Zimmermann), Henze is still unable to advance into a world free of those traditions and associations which, for a German of his generation and experiences, remain profoundly disquieting. 'The Germans are still hated in Europe', Henze wrote in the 1990s, 'still the object of contempt and mistrust. More time is needed: at least two more generations must come and go before the Germans' reputation is more or less restored and the events of 1933 to 1945 are mercifully forgotten.' He then recalls that 'for me, German art – especially the middle-class, nationalistic art of the nineteenth and early twentieth centuries – became insufferable and suspect. For a time I was unable and unwilling to take any interest in it' (p. 53). Eventually, however, he was unable not to be interested, and influenced, by it – while seeking to transform, and even redeem it.

Describing his preparations for the composition of the opera *The Bassarids* (1964–5), Henze writes that 'both Auden and Kallman were keen that, as a relatively young German composer, I should learn to overcome my political and aesthetic aversions to Wagner's music, aversions bound up in no small measure with my many unfortunate experiences in the past'. He then provides a semi-comic account of a performance of *Götterdämmerung* in Vienna, which 'seemed to go on for ever' (perhaps the similarity to Stravinsky's account of attending *Parsifal* at Bayreuth in 1912 is intentional):[3]

> Of course, I was perfectly capable of judging the wider significance of Wagner's music...But I simply cannot abide this silly and self-regarding emotionalism, behind which it is impossible not to detect a neo-German mentality and ideology. There is the sense of an imperialist threat, of something militantly nationalistic, something disagreeably heterosexual and Aryan in all those rampant horn calls, this pseudo-Germanic *Stabreim*, these incessant chords of a seventh and all the insecure heroes and villains that people Wagner's librettos. (pp. 206–7)

Since Henze's critique includes technical as well as ideological aspects, it is all the more ironic that he should, in the end, seek to define his later, most mature style in relation to those very traditions excoriated here. After all, he has made no claims about reconciliation, of purging the past musically in precisely the way he declares to be impossible, for the moment, culturally. Understandably, therefore, Henze's route to Wagner seems to have been defined as much by opposition as affinity. Here is a particularly crucial text, the composer's account of the genesis of his own *Tristan*:

> One morning, early in 1972, I composed a lengthy piano piece within a few hours. The thematic material which figures prominently in it – steps of a semi-tone and sixth, and on the vertical plane, chords of the fourth and especially diminished fifths – represents distant recollections of something concrete: the music of Wagner's *Tristan*. Like Wagner's, my harmony seems to strive towards an incommensurable goal, whose attainment is constantly deferred while new questions present themselves. Wagner's music has, however, something glowing and exclusive, total and ceremonial about it. Mine, on the other hand, is cool as though it is early in the morning, and the questioning and longing are muted, seemingly coming from afar – it appears to have something marble, monumental and impersonal about it.[4]

Heard in these terms, Henze's *Tristan* becomes a 'cool', Apollonian deconstruction of Wagner's Dionysian music drama: or it would assume this character, were not that striving 'towards an incommensurable goal' such a potent counterweight to its would-be monumental 'impersonality'. There is certainly little sense of 'homage' to an idealised Master in a work which is almost Zimmermann-like in its embrace of heterogeneity. Apart from the touchingly ironic superimposition of a child's voice reading (in English) Gottfried von Strassburg's description of a passionate encounter between Tristan and Isolde onto quoted Wagner (the opening of Act 3), allusions to Chopin and Brahms reinforce the impression of socio-political purposes in which various icons of orthodoxy are paraded and ritually demolished, to intensify the looming shadow of catastrophe, of breakdown. In Henze's carefully constructed scenario, contemporary horrors in Chile are placed alongside personal memories of death in Venice, and the idea of 'Liebestod' dissolves into unambiguous lament, not exultant celebration.

A role for Wagner in late-twentieth-century compositional practice becomes more plausible if his importance for early twentieth-century radicals is recalled. The technical essence of that importance extends far beyond the psychological frisson of merely quoting, or parodying, the opening statement of *Tristan*, or some other emblematic Wagnerian fragment: and several musicologists have tried to define Wagner's importance in terms of a special kind of progressive thinking promoting the transition from tonal to post-tonal musical syntax. For example, Nicholas Baragwanath has suggested that the symmetrical structures which can be abstracted from Wagner's music dramas have profound significance for the abandonment of hierarchical, rooted harmonic thinking: and they

> also suggest an essential, specific continuity between Wagner's music and that of the early twentieth century. It seems almost as if such abstract designs were able to realize their potential only once freed from the confines of the tonal system. That so many composers around the years 1908–14, separated by national boundaries yet united through a passion for Wagner, should have arrived almost simultaneously at such similar musical 'discoveries' is perhaps more than coincidence.[5]

The urge to streamline cause and effect in such thinking merits a cautious response, not least because of the broader tendency in nineteenth-century music to explore the extended tonal relations of hexatonic and octatonic systems.[6] In any case, the response of post-1945 composers to Wagner probably owed more to the kind of features praised by Boulez – the 'ductility, or pliability' of the material in the *Ring*, the 'perpetual state of "becoming"' and the 'emphasis on *uncertainty*' in *Parsifal*[7] – than to dialogues between symmetrical and hierarchic processes. This in itself might not have been a technical feature sufficiently seductive to draw Henze back to a composer who stood for so much that he feared and despised. But an examination of Henze's 'rhetoric of lament' suggests that, along with the possibility of exorcism though deconstruction, there was the more positive prospect of exorcism through transformation.

Aspects of the *Requiem*: Mozart, Wagner, Henze

The Lacrimosa of Henze's *Requiem,* for piano, trumpet and large chamber orchestra, completed in 1992, begins with a solo trumpet ascent from D to A (Ex. 8.1a). The three intervening pitches are not tonally diatonic, although on its own the sense of a proposition in a chromatic D minor, moving from tonic to dominant, is difficult to resist, and is certainly more plausible, aurally, than the argument that the phrase composes out a symmetrical pitch-class set: D, E♭, F♯, A, B♭ [01478] (Ex. 8.1b).

'Lacrimosa, chromatic D minor' suggests a Mozartian association, and bars 5 to 8 of the Lacrimosa of Mozart's *Requiem* project a stepwise ascent from low D to high A in the choral sopranos, with a final two bars of chromatic harmonic support which includes E♭, F♯ and B♭ (Ex. 8.1c). Should we suspect a not-so-subtle case of derivation? Henze says nothing about Mozart in his own discussion of *Requiem* in *Bohemian Fifths*, and the only composer mentioned is Beethoven, the 'pastoral' rhythm' of whose Agnus Dei (*Missa solemnis*) is given 'virtually the status of a quotation' in Henze's Agnus Dei. But what Henze writes about the work more generally leaves no doubt that allusion and past-consciousness reach as deep into its fabric as is the case with many of his other compositions.

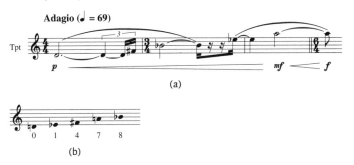

(a)

(c)

Ex. 8.1 (a) Henze, *Requiem*, Lacrimosa, initial trumpet phrase
(b) Henze, *Requiem*, pitch-class set for initial trumpet phrase
(c) Mozart, *Requiem*, Lacrimosa, bars 5–8

Writing in the spring of 1991, Henze said that *Requiem* 'involves what, for me, is a new and freer approach to chromaticism that sometimes suggests a return to the harmonic world of Wagner's *Tristan und Isolde*', and what follows merits quoting at length.

I use this harmonic language much as a poet integrates a particular foreign idiom into his personal style for his own specific ends. I evoke feelings that are familiar not only to myself but also to my listeners as a result of our shared but solitary experience of Wagner's chromatic language. I work with brief quotations often consisting of no more than a couple of syllables or, rather, of a few notes that are capable of directing the thoughts of my more knowledgeable listeners in the direction that I desire, affording them the best possible opportunities to draw all necessary comparisons and, hence and above all else, allowing them to experience the interconnections for themselves. This is why I have increasingly chosen to call up harmonic (and melodic) gestures from German Romanticism in my own more recent music – not because I am a Romantic composer, but because I adopt a specific, modern approach to the expressive language of nineteenth-century music and do so, moreover, from an analytical standpoint. It is as though I were introducing words from earlier centuries into my spoken language: one recalls them, even though they are no longer used. They mean something, but precisely what that meaning is seems to have slipped from our grasp. We have to descend into the depths of oblivion in order to find the answer. I work with the echoes left in my psyche by all that is German, especially German folk-tales. The result is sounds and images, an interplay of light, all of which I bring to the surface, effortfully but with the best of intentions, in order to place them within my own poetic context. They help me to tell my story. (pp. 57–8)

This passage is characteristic of a text whose constructions of personality and aesthetic intent are as artful as they are elusive, and in which the slippage between 'we' and 'I', the factual and the fanciful, renders explanatory interpretation perilous. In particular, the references to Wagner and nineteenth-century romanticism could almost be calculated to reinforce the music's 'specifically modern approach' – its actual distance from Wagnerian, nineteenth-century qualities – and to downplay, if not to ignore, aspects which bring Henze much closer to the techniques of his more consistently progressive contemporaries: Stockhausen's Moment-form or Boulez's serial multiplications. To provide a deliberately naive comparison: a 'Wagnerian' continuation of the Lacrimosa's opening phrase could be a sequential repetition, especially if Henze has noted the degree of contact between the ascending minor sixth A/F which opens Mozart's Lacrimosa melody and provides the first two notes of *Tristan*. But Henze actually proceeds by contrasts far more absolute than those possible with sequence. From bar 4 polyphony replaces monody (Ex. 8.2), and it is immediately much more difficult to describe the resulting texture in terms of directed motion. Nevertheless, proliferation of textural strata does not eliminate the possibility of some lines being more sustained, and in this sense stable, than others: in bars 4 to 7, the first orchestral trumpet takes over the soloist's high A, and 'answers' the soloist's leaping ascent with a stepwise descent – A, A♭, G, G♭, F. To point up the distinction between such an obvious *Hauptstimme*, with its stark delineation of the lament topos, and a decorative *Nebenstimme*, Henze has the lower violin line (players 2, 3 and 4) starting on the same A and moving more rapidly around the two semitones above it. But when the *Hauptstimme* begins to move, in bar 6, the violins unite with a much more sharply articulated ascending counterpoint, elaborating the basic D/A ascent and extending it in ways which the solo trumpet is also beginning to explore.

This brief analytical exercise is intended to underline the point that in such modernist contexts there is a world of difference between the systematic functional elaborations of tonal Background into Middleground and Foreground, and the separation of notional frameworks (others could well be proposed for this passage)

Ex. 8.2   Henze, *Requiem*, Lacrimosa, bars 4–7

from the actual, atonal musical surface. For example, while it is possible to propose that the upper-voice framework A in bars 4 and 5 of Henze's Lacrimosa is underpinned by an F, to anticipate the more sustained bass F in bar 6, the departures from and returns to that pitch-class are governed by concerns for linear independence within a relatively uniform tonal colour (the string writing, in particular).

Other elaborative procedures in this continuation include the shadowing of the *Hauptstimme* descent, at the minor third below, in double bassoon and double bass (bars 6–7): and although there is only fragmentary representation of a bass line in the continuation to bar 14, the stepwise focus around C♯, D, D♯, E and F is clear, reinforced as it is by the solo piano. These are some of the ways in which Henze elaborates a texture whose primary expressive purpose is to represent a transformation from self-possession to breakdown ('like a scream' at bar 14). With

Ex. 8.2   (cont.)

this dramatic trajectory it is perhaps fitting that the solo trumpet line should sound as much in conflict with already conflicting orchestral lines as in harmoniously balanced counterpoint. While the separate strata — strings, woodwind, brass, piano with trumpet — might be quite conventionally balanced as contrapuntal designs in themselves, their combination (even when there is a strong degree of convergence, as in bars 12–13) promotes a move from resolution to disintegration.

Such qualities are strongly implied by the composer's account of the movement as a portrait of a suffering, weeping individual...We do not know the reasons for the man's weeping, do not know the nature of the pain that arises from the musical textures necessary to depict it. All that we can do is follow the course that is taken by this weeping and grieving, emotions depicted by a solo trumpeter with assistance from all the other performers, swelling, abating, welling up once again and finally breaking off for ever with an expression of utter despair. (p. 471)

Furthermore, 'all the other performers' assist the solo trumpeter by making harmonious integration and consolation – what Henze refers to a little later as 'divine or artistic comfort' – impossible. Yet choices have to be made, even when depicting sorrow and pain, and the final stages of the Lacrimosa (from one bar before Fig. 13 to the end, too densely scored to be reproduced here) do suggest a conclusion on the basis of the initial premiss.

On the one hand, there are features which relate to a chromatic D minor, with D and A emphasis, and include, after the cellos' descent to a bass A at the double bar, the piano's A- and D-based clusters, reinforced by the celesta. In combination with these, the trumpet's frantic final phrase plunges to low A, then rises to the high D, in what almost amounts to a triumphant enjoyment of pain. D-emphasis is supported at the end by horns, oboe, cor anglais and flutes. But what counters the D minor tonal tendency most decisively is the absence of D from the bass. In pitch-class terms, D is put at the centre of a symmetric cluster – B, C, D, E, F [01356] – whose spanning tritone is graphically reinforced by the timpani's final glissando. At the very least, as the sustained horn dyad suggests, D and E are competing, yet homogeneously superimposed quasi-tonics.

One of Henze's most decisive declarations is that 'my music draws what strength it has from its inherent contradictions' (p. 56). Yet, while this comment could obviously refer as much if not more to grand work-spanning expressive characteristics as to local details of texture and harmony, he goes on to say that 'in the course of my development, my works have become more and more multi-layered', and that the 'superimposed layers of music should be seen and heard as precisely that, with all their comings and goings, their appearances and disappearances, the increase and decrease in their presence and density producing a constant fluctuation in intensity and light and thereby ensuring excitement, surprise, and variety' (pp. 56–7). This combines a bold prescription for listening with the promise of a specific perceptual result, as if there is something in the music guaranteed to ensure that other (tonal, hierarchic) ways of hearing will not interfere with or confuse the response. That this result cannot be guaranteed is evident in the fairly common critical complaint about the obliqueness, the greyness, of Henze's harmony.

No self-analytical statement in Henze's autobiography is more crucial than the remark that 'in my polyphonic writing...I had to be on permanent guard not to

Ex. 8.3   Henze, *Requiem*, Agnus Dei, beginning

overload the textures and provide too much information' (p. 422): the point being
that 'overload' tends to intensify homogeneity, rather than 'inherent contradictions' — the complementary, competing strata inherent in a properly functioning
musical modernism.

One example of layer-superimposition which balances similarity and diversity can be found in the contrast between strings and piano at the start of the Agnus
Dei (Ex. 8.3). Again, the foundation is an initial fifth, D/A, and the simplest, least
independent stratum is that in the double basses, whose A is doubled by the violas,
the semitone D♯ to E by the violins. The tripartite viola stratum starts from that
shared A, but evolves into a sequence of triads (F♯ major, B minor, diminished — C,
E♭, F♯). The cello stratum also involves three-part stepwise movement, but the harmony is less consistently triadic, the upper line finally flowering into a melodic
shape whose focal D♮ is dissonant with the lines of the other strata. Finally, the

Ex. 8.3   (cont.)

violin stratum has a melodic shape spanning the octave D♯ which certainly does not 'fit' with the other main melodic strand in Cello 1.

Is this the kind of 'inherent contradiction' to which Henze refers? The closeness of register and homogeneity of timbre enforce an instability in which any sense of a coordinating bass descent – D, C, B♭, A♭, G – is suppressed. But is there 'too much information', and therefore textural 'overload', in this passage? Is the effect of a rapt floating calm, or of an opaque, inchoate flux? The rhythmic oscillations, and use of immediate repetition within the most continuous strata, inhibit definition and sense of motion, and these characteristics persist in the piano's antiphonal response, where there is a tendency to merge the initially distinct material for the two hands. Even at the other expressive extreme of *Requiem*, in Rex tremendae (1991–2), the initial separation of solo trumpet from punctuating, perfunctorily accompanying ensemble gives way to a more uniform textural density in which the ensemble does its utmost to reinforce the trumpet's dramatic purpose. This is not the kind of information overload that generates expressive ambiguity, still less incoherence. But in the absence of that ambiguity, the texture, the information, could be rather more dense than it needs to be. If some of those thickenings and doublings were deleted, would the result be too thin, too understated, to suggest 'the voice of a ruler or commander relayed through the trumpet's amplifying bell in what seems to be an agitated, fanatically incendiary speech delivered in a rasping, peremptory tone and using a vocabulary which, vulgar to the point of sounding comical, is aggressively petty bourgeois' (p. 470)? This is a particular problem for a composer who finds tradition-evoking Germanic expressionism culturally distasteful, yet whose own expressive aspirations seem to demand not so much its evocation but its transcendence.

Wagner, Britten, Henze

If Henze's aim were to transcend the Wagnerian, and the Dionysian, not so much by subverting their most important elements as by shunning them altogether, cultivation of the Italianate and the Apollonian might prove an effective tool. The more consistently dance-like — at least if avoiding swaying waltz-like rhythms evoking *Parsifal*'s Flowermaidens — the more clear-cut and regular in phraseology, the less debilitating any conformity to the principles of Wagnerian musical prose would be. Another strategy would be to aim at a specifically non-Wagnerian kind of opera — and Henze's sympathy for the achievements of Benjamin Britten gave him a very concrete example of what viably un-Wagnerian opera after Wagner could be like. But Henze was drawn to elaborate depictions of the Dionysian, and it was therefore a stroke of genius to use the Wagnerian potential of *The Bassarids* (as Auden saw it) as the basis for a declaration of post-Wagnerian intent, since among many other things *The Bassarids* is, in outline, a four-movement symphony, where 'Mahler's influence is greater...than even in my Sixth, Seventh or Eighth Symphonies' (p. 208).

For those who believe that Wagner, with his music dramas, created a new genre of 'symphonic opera', and that Mahler, of all composers after Wagner, came nearest to writing dramatic symphonic works of the kind Wagner might himself have contemplated (in spirit, if not in style), *The Bassarids* is indeed a statement of conscious 'going-beyond'. As Henze observes, 'it is certainly not Wagner's compositional method that is taken up and developed here; for that, my piece is far too close to the older type of number opera' (p. 207). At the same time, however, *The Bassarids* appears to attach even more importance to an all-embracing symphonic framework than Berg did in the alignments between particular instrumental genres and operatic through-composition in *Wozzeck* and *Lulu*. It can therefore be seen as a grandiose attempt both to transcend and to subvert the Wagnerian style. Not only does *The Bassarids* end with a Passacaglia, the kind of instrumental form which Wagner's musical prose had no room for, but it ends with a male God asserting control. In what seems like a conscious inversion of the climax of *The Ring*, it is the palace of the human rulers which is burned, while Olympus, the equivalent of Valhalla, remains secure.

The character of Dionysus, central to *The Bassarids*, is one to which Henze was profoundly drawn, and the main reason for his failure to escape the lure of Wagner in general and *Tristan* in particular is the defiant Dionysianism embodied in the style and structure of so many of Henze's works. For much of the twentieth century, as for the nineteenth, the topic of a doomed and desperate love, defying social conventions, could be held to point in the direction of homosexuality, and since Henze's *Requiem* is inscribed 'in memoriam Michael Vyner', the London Sinfonietta's artistic director, who died of AIDS, it is by no means inappropriate to consider that work against the background of other celebrations of homosexual or pederastic obsession. A prompting for this approach comes from Timothy L. Jackson's controversial study of Tchaikovsky's Sixth Symphony as 'an erotic drama of doomed homosexual love richly adorned with intertextual references to opera, specially to Wagner's *Tristan*, Bizet's *Carmen*, and Tchaikovsky's own operas'.[8] The analogy is initially strengthened by the degree to which Tchaikovsky seems to have thought of the symphony as a Requiem (p. 44): but to follow Jackson's interpretation is to encounter one fundamental distinction between the tone of these two works.

At the heart of Jackson's reading is the belief that Tchaikovsky composed what amounts to a 'deformation' of *Tristan*'s Schopenhauerian ethos:

> There can be no doubt that for Wagner, Tchaikovsky, and many later nineteenth- and early twentieth-century composers, register had profound symbolic and metaphysical connotations. Employing Schopenhauerian terminology, we may conceive the phenomenal world as basic reality...If basic reality – the phenomenal – corresponds to the lowest register, and transcendental reality – the noumenal – is associated with the highest register, then the emphatic *ascent* (the musical-rhetorical figure of *anabasis*) in the *Tristan Liebestod* from the very lowest to the very highest registral bands may represent the arduous path from the everyday world to the higher plane of the visionary, i.e. from the illusion of the phenomenal to the ultimate reality of the noumenal. In the *Pathétique*'s critical deformation of *Tristan*, the converse, i.e. the striking *descent* (*catabasis*) from the highest to the lowest register, signifies numbing collapse.

Jackson later reinforces the point: 'In *Tristan*, the lovers, although condemned on earth, experience transfiguration in the realm of death...But through critical deformation of *Tristan* in the *Pathétique*...the homosexual condition proves "incurable": there can be no transfiguration; rather, the lovers are condemned to the eternal "darkness" of their "illness" and the nihilistic oblivion of death' (p. 69).

The ending of Henze's *Requiem* is closer in spirit to that of *Tristan* itself than to Tchaikovsky's symphonic 'descent': and despite his eagerness to impose a singular master trope on the whole of music history after Tchaikovsky, Jackson concedes that whereas Berg's *Lulu* analogously associates an 'unhappy and finally fatal' narrative about same-sex love with '*Tristan*-deformation' (p. 97), Britten's

Death in Venice, which also uses the *Tristan* chord to represent 'Aschenbach's un-satisfied homosexual yearning for Tadzio', is more ambiguous. Since 'it can be shown that the opera's final measures provide the strategically withheld resolution to the "*Tristan-Pathétique*" chord... perhaps, in the closing scene Britten also reverses the tragedy of Tchaikovsky's *Adagio lamentoso*, transfiguring homosexual pathos in post-mortem resolution of the "dysfunctional" seventh chord.' Leaving aside the technical loose ends of this interpretation, it can at least be acknowledged that the spirit of delicate transfiguration suggested at the end of Britten's last opera is taken up and made more decisive and affirmative at the end of Henze's Sanctus, which he describes as a hymn to the 'holy' mystery of creation.[9]

The grand impersonality of these images is a useful reminder that Henze's own relationship to Michael Vyner was not that of Aschenbach to Tadzio, still less that of Tchaikovsky to Vladimir Davidov. But Jackson's description of Britten's 'transfiguring homosexual pathos in post-mortem resolution' is still relevant to the tone and character of Henze's Sanctus, where the solo trumpet climbs to its highest register, and the Schütz-inspired spatiality of the two echoing trumpets, as well as the potent decorative flourishes of the rest of the ensemble, create a sense of striving for transcendence. What is not achieved is any breakthrough into Apollonian serenity or detachment. In the context of *Requiem*, such a mood would seem positively blasphemous. Only very rarely, as in the setting of the Hafiz/Rückert 'Das Paradies' which forms the last of the *Sechs Gesänge aus dem Arabischen* (1999) does Henze approach a calmer spirit: and even this does not completely banish all fear of the dark. As for the very different spirit in which *Requiem* ends, Henze's description echoes the final words of *The Bassarids* about 'incomprehensible mysteries, not for mortals to know'. But one suspects that the composer is less interested in the vision of a god required by the opera's subject-matter, more aware of 'the presence of higher powers... which we do not and cannot understand' (Henze, 'Language', p. 22), and in which that 'mystery of creation' is enshrined. The great achievement of Henze's *Requiem* is to create the feeling that such matters are not demeaned by the music which evokes them.

Given the Wagnerian theme which runs through this chapter, it is tempting to consider *Requiem*'s concluding Sanctus as equivalent to Isolde's 'Verklärung' — otherwise known (not by Wagner) as the 'Liebestod'. This is only conceivable in the wider context of a view of *Requiem* which sees it as sharing something fundamental with Wagner's 'Handlung', as defined with special clarity by Thomas Mann. In *Tristan*, Mann wrote, 'there is no God — nobody mentions him, nobody evokes him. There is only erotic philosophy, atheistic metaphysics, the cosmogonical myth in which the longing motif summons the world into being.'[10] Yet the absence of God is not the absence of religion. Joseph Kerman has argued that *Tristan und Isolde* 'is a religious drama' in which 'the fundamental sense is of a progress towards a state of illumination which transcends yearning and pain',[11] and Michael Tanner concurs, declaring that 'while not being Christian, *Tristan* is in certain ways decidedly religious; in the need, above all, of its two central characters to transcend themselves'. Since Tanner accepts the interchangeability of 'religious' and 'metaphysical', it becomes possible to equate Mann's 'atheistic metaphysics' with what Tanner defines as the work's 'curious tendency... to become ever more overwhelmingly sensuous the more it is concerned with transcendence'.[12]

Whether or not Henze would accept 'atheistic metaphysics' as a description of his attitude to the 'mystery of creation' in *Requiem*, it is difficult to resist the feeling of sensuality fuelling transcendence in the shape and style of the solo trumpet's final melodic surges in the Sanctus. This is not to make the tasteless proposal that the trumpet is some kind of embodiment of the voice and character of *Requiem*'s dedicatee, still less of its composer. If the composer has a role in this drama, it is as likely to be that of the Marke-like compassionate observer: only, in this case, Henze is both observer and composer, Marke and Wagner.

If the endings of Wagner's *Tristan* and Henze's *Requiem* are seen as un-equivocally affirmative – and the fulfilment of Dionysian ecstasy rather than its rejection – other comparisons may be made, and other similarities adduced. But not all commentators have been willing to accept Wagner's own description of the 'Verklärung' as a 'blessed fulfilment of ardent longing'.[13] For Robert Gutman, it offers 'a kind of purging, but no true catharsis',[14] while for John Deathridge 'the most important thing about Isolde's death scene is that, gradually and al-most imperceptibly, it seems to separate itself off from the rest of the opera':[15] and Deathridge underlines what for him is the 'postmodern' quality of Wagner's work by challenging all those super-integrationist readings of the 'Verklärung' which attempt 'to domesticate... the work's subversive close'. As he concludes,

> if analytical propriety can make out a seemingly good case for the inherent unity of the *Liebestod* with the rest of *Tristan* it is again the expressive char-acter of the music, as well as its tonal structure, which exposes the spirit of contradiction, the difference in sameness, that the comforting view of organic wholeness usually fails to confront in the looking-glass world at the centre of the opera. (p. 117)

The 'spirit of contradiction' is also apparent in the way that, in the drama as a whole, non-conformity is symbiotically matched by separation. In conform-ing to their transcendent impulses, the lovers achieve a resolution, but against the silent background of the grief and sorrow of the 'conventional' society that remains. (Arthur Groos has written persuasively about 'the mutual unintelligibil-ity of the lovers and the feudal world'.[16]) In this reading, the ending of *Tristan* is so poignant and powerful not because Isolde 'triumphs', but because her ful-filment and Marke's regret are indissolubly fused, yet unmistakably distinct. The 'Verklärung' is, therefore, as much the fantasy of a deeply isolated persona as that celebration of sublime spiritual fusion of which the music seems to speak. If the infinitely delayed, opulently celebrated B major resolution is at the same time 'inconclusive, equivocal', as Gutman claims (p. 359), this can only be because it represents Isolde compensating, as she dies of grief, for her failure to cure Tristan a second time. The combination of Isolde's blissful self-absorption and the compliant sorrow of King Marke suggests that the ending offers a dialogue between fulfilment and regret, rather than an unambiguous embodiment of Wagner's 'blessed fulfilment of ardent longing'.

For Henze, with his post-tonal language and commitment to contradiction, it might be expected that such a sense of symbiosis, of dialogue, would be enhanced and intensified, projecting not so much a 'deformation' of *Tristan* as a reformulation of its more traditional, more conventional dramatic and tonal ambiguities. The problem is that Henze is celebrating the memory, and remembering the suffering, of real people, and the effect of the Sanctus's conclusion is more that of a triumph over superhuman odds than a precarious balance between doubt and certainty, regret and joy. This music has more of that 'glowing, ceremonial' quality that Henze seems to dislike in Wagner, less of the cool impersonality which was his answer, in theory, to Wagner. Of course, it could be argued that while, on the one hand, the solo trumpet rises unequivocally and triumphantly to its top C in a context which could support a tonal, or at least modal interpretation, the ostinato-dominated accompaniment, quite devoid of counter-melodic voices save from the two other trumpets separated out in the hall, refuses to accept the soloist's 'resolution', preserving an element of resistance to the end. A pure C major ending is not possible within the parameters of Henze's language anyway, and it could just as well be argued that the accompaniment provides a stable background which throws the soloist's triumphant move to closure into the most effective relief. If Henze is to avoid that 'silly and self-regarding emotionalism' he so disliked in *Götterdämmerung*, he must never allow the prose-like tendency inherent in post-Wagnerian music to lose all contact with classical disciplines. As a result, the element of regret that can be sensed alongside fulfilment at the end of *Tristan* – or Mahler's *Das Lied von der Erde* – is less apparent here than elsewhere in *Requiem*.

The German labyrinth

The place that Germany represents for Henze invites a constant process of construction and reconstruction, alienated as he is by the horrors of political and social history, while engaged by artistic traditions that leave central genres like symphony and opera open to interrogation and continuation. As seen in earlier chapters, musical life in Germany after 1945 has been broad enough to accommodate such different attitudes to tradition as Kagel's oratorio *Sankt Bach Passion* and Stockhausen's opera-cycle *Licht*. The primary synthesising force appears to have been an aesthetic preference for the 'inclusive' rather than the 'exclusive', as in Wolfgang Rihm's notion of *Inclusivsmusik*. The appeal of this lies in its very flexibility, and in the degree to which composers can be associated with it even – especially – if they would prefer not to be. Thus, while there is a very great difference between the collage-technique of Zimmermann's *Requiem for a Young Poet* and the determinedly self-referential ethos and processes of *Licht*, the concept of inclusiveness can be adapted to acknowledge Stockhausen's manipulation of multimedia, as well as the inescapable associations created between his *magnum opus* and other operatic representations of a world-view.

In most cases, nevertheless, inclusiveness is not synonymous with allusiveness, but requires some specific representation of and tension between distinct 'voices' within a single work. With Helmut Lachenmann, for example, there has been an emerging awareness of 'the impossibility of ignoring the historical connotations of any music, even that so removed from convention as his own, and that to shut out the past was analogous to an attempt to forget history, and thus be condemned to repeat its mistakes'. Writing of Lachenmann's 'breakthrough' work, the Clarinet Concerto *Accanto* (1975–6), Ian Pace observes that it 'enters into a dialogue with Mozart's Clarinet Concerto', but that 'only very brief fragments or snatches of harmony of the Mozart can be discerned'. Pace also stresses Lachenmann's concern 'to temper any sentiments of nostalgia with their opposite extreme, thus avoiding the pitfalls of many other works making use of quotation, which appeal to an audience primarily because they enable one to bask in the familiar'.[17]

Here a refusal 'to shut out the past' is conceived less as a means of embracing diversity and devising continuities than as a way of dramatising distance, to make the audience more vividly aware of how time passes. By contrast, York Höller aims to achieve as complete and natural a synthesis as possible between quoter and quoted: to contextualise nostalgia, and to make it feel at home rather than estranged. That is the view of Jürg Stenzl, who sees Höller's opera *The Master and Margarita* (1984–8) as 'championing the art of synthesis'. The result is 'not an accumulation of different operatic legacies exploited for their "post-modernism": the few quotes (Berlioz, Busoni, Ravel) are very discrete and the allusions to ancient music... are perfectly integrated. Trapped in a crumbling contemporary world, Höller creates another; the work of art proffered as "world" in which all contradictions are reconciled.'[18]

As I have argued elsewhere,[19] such a determined synthesis risks depriving the music of links with its modernist inheritance, promoting a 'new classicism' instead. In not wishing to exclude Höller from all contact with that 'crumbling contemporary world', I also question whether he has been quite as decisive in reconciling 'all contradictions' as Stenzl claims. Nevertheless, Höller aspires to a higher degree of integration and synthetic stability than the iconoclastic Lachenmann, and to this extent his work can be aligned with the prevailing Germanic image of inclusion that embraces the music of the term's inventor Wolfgang Rihm. In no work of Rihm's is the symbiosis of accepting yet resisting associations with tradition more effectively wrought than his *Deus Passus: Passions-Stücke nach Lukas* (2000).

Rihm is both prolific and uneven, and there is an abiding paradox about a composer who proclaims himself strongly influenced by such radicals as Feldman, Nono and Lachenmann, yet risks lapsing into a neutral non-radicalism by shunning the obvious extremes which such allegiance might be expected to promote. What makes *Deus Passus* so impressive is that these risks have been turned to positive account, not least in choral writing whose solemnity manages to evoke both Handel and Hindemith, while having a harmonic tension very different from either.[20] As Rihm's title suggests, his treatment of Christ's suffering and death is more fragmentary than those precedents, from Schütz to Penderecki, which inevitably come to mind. Although Rihm shuns the unguarded pathos that helped to popularise Penderecki's *St Luke Passion* in the 1960s, his music moves very convincingly between austerity and expressiveness. Explicit personification is avoided in one respect: Christ is not portrayed by a single singer. But there is still plenty of vivid characterisation, and while Rihm, like Penderecki, replaces Bach-style chorales with such meditative texts as the *Stabat mater*, his treatment is economical rather than expansive, and as likely to resort to chilly understatement (the choral mutterings of 'Barabbas' and 'crucify') as to hectic clamour. Nowhere is Rihm's concern to dramatise tension between old and new, religion and politics, more evident than in his decision to end *Deus Passus* with a setting of Paul Celan's 'Tenebrae'.[21] To some it will smack of callow political correctness to pick this unsparing, post-Holocaust reversal of the conventional relationship between praying humanity and listening God (God being exhorted by Celan to 'pray to us'). This text certainly threatens to render the preceding Gospel text irrelevant, and that could be the whole point, since Rihm's music is equal to the angry sorrow as well as the ritualistic gravity of Celan's lines. As a result, *Deus Passus* is an impressive vindication of the rewards of confronting precedents and traditions in ways which reinterpret rather than reject them: it embodies another Rite of Transformation.

9 Modernism, lyricism

Shadow and symmetry

The world described in Elizabeth Bishop's poem 'Insomnia', set by Elliott Carter in *A Mirror on which to Dwell* (1975), is inverted, mirrored: 'left is always right'. The moon has a floating-in-space perspective, placed between the earth and the rest of the universe. But the last three lines of the poem suggest another perspective:[1] the human presences represented by 'we', 'you' and 'me' are separate from the moon's 'she'. It is 'we', or maybe only 'me', who see the moon reflected in the bureau mirror, and this mirror, like the no less reflecting 'body of water' mentioned later, represents earth, gravity. The world of the poem extends a million miles out into space from the room with a bureau. Yet the 'me' inhabiting the room feels kinship with the moon's inverted world of unreality, in which matters of virtual, spatial experience, 'where the shadows are really the body...where the heavens are shallow as the sea is now deep', intersect with human experiences: 'where we stay awake all night...and you love me'. None of this, the poem gently implies, corresponds to reality.

If, as this reading suggests, the poem reflects a situation in which you do *not* love me, its ending is touched with regret. But there is no breast-beating declaration of sorrow, and, for Carter, the predominant mood is indicated by the marking 'tranquillo' which governs the vocal line, save for the contrasting segment of the middle stanza (bars 16–22), whose atmosphere is more good-humoured than angry. But how much of a reading of the text like the above can be captured by the music? An account of Carter's setting without reference to the text would probably begin with the character of the instrumental writing, so clearly stratified between the flickering, fragmented viola and marimba parts and the sustained lines in violin and piccolo. However, Carter has no intention of preserving such a simple opposition unvaried throughout the movement, and contrast comes near the midpoint. After bar 21, the viola participates in the more sustained counterpoint and the marimba is virtually silent, before a brief return to the original textural pairings in the last two bars.

The image of floating in space is no less appropriate to the music than to the poem, given Carter's emphasis on relatively high register and flexible rhythm, and his avoidance of treble/bass polarity, even though there could be a gently ironic hint of traditional earth-bound cadencing at the end in the way B and F♯ are treated. Further, the effect of the opening, as the instruments fan out from a

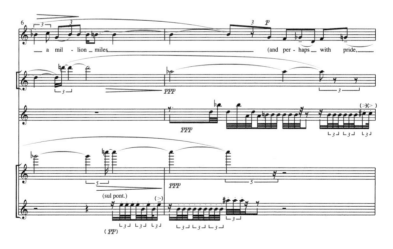

Ex. 9.1   Carter, *A Mirror on Which to Dwell*, 'Insomnia', beginning

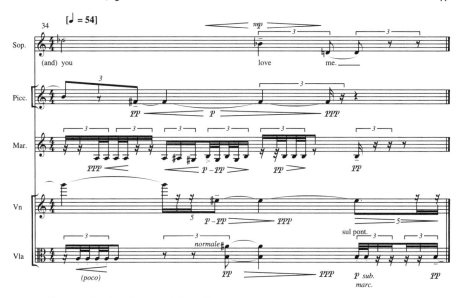

Ex. 9.2   Carter, 'Insomnia', ending

collection of shared pitches, is comparable to the ripples in water when a stone is dropped onto a still surface. If music can suggest floating by resisting gravitation, it can also – as noted in Chapter 2 – represent mirroring by the use of inversional symmetry. Carter's setting of the poem's first two lines (bars 4–6) does this explicitly, and the absence of the axis of symmetry – A – at a point when the persistence of E above is still hinting at a degree of 'inverted' rootedness, offers a delicately ironic response to the poetic word-play (Ex. 9.1). To the extent that the poem is about perception split between overlapping manifestations of the real and the unreal, the music can respond by using processes in which contrast does not exclude degrees of similarity, of shadowing. Shadowing seems to be the decisive image at the end, both poetically and musically, as closure is achieved through an appropriate combination of real and unreal, 'body' and 'shadow'. A more technical way of describing this is to talk of the combination of convergence and divergence. Several lines move onto the relatively stable interval of the perfect fifth, B/F♯, while other voices diverge, touching in the 'shadow' fifth, A♯/E♯ (Ex. 9.2). The element of reductiveness evident in any such analysis can be defended on grounds of interpretative validity. While the convergence/divergence model fits with the specifics of the text, it could function in many other contexts too. It is a regular feature of Carter's style and technique, not a purely local response to a single verbal stimulus.[2]

Bishop's poem is not a straightforward narrative account of an insomniac state of mind, but it does not move a great distance away from simple propositions and statements. Paul Celan's poetry is more radical, its distinctiveness stemming

Ex. 9.3　Birtwistle, *Pulse Shadows*, 'Night', ending

from the way in which phrases freighted with expressive significance − 'message of comfort', 'sign of eternity' − are placed in enigmatic contexts that destabilise them both syntactically and semantically. John Felstiner has described Celan as a poet whom 'negation and paradox' serve as 'a basic stylistic principle', while, at the same time, 'the urge towards transcendence and resolution of paradox' are present, in 'an art of contrast and allusion that celebrates beauty and energy while commemorating their destruction'.[3] There is no shortage of musical imagery, or of the kind of formal devices alluding to refrain structures ('psalm-like incremental repetition'), to attract composers to Celan, and Harrison Birtwistle proves well suited to depicting something analogous to what Felstiner terms the 'abysses' which open between Celan's 'ritual forms' (p. 167). Yet even in this post-Holocaust world there can still be hints of the delicate balance between fixed and floating, body and shadow, comparable to that devised by Carter in his Bishop setting. The composer can adapt the archetypal modernist technique represented by the convergence/divergence continuum, as the following analysis of 'Night' from Birtwistle's *Pulse Shadows* (1989−96) indicates.[4]

If the poem's title is the setting's keyword as far as its dark, drifting atmosphere is concerned, Birtwistle's approach to the last word, 'target', indicates something basic about his compositional technique (Ex. 9.3). Even though the full possibilities of Celan's meaning cannot be reduced to the single image of a stone as the 'target' or goal of motion, Birtwistle's setting of that final clause reflects the similar/separate image by beginning and ending on the same note, and moving

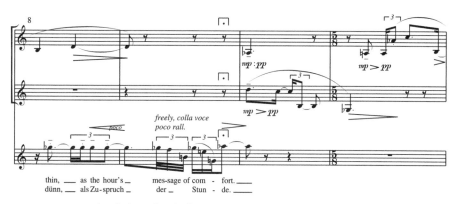

Ex. 9.4   Birtwistle, *Pulse Shadows*, 'Night', bars 4–11, voice and clarinets only

in the space between the two Cs by means of the disguised, and therefore unstable symmetry resulting from the mirror set-class sequence of four trichords in the vocal line – [027: F, G, C], [016: A, A♭, E♭], [016: G, G♭, D♭], [027: C, D, G]. (The wider function of the setting's final section as a winding-down from the C over F emphasis at bar 34 is discussed below.) The instrumental accompaniment for this final phrase also deploys a similar/different polarity in relation to the vocal line. The two clarinets conform at the set-class level, with [016: C, B, G♭], while the string trio has 'shadow' trichords, in which one of the sequence of pitch classes from the 'parent' trichords of the vocal line (as well as one or two of the actual pitch-classes) is changed: [027] into [024] – C, D, E in the cello, and [026] – E, D, B♭ in the violin: [016] into [015] – B♭, A, F in the double bass.

A fuller analysis of this passage would deal with vertical and well as horizontal factors, and also comment on the degree of stabilisation provided by the emphasis on common pitch-classes between the lines, especially the Cs in voice, clarinet 1 and cello, and the Fs (voice, bass). Easier to fit into a hermeneutic narrative is the way the images of pulsing, drifting and shadowing which pervade

Ex. 9.5   Birtwistle, *Pulse Shadows*, 'Night', bars 16–18, 20–4, 29–34, voice only

Pulse Shadows as a whole are deployed in 'Night' in a kind of 'poetics of invariance'. There is also an approach to voice-leading in which surface polarities of step and leap contribute to somewhat larger-scale motions that reflect associations with tonal goal-directedness. To claim that the first vocal phrase (bars 5–10) prolongs the progression from G up a semitone to Ab is not to argue that it does so in an orthodox tonal context, and the voice's climactic ascending minor ninth in this first phrase is as much the motivic complement of the descending ninth (C to B) in the clarinets – the recurring focus of the instrumental counterpoint to the vocal line – as it is a structural, contrapuntal feature of the kind revealed by Schenkerian analysis (Ex. 9.4). It is perhaps to balance the enigmatic quality of the text that Birtwistle imposes such overt musical invariants, musical discipline being proposed as the corrective shadow of poetic licence. How this works in the vocal line is shown by the G to F prolongation of bars 16–18, balanced by the F to E progression of bars 20–25. The next vocal phrase (bars 29–34) then reflects the first by moving to closure with a flourish embodying an ascent, here to the high C ('stars') (Ex. 9.5). The C is extended by Clarinet 2 and supported by F in the bass, a stable fifth (though not a 'tonic') which then survives the fragmentation process leading to the end.

Perspectives on Carter

It is always tempting for the interpretative musicologist to seek out connections between earlier and later procedures in a composer's work, for such

Ex. 9.6   (a) Carter, Piano Sonata, 2nd mvt, ending

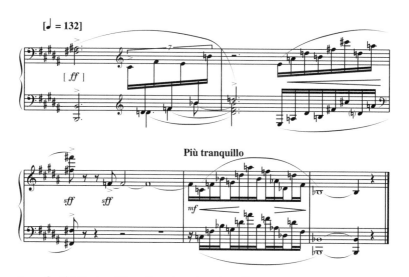

Ex. 9.6   (b) Carter, Piano Sonata, 1st mvt, ending

connections promote those dialogues between consistency and change which offer special aesthetic satisfactions. Since the difference between earlier and later styles is considerably greater with Carter than with Birtwistle, it is instructive to compare the shadowing effect at the end of 'Insomnia' with a much earlier manifestation of closural shadowplay with fifths, as relatively stable intervals. For example, at the end of its final movement Carter's Piano Sonata (1945–6) resolves its extended B major tonality onto a tonic chord which piles up fifths (and thirds) onto the tonic B, but in such a way that B's fundamental status is enhanced rather than undermined

(Ex. 9.6a). Appropriately, given the sonata's allegiance to aspects of traditional tonal syntax, the piling up does not extend beyond the diatonic scale degrees of B major itself, and the A♯ therefore has no E♯ in support. (At the beginning of the work, A♯ and E♯ have been introduced quite traditionally as neighbouring notes of the more fundamental B and F♯. But the sonata's first movement ends – stably enough, in context – not with F♯ moving to B but with F♮ moving to B♭ (Ex. 9.6b).

It was part of Carter's declared desire to respond more appropriately – as he saw it – to the contemporary world 'in a less oblique and resigned way' than that implied by a 'neo-classic aesthetic'[5] that such well- tried resolutions and formal routines should be transformed into something altogether more multivalent and challenging. Yet his motivation for this change was far from purely aesthetic. He came to regard those 'neo-classic' routines as evading confrontation with fundamental facets of human nature – to do with 'physical and intellectual violence' – of which anyone who had lived through the 1930s and 1940s could hardly have been unaware. In formulating this position, Carter can easily be accused of ignoring the degree to which neoclassical works like Stravinsky's *Oedipus rex* or *Orpheus* confront violence in ways which are anything but 'oblique and resigned'. But he needed to rationalise what for him was a leap into the unknown, something likely to arouse incomprehension, if not contempt, in the broad mass of music lovers. Looking back from his own special position in the 1980s, Philip Glass gave a hint of such contempt when he proclaimed 'the failure of modernism', as something which 'had become truly decadent, stagnant, uncommunicative...composers were writing for each other and the public didn't seem to care. People want to like new music, but how can they, when it's so ugly and intimidating, emotionally and intellectually?'[6]

Glass toned down this judgement later on, but those earlier remarks can still be expected to command wide assent, even when applied to such a respected figure as Elliott Carter. Carter's equally celebrated declaration of those respects in which the qualities of 'serious music' reach 'far beyond the range of popular or folk music'[7] provides further evidence of the impulses which fuelled his creative drive. What is striking, in the circumstances, is that his music stayed so free of the anguish and pathos that was second nature to much European avant-garde and expressionist composition after 1950. Even in the Double Concerto (1961) and the Piano Concerto (1964–5) which, according to Carter himself, confront disintegration and entropy most directly,[8] the avoidance of lamenting 'espressivo' and the solid strengths of the formal designs suggests sympathy with a 'classic' stoicism, and a rejection of post-Bergian chartings of social and psychological trauma, even when those chartings aspire to exorcise trauma and lead on to something more stable and serene.

Like other composers aligned with a modernist aesthetic, Carter tends towards the Dionysian and the dithyrambic, and his Apollonianism, like Schoenberg's, is primarily a matter of using constructivism to control and counterbalance the explosive aspects of expressionism. In consequence, the aspects of 'passion and tragedy' which can be heard in the Piano Concerto are complemented by the spirit of joy that emerges from the turbulent complexities of the Concerto for Orchestra (1968–9) and many other works.[9] As I have argued elsewhere,[10] Carter is a modernist who brings expressionism and classicism into conjunction and equilibrium, rather than, as David Schiff contends, a composer whose modernism was eventually 'absorbed' by classicism. The difference is not a mere matter of semantics, but involves vital perspectives on the humanity and social percipience of some of Carter's most complex and ambitious instrumental compositions. Their range of allusion is immense – from the Double Concerto's associations with Lucretius' *De Rerum Natura*, 'which describes the formation of the physical universe by the random swervings of atoms' (Bernard (ed.), *Essays*, pp. 260–1), and – eventually – the reversal of that supremely organic process, to the parallels between a modern urban cityscape (as depicted in Hart Crane's poem 'The Bridge') and *A Symphony of Three Orchestras* (1976). Even if neither the natural nor the metropolitan worlds are places of comfort and joy, from Carter's perspective, his music radiates stoic endurance and exuberant acceptance, rather than gloomy disaffection.

Schiff claims that, in many of the major instrumental works composed between 1959 and 1976, 'stratified textures are used to heighten the alienation of the protagonists, the sense that they were playing different pieces at the same time without mediation'.[11] Here Carter is at his most Ivesian, but unlike his great American predecessor, he seems to have had no need of transcendentalist philosophy, or of pictorial contrasts between the chaos of the city and the tranquillity of life in rural New England. For Carter, a rationalistic stoicism is the most effective counter to the turbulence of contemporary life, and naive programmaticism, together with the risks to textural coherence found in Ivesian depictions of modern civilisation, are to be avoided at all costs. Metaphors of social confrontation and interaction can be most fruitfully explored in contrasts of mood and tone between the dramatic and the lyric, whether in purely instrumental structures or in settings of relatively complex and elusive poetry – by Elizabeth Bishop, Robert Lowell and John Hollander among others. Only late in life, in the short opera *What Next?* (1997–8), did Carter's search for new generic possibilities lead him to risk a direct representation of the conjunction between psychological disorientation and urban malfunction, as a family party explore reality and imagination in the aftermath of an automobile accident, and search, like comic shadows of the single, traumatised character of *Erwartung*, for the truth in a situation where any clear, unambiguous outcome is inconceivable.

In the light of these issues, it is all the more important to reaffirm the essential humanity of Carter's musical world, and the communicative potential of his compositional processes. These come together in an expressive rhetoric that is celebratory in essence, and also 'civilised', in that even the most expressionistically fractured superimpositions contribute to a discourse, a process of exchange and interplay, of oppositions mediated by a willingness to coexist. Passages which, for Schiff, represent Carter's 'modern' side – 'an entropy-haunted collage, fragmented, unpredictable, and at times chaotic'[12] – are balanced, not by the factitious purity of a classically integrated synthesis which, in music, has only been achieved in relatively small-scale tonal structures, but by giving the unpredictable fragmentation a more genial aspect, a less turbulent tone. Hence the importance of not ending with the proclamation of singular victories: a gentle, even an exhausted, dissolution is preferable.

The special quality of Carter's achievement emerges potently in *Syringa* (1978), for mezzo soprano, bass, guitar and ten instrumentalists. This is one of his most difficult and neglected compositions, and it tackles an archetypal dramatic and poetic theme, described by the composer as 'a familiar, many-sided, affecting subject: Orpheus and the power of music'.[13] Apart from its resonance in a chapter also concerned with another Orpheus-obsessed composer, Birtwistle, *Syringa* is a distillation and an intensification of Carter's modernist 'project', its apparent disregard for easy accessibility reinforcing its status as an emblematic statement about the modern world and music's role within that world.

Syringa's superimposition of two voices and two texts (verse in English by John Ashbery, various texts in classical Greek) prompts a critical exploration of how it moves along the continuum between opposition and fusion. Lawrence Kramer is in no doubt that the work is not 'a traditional composition', which 'might oppose these two voices through contrastive statements and developments':[14] 'the voices are not *opposed* to each other at all, but *posed against* each other. Neither dialectical nor competitive, they combine without blending to form a singularity, a kind of third voice, which is the integral voice of the work – the voice one hears in how the music sounds, how the poem reads.' By way of such strategies, and perhaps with a hidden agenda to do with what he sees as Carter's ultimately 'classical' aesthetic (not that he speaks of it as such), Kramer seems reluctant to allow for any element of tension between the speech-like Ashbery setting and the more declamatory Greek. He claims that 'Carter underscores the radical oneness of this voice by allowing the expressive repertoires of the mezzo and bass to overlap.' But overlap is less common than differentiation, complementation, 'radical oneness' displaced by uncompromising duality.

Kramer's interpretation stems from his reluctance to close off the interpretative options which result from a different kind of 'radical oneness', as in his observation that

Carter's polyvocality diverts emphasis from the linear progression of his music to its vertically generated duration...A mature piece by Carter essentially consists of a referential sonority that sustains itself continuously...Each moment, each texture of a composition merges seamlessly into the next (no matter how different) within a rhythmic whole that does not guide the ear but envelops it. (pp. 214–15)

As a result 'the polyvocal whole composed of these voices absorbs their linear impetus into the resonance of a temporal order that persists instead of progressing', and Carter continually superimposes 'different metrical structures, all of which are themselves in constant change. Given so many shapes, polyvocally fused together, time loses the quality by which we customarily identify and measure it – its periodicity. What remains is a kind of eddy, full of complex swells and pulsations' (pp. 219–20).

This goes too far in rejecting the possibility that this 'constant change', those 'complex swells and pulsations', could retain any remnant of periodicity and progression. To deny Carter this ultimate ambiguity, this ultimate tension, impoverishes the work: and even if Ashbery's poem on its own discloses none of the conflicts necessary for a sense of ambivalence, Kramer's understanding of the way 'its two voices compose only one utterance – just as, say, Carter's Third Quartet is not itself a pair of duos, but music polyvocally *composed* of duos' (pp. 206–7) – strains for a contrived effect of comparability in which the expressionistic dynamism of the quartet's music is sacrificed on the altar of 'postmodern' paradox.

Kramer is on firmer ground when he notes the differences between the Ashbery setting, for soprano, which 'sustains a feeling of unforced contemplativeness' and the bass's 'agitated, complex, mournful vocal line in ancient Greek, in a melismatic style that suggests an archaic litany' (p. 207). The element of conflict here is undeniable, evoking one of modern music's archetypal oppositions, that between the speaking Moses and the singing Aaron in Schoenberg's opera. While Carter rejects the blatant polarity of song and speech-song in favour of two complementary kinds of lyric writing, there is an unambiguous divergence between the dithyrambic declamation of the bass and the flowing musical prose of the mezzo which creates a strong expressive charge. It is not so much that the potential dialogue is 'unachieved', as Kramer has it – 'the bass is trying to "reach" the mezzo, who is most often deaf to his music' – or that 'the disposition of forces tends to isolate the mezzo in her serenity and detachment against a troubled, sometimes violently agitated background' (p. 210). Orpheus and Eurydice are not as consistently indifferent to each other as this scenario seeks to suggest. As Kramer notes, 'the meditative voice does not want to sing because song is the instrument of regret, even of wild grief': hence 'the impression that...what she

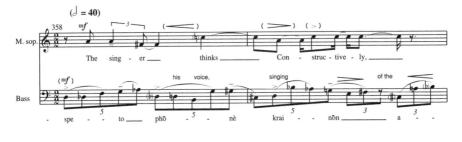

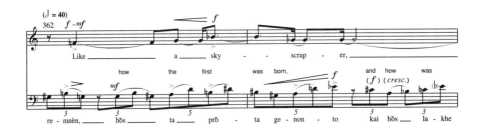

Ex. 9.7   Carter, *Syringa*, bars 358–69, vocal parts only

is doing is closer to recitative – the musical equivalent of speech – than it is to song' (p. 211). David Schiff has claimed that the mezzo's line shadows Ashbery's own 'flat, commonsensical' reading of his text (Schiff, *Carter*, p. 179). Yet Carter's decision to set this text at all – to fixed values of pitch and rhythm (even if the latter are to be flexibly interpreted) – indicates a concern to resist the claims of a more explicit difference, and a preference for the idea of a musical dialogue to offset the dramatic circumstance of searing separation.

At one point Ashbery's poem alludes to the always fraught relationship between the rational and irrational, the constructive and the intuitive, within the creative persona of the singer/composer: 'The singer thinks/Constructively, builds up his chant in progressive stages/Like a skyscraper, but at the last minute turns away./The song is then engulfed in an instant of blackness...' Simultaneously, Carter aligns Greek texts about the beautifully accompanied solemn song 'of the immortal gods and dark earth', and the settings sensitively balance similarity and difference (Ex. 9.7). Both lines feature smaller intervals, and have occasional minor seconds and minor thirds in common, but the smaller-scale rhythmic differences between triple and quintuple divisions of crotchet and mimim is affirmed, while the instruments (not shown in the example) touch in allegiance to both. Here, as throughout, pulsation – and the ultimate generic allusion to song's complement, dance – cannot be denied, any more than dramatic dynamism, as Carter's dialogue with the Orpheus myth unfolds in rich multiplicity. It is therefore perfectly possible to contemplate a Kramer-countering, formalistic analysis of *Syringa* which charts the motivic process – and progress – found when the pitch-class sets used for various verbal repetitions and associations across both texts are identified. Carter's varied invariants, and the degrees of constancy revealed through the interaction of change and stasis as *Syringa* unfolds in time, may not be as explicit as some of Schoenberg's more traditionally thematic demonstrations of developing variation. But they stem from a comparable concern to preserve that appeal 'to a longer span of memory and to a more highly developed auditory memory' which prompted Carter's turn away from neoclassicism in the 1940s. Even if he risks succumbing to that very 'obliqueness' he condemned in neoclassicism, there is a compensating immediacy to the urgent flow of *Syringa* as the music aspires to, yet distances itself from, the purer lyricism of simple song forms.

Angles on Birtwistle

Harrison Birtwistle is most distant from Carter at points like the profound – if restrained – pathos which ends the opera *The Mask of Orpheus* (1973–5, 1981–3), its subtly centred drifting standing as an antithesis to Carter's typically volatile, unstable flow. In *Syringa*, the archetypes of Apollo and Dionysus cannot be directly mapped onto the mezzo and bass voices any more directly than they can onto the *Sprechstimme* baritone and lyric tenor in Schoenberg's *Moses und Aron*.

Birtwistle's music drama has less equivocal, if no less multivalent, characterisation, but other, less ambitious works embrace the archetypes more directly. For example, Birtwistle has called *Panic* (1995) a 'dithyramb', and Robert Adlington has noted a precedent in *Punch and Judy* (1966–7), in 'the sinisterly celebratory build-up to Punch's first murder of Choregos. Its raucous combination of high winds, bawling toy trumpet and percussion, the latter two following their own tempos, directly foreshadows *Panic*.'[15] Jonathan Cross emphasises *Panic*'s

> primordial expressivity. Its power, its excitement, even its danger, come from its predominantly Dionysian directness, from the pleasure it takes in the immediate (sonic, rhythmic), from its celebration of the rough bodily physicality of its soloists seemingly uninfluenced by the rational Apollo. It is this powerfully erotic aspect of the work which is the source both of its strength and its discomfort. It is this which places *Panic* in direct line of succession with other Dionysian dances of the twentieth century such as *The Rite of Spring*.[16]

In identifying Apollo with rationality rather than with poise or serenity, Cross acknowledges the modernist, constructivist mode of Apollonianism (relevant, as seen earlier, to Schoenberg and Carter), and he also devises a 'classical' continuum which functions even for those compositions by Birtwistle, like *Panic*, in which there is virtually no repose or lyricism, still less the kind of 'absolute tranquillity' found by Michael Hall in the 'stasimon' section of the predominantly 'raucous, turbulent' *Tragoedia* (1965).[17] Birtwistle is in any case scarcely likely to associate Apollo entirely with benign, peaceful gentility, since in *The Mask of Orpheus*, having presided over the birth of Orpheus, and teaching him to sing, Apollo eventually becomes jealous of the singer, and destroys his own creation.

As many commentators have observed, multiplicity is fundamental to the 'lyric tragedy' of *The Mask of Orpheus*, and one effect of splitting each principal role (Orpheus, Eurydice, Aristaeus) into three is to enhance the mythic interactions of which the contending spirits of the Apollonian and the Dionysian – each appropriately protean in character – are a vital part. So, even if Orpheus himself remains 'the disciple of Apollo...the very embodiment of reason', who 'has cut himself off from the natural, sensuous side of life',[18] this simply renders him the more vulnerable to the predations of intuition, instinct, and all the dark forces embodied by Dionysus. Further, given the associations between Orphism as a cult and Dionysiac rites,[19] Orpheus himself must be represented as not wholly rational, but seeking 'spiritual ecstasy'. Nor is Orpheus shown as a 'character', a single human identity, in the way that (despite the masks) Stravinsky presents Oedipus. Birtwistle's generic allusions, like his characterisation, stress the archetypal more than the specific, the multiple rather than the singular. To a degree, this is the logical result of a composer who consciously distances himself from 'the audience' (Hall, *Recent Years*, p. 128), but who is no more anti-social than the great dramatists

of ancient Greece who matter so much to him. In demonstrating that a living continuity can be created between such ancient archetypes and present-day dramatic
themes and topics, Birtwistle, like Stravinsky before him and Carter alongside him,
has reinforced the claims of serious, progressive, modernist art to be considered a
force, not merely a presence, within contemporary culture – not least because it
attempts to detach itself (even to signify alienation) from social, political polemics
and propaganda.

Carter's preference for an oblique yet essentially optimistic approach to
contemporary cultural concerns can be inferred from his *magnum opus* of the
1990s, the three-movement *Symphonia: Sum Fluxae Pretiam Spei* (1993–7). As
David Schiff observes, Carter interprets his own willingness to undertake such a
'monumental' task ironically, linking the project to Richard Crashaw's celebration
of the 'bulla', or bubble, not solely as a symbol of ephemerality, but as 'an emblem
of art; the bubble is a transient mirror of human existence' (Schiff, *Carter*, p. 317).
In Schiff's reading, *Symphonia*'s initial 'Partita' ('game' in Italian) is 'a lesson in
the pleasures of modernism... angular, brash, chaotic, unpredictable' (p. 318). Then
comes the 'solemn ritual and anguished meditation' of the 'Adagio tenebroso',
whose 'desolate, pain-filled landscape' seems 'to encompass all the suffering of
the twentieth century' (p. 319). In this music, whose 'broken chain of expressive
phrases seems to reject the possibility of Beethoven's prayer of thanks' (p. 321),
Carter comes as close as he has ever done to a Birtwistle-style lament, even if
there is a measure of consolation in 'expressive phrases' which resemble those
in the solo oboe piece (a memorial to Stefan Wolpe) 'Inner Song' (1992), to be
discussed in Chapter 11. Finally, 'Allegro scorrevole' provides a very un-Birtwistle-
like release, floating away into space. Not that all conflict is absent: 'the light,
fast motion is opposed by a more traditional lyricism which is finally overcome'
(p. 322).

Even if, as Schiff suggests, the central panel of *Symphonia* encompasses
'all the suffering of the twentieth century', it scrupulously shuns the kind of direct engagement with particulars of contemporary history found in Dallapiccola's
Il Prigioniero, Schoenberg's *A Survivor from Warsaw*, Nono's *Intolleranza 1960*
or Britten's *War Requiem*: and Birtwistle too has been inclined to accept that
'engagement' is possible without lapsing into documentary polemic. *Pulse Shadows: Meditations on Paul Celan* (1991–6) can be interpreted as reading Adorno's
declaration about the difficulties faced by art after Auschwitz as a warning of the
dangers of triviality. But (again like Carter) Birtwistle does not aim to banish the
playful, the dance-like from music: rather, he seeks to establish connections with
the rituals of ancient classical tradition without the ironic context of the Ashbery/
Carter *Syringa*, of the allusive refinements of Crashaw's 'bulla'. In *Pulse Shadows*
the primary quality is not the superimposition of old and new worlds. Rather,
the juxtaposition and interlacing of two cycles – nine movements for string

quartet, nine settings of Celan for soprano and ensemble (which can be performed separately) – invites meditation on the aesthetic topic of connection and separation, as if in the blinding light of that disorientation and confrontation between reality and imagination found in Celan's post-Auschwitz poetry.

The regular alternation – in the complete version – of vocal and instrumental movements can make *Pulse Shadows* seem like a kind of magisterial corrective to the surrealist flippancy of Boulez's *Le Marteau sans maître*, a score whose musical character is of seminal significance for Birtwistle, even if its poetic subject-matter is alien. One key to the relation between the poetic and the musical in *Pulse Shadows* can be found in the function of the two sub-cycles provided in the quartet movements – five Fantasias and four Friezes. As Stephen Pruslin reports,

> like many of their painted or sculpted counterparts, these musical friezes form a continuum of 'frozen sections', each representing a single idea. This is a music of exposition, not development, although the latter can be sensed gradually in retrospect as the cycle unfolds. Sometimes, a figure introduced right at the end of a movement becomes the entire basis of another one. In performance, this can create the impression that a long, continuous frieze has been 'sliced', and its component panels dispersed. The territory treated strictly in the four Friezes is explored more freely in five Fantasias that evoke the world of early English viol music, suggesting that an important ancestor of the present quartet-cycle is the whole series of pavans by one of Birtwistle's favourite composers – John Dowland's *Lachrymae or seaven teares*.[20]

Pruslin's account invites the conclusion that Dowland, Birtwistle and Celan all share a concern with what might be called the ritual of lament. There is also the implication that the contrast between frieze and fantasia might mask a degree of shared background in the early English pavan, and there are places where Birtwistle seems to have chosen two different titles simply to highlight the arbitrariness of attempted distinctions between them.[21] Thus 'Fantasia 1', written during the final stages of the work's evolution, begins with exemplary strictness, to the extent that the initial uniformity of its quintuplet reiterations transmutes into the quintuplets of a melodic line which is passed from instrument to instrument in an imitative fashion that seems intended to mirror the contrapuntal and motivic characteristics often ascribed to Celan's verse. Although this melodic material attains the relative freedom of a cadenza-like statement in the second violin at the movement's centre, it is followed by a final section whose fragmented gestures (marked 'savage' in several places) attain closure under the control of a decisive rhythmic unison.

Countering this sense of convergence between two generic prototypes is the ambiguity arising from the circumstance that, in one movement at least – 'Frieze 1' (1991) – the tone is more of celebration than lament. Written for the ninetieth birthday of Universal Edition's Alfred Schlee, 'Frieze 1' makes something more jaunty and mechanistic out of a D-centred Cantus that could have been derived from 'White and Light', the first Celan setting, made two years before in 1989. Yet 'Frieze 1' is by no means straightforwardly lighthearted: it reaches its extraordinary climax with the cello attempting to project a high and somewhat desperate song against the dance patterns of the other instruments before the texture fragments, and sustained melody, now in the first violin, floats away into inaudible heights, gruffly punctuated below.

Celebration and lament, as generic prototypes, can be felt to converge with the dithyramb, and this convergence is salient to 'Fantasia 1', which begins 'with maximum force and intensity', generating wildly improvisatory melodic flights out of its reiterated chords, before free, recitative-like song (Violin 2, bars 19–20) yields to brief but explosive dance patterns. As these patterns quieten and die away the first Celan setting, 'Thread suns', begins, perhaps placed here because of the degree to which the text (the shortest of the nine) introduces two basic images – of the 'grey-black wilderness', and of music as something which survives: 'there are still songs to be sung on the other side of mankind'. What Celan means by his implied distinction between that 'other side' and the alternative is not spelt out: but we can deduce that there is a 'side' of mankind for which song is no longer possible. Birtwistle's setting is projected from an initial pair of notes – B, A – which act as a recurrent pivot for phrases which flexibly reflect the poetic imagery – ascending to the upper register on the word 'high', moving still higher on 'light' (there is a comparable effect at the very end of the work), and with an elaborate yet tense melisma on 'sung' before returning to a variant of the initial shape with a final descent from B to C. The accompaniment progresses from lyric support to mechanistic punctuation as a link to 'Frieze 1'.

After 'Night', the movement discussed earlier, *Pulse Shadows* ends with 'Todesfuge – Frieze 4', and 'Give the Word'. By, for the first and only time, giving a quartet movement the title of a Celan poem, Birtwistle suggests a degree of convergence between the work's two independent yet associated cycles. And just as his final setting, of one of Celan's most enigmatic poems, 'gives' little in the sense of obvious and straightforward meaning, so allocating the title 'Todesfuge' to a purely instrumental movement indicates that, in at least one case, Celan's purpose is better served by allusion than by direct musical setting.

Celan's 'Todesfuge' (1952) is a relatively early poem in which, as Michael Hamburger says, 'the personal anguish was transposed into distancing imagery and a musical structure so incompatible with reportage that a kind of "terrible beauty" is wrested from its ugly theme.... The power and pathos of the poem arises from the extreme tension between its grossly impure material and its pure form'. Hamburger also points out that Celan turned against 'Todesfuge' in later years, 'because he had refined his art in the meantime to a point where the early poem seemed too direct, too explicit'.[22] Even so, that relative directness — and the ambivalence provided by Celan's suppressed alternative title, 'Tango of Death' — is seized on by Birtwistle as a pretext for the kind of allusions to a traditional musical genre, and texture, which he would normally take considerable pains to avoid. As Hamburger says, the poem can be aligned with certain elements of fugal structure, if only through incantatory repetitions which appear to overlap, contrapuntally. Nevertheless, the impact of the poetic structure is more fully revealed by the use of contrast aligned to similarity, as in the devastating final couplet:

> dein goldenes Haar Margarete
> dein aschenes Haar Sulamith
>
> your golden hair Margarete
> your ashen hair Shulamith

And this is precisely the kind of modernist trope, embodying an unresolved tension between difference and similarity, with which Birtwistle is very much at home. It follows that Michael Hall's reading of this movement as seeming to epitomise, 'like Beethoven's *Grosse Fuge*, the will to overcome adversity'[23] tells only half the story.

The musical content of the poem involves an interaction between the repetitive/imitative form and certain musical images in the text itself — the activity of playing (including the instruction, 'stroke your strings'), singing and dancing, which come together in the poem's most chilling phrase — 'sweetly play death' — and not forgetting the sound of whistling, which Birtwistle might be recalling in the muted harmonic of the cello subject at his fugue's beginning (Ex. 9.8). Combined with the fierce (tango-like?) fragments of the viola subject (for this is in one sense a double fugue), the possibility is there for recalling Celan's terrifying verbal picture of the man who 'whistles his Jews out in earth has them dig for a grave/he commands us to strike up for the dance'.

For a dedicated modernist to compose a fugue which is not simply a parody is a formidable challenge, and it is tempting for the critic to opt for the sentimental, even tasteless declaration that composer keeps faith with poet in writing music about the impossibility of fugue after Auschwitz. Alternatively, Birtwistle composes not an utter negation of fugue, an anti-fugue, or even a shadow-fugue, but an imaginary fugue, a structure which recaptures the cumulative quality of Bach's or Beethoven's fugal movements, while reinterpreting contrapuntal art in terms of the complementary strata of atonality, not the interacting lines of tonality. The vital elements are the two initial subjects in cello and viola, which can easily be derived from the generative material of *Pulse Shadows* as a whole, as set out in 'White and Light' and 'Frieze 1', with the almost stepwise descending shape in

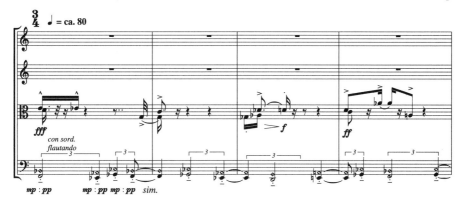

Ex. 9.8   Birtwistle, *Pulse Shadows*, 'Todesfuge – Frieze 4', bars 1–7

bar 5 of the viola theme having the closural potential of a codetta. When Subject 2 is passed to Violin 2 in bar 6, the viola introduces a third related idea, more 'pulse' than 'drift', which behaves rather like a counter-subject.

The movement then explores these three strands of material, exchanging and developing them in constantly varied combinations, and with the use of imitation (the codetta theme from bar 29) and stretto (Subject 2 from bar 33) that illustrate how close Birtwistle's normal compositional procedures are to those of 'traditional' counterpoint. A new level of tension is reached after bar 56, when Subject 1, whose drifting rhythms have provided the most connected strand in the texture, disappears. A counterpoint of demisemiquavers, whether derived from the original counter-subject or devised to contrast with the predominant thematic characteristics of Subjects 1 and 2, builds to three dramatic passages of stretto-like imitation (bars 81–5). The true climax involves the separate lines converging, rhythmically, in material reminiscent of the pulsing Subject 2 (bars 86–91), then, very briefly, of Subject 1 (bar 92) and the codetta (bars 93–4) (Ex. 9.9). Finally,

Ex. 9.9   Birtwistle, *Pulse Shadows*, 'Todesfuge – Frieze 4', bars 84–94

Subject 1 is heard again (bars 95–6), at which point the setting of 'Give the Word' begins.

Having read Michael Hamburger on Celan, Birtwistle might have thought of his fugue-material as in some ways 'grossly impure' – or as different as possible from the purity of the form as such, thereby creating a disparity between structure and content explosive enough to do justice to the associations of the movement's title. The music relishes its relation to traditional fugality. 'Shadows' here have nothing to do with 'anxiety of influence'. There are no coy allusions to romantic dances of death: the association, even in the chant-like cello subject,

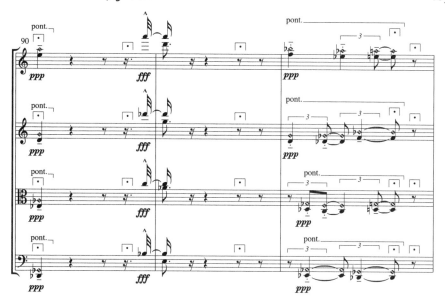

Ex. 9.9   (cont.)

is unmistakable. And so this composer's idea of fugue, represented by the long-drawn-out harmonics of Subject 1, 'give the word' to the final movement by continuing as a barely-audible background to the end. The voice synchronises mainly with these quartet chords, while the ensemble unfolds an invention polarised between the fractured pulsations in cello and double bass and the drifting lament in clarinets and viola. Whatever the poem is about, it seems to accept the involvement of humanity: 'All come, Male or female, not one is missing...A human being comes', and the human voice stutters its way through expanding permutations of its initial cell, the sung notes which end each phrase suggesting an aspiration towards resolution which is reinforced by the final, if displaced, high A♭ on the word 'light'. This displacement underlines the singer's aspirational divergence, however. The instruments simply continue working the patterns with which they began, their dedicated, drifting consistency highlighting the voice's isolated instability. Triumph and non-triumph. A fitting conclusion. The human being has come – but to where, and to what?

10 Experiment and orthodoxy

Minimalism, modernism, classicism

In its earliest and most authentic musical manifestations during the 1960s and 1970s, minimalism – Keith Potter declares –

> owes more to non-Western music, jazz and rock than to 20th-century Modernism or any other Western art music, at least since the Baroque period. Openly seeking greater accessibility, it is tonal or modal where Modernism is atonal, rhythmically regular and continuous where Modernism is aperiodic and fragmented, structurally and texturally simple where Modernism is complex.[1]

These distinctive, non-modernist qualities are still apparent in a relatively recent work like Steve Reich's *City Life* (1995), referred to in Chapter 1. Yet historians of contemporary music have tended to stress the ways in which minimalism has evolved – or declined – as it has sought accommodations with more mainstream compositional techniques, and with the established genres of instrumental and vocal music. Just as Cageian experimentalism has had to be constantly alert to the consequences of finding itself accidentally absorbed into the mainstream musical world of conventional concerts and commercialism, so minimalism has survived as much through adaptation to and alignment with what it originally opposed as through the renewed assertion of difference and distinctiveness. This process can be regarded either as a reprehensible surrender to the lure of commercial success or as a demonstration of the flexible power of the original initiative in radically and permanently changing the nature of modern music. If, this latter view concludes, the result is a more pluralistic range of possibilities than formerly obtained, so much the better.

The dialogue between tradition and innovation has also inflected the critical debate about the ways in which minimalist composers have confronted contemporary cultural possibilities. A notable example of such inflection, if only on account of its length, is John Richardson's book (published in 1999) about Philip Glass's opera *Akhnaten*. Composed in 1983 as the last of a trilogy of 'character operas' – the others were *Einstein on the Beach* (1975–6) and *Satyagraha* (1980) – *Akhnaten* is the most traditionally operatic of the three, indicating that 'approach to more conventional instrumental forces and linear narrative'[2] which continues in Glass's later works. Given the range of memories and allusions which any late-twentieth-century engagement with convention was likely to bring with it, it is to be expected that Richardson's analysis will centre on notions of ambiguity: 'probably the most distinctive feature of the music of *Akhnaten* is its ambiguous tonality', and the 'ambiguity between old and new extends to broader considerations of form',[3] when Glass has recourse to traditional compositional genres like chaconne and lament.

For Richardson the outcome of these various ambiguities is not a reinforcement of the instabilities inherent in modernism, but the 'harmonious combination of old and new': as such, it is 'a distinctive feature of the postmodern ethos' (p. 66). As his analysis advances into detailed interpretation, however, he cannot exclude responses which involve the interaction of 'harmonious' postmodernism with the very forces it sought to reject: for example, Glass's music for the funeral of Amenhotep III has 'a power... that modernism never knew, although the long, dissonant tones sounded in the bass and the tritone-based melody sung by Aye later in the scene hint at some sense of agency from precisely this direction' (p. 113). It is these darker aspects of what Glass himself regards as a 'tragic' opera that bring the atmosphere and even the techniques of modernism back into the picture. Richardson claims that the music in Akhnaten's 'Hymn to the Sun' is 'archeological... not because it deals with real archeological artifacts from ancient Egypt but because it treats the entire history of Western classical music as an archeological site, digging up signifiers from the musical past and, by the very act of representation, uprooting them from the semantic field that formerly nourished them' (p. 201). To the extent that this compositional strategy involves 'leaving discontinuities and anomalies in sight, rather than seeking to incorporate them into an integrated, internally consistent whole' (p. 10), it can be regarded as modernist – at least as that term is defined in these pages: and Richardson reinforces the general significance of the point by adding that 'Glass remains controversial not because he broke with tradition in the first place... but because works like *Akhnaten* problematize the very act of breaking with tradition upon which the whole concept of avant-gardism hinges' (p. 202).

The implication that the Glassian form of problematisation requires a more uninhibited confrontation between the traditional and the innovatory than the avant-garde would ever permit can stand, if it is accepted that 'avant-garde' identifies one extreme of modernism, where aspirations to purity and integration mirror the corresponding aspirations of classicism at the other extreme of the aesthetic spectrum. It is also clear, however, that retreat from purer forms of experimentalism and minimalism brings with it the dangers and delights of a fuller engagement with the modernist mainstream and its own preoccupations with history as archeology. As the following discussion of Louis Andriessen and John Adams aims to illustrate, the minimalist or post-minimalist approach becomes decisive in its resistance to complexity, whether as rhythmic fragmentation or as contrapuntal 'prose' – the kind of complexity which seeks to shun all explicit patterning and connected process. As noted in Chapter 9, Elliott Carter's route to a modernist dialogue between the expressionistic and the classical has not involved any links with the sort of procedures which Glass and others have employed with such resourcefulness. The inescapable twentieth-century spirit of Dionysus can still create associations of mood where there are none of technique. Nevertheless, manifestations of this spirit which evoke aspects of minimalism and classicism have close, if often uneasy, associations with Stravinskian rituals, and these echoes of Stravinsky are central to the work of Louis Andriessen.

The Dionysian clockwork

> There are bells for marriage and bells for death. But they are all played on the same bells. That is why the silence at the end of *Les Noces* is the same as the silence at the end of *Requiem Canticles*.[4]

The epigrammatic, allusive style of the book about Stravinsky by Louis Andriessen and Elmer Schönberger is not to all musicological tastes. But its concluding celebration of bells resonates to stimulating effect when Andriessen's own compositions from the 1990s are considered: for example, the ending of the *Trilogy of the Last Day*'s concluding 'diabolic scherzo', 'Dancing on the Bones'. Here a sinisterly simple, blithely modal vocal melody, gleefully detailing the physical indignities of dying, precedes a less explosive but still highly dissonant coda which evokes the Postlude of Stravinsky's *Requiem Canticles*, not just by bell-like chords, but by harmonically centring on the pitch-class F. One essential Stravinskian quality nevertheless remains unattainable – at any rate, by someone whose thinking is more Marxist than Christian. Andriessen's bellwork, like his clockwork, retains rather more of Dionysian abandon than of Apollonian serenity. This dance of death refuses to dissolve itself into a ceremonial, ritual procession. There is not the slightest whiff of incense: and so it cannot be said that the silence at the end of Andriessen's trilogy is exactly the same as the silence at the end of *Les Noces* or *Requiem Canticles*.

The 1990s was a productive decade for Andriessen, with the completion of three substantial scores: *Rosa (a horse drama)* (1993–4), *Trilogy of the Last Day* (begun in 1993, but mainly composed in 1996–7), and the opera *Writing to Vermeer* (1997–9). All three offer a characteristic blend of the spontaneous and the self-conscious, as fully-fledged responses to the now-constant cultural fact that 'all interesting music deals with existing music, and that you are always in a polemical relationship with existing music'.[5]

During the conversation from which these words come, Andriessen rapidly replaced 'polemical' with the more ideologically loaded 'dialectical':

> 'Dialectical' is a word I like to use very much. I would say that I deal with
> Bach in a dialectical manner, because I'm a totally different person and I can't

write his music. I use his harmonies sometimes and his attitude towards composing and his ways of thinking about musical material, but in a totally different way...Apart from Stravinsky, Bach is the main composer I study all the time – every day, in fact. It's very strange and it's getting worse; I'm doing it more and more. At the moment I'm writing an opera with Peter Greenaway [*Rosa*] and I am trying to make a form similar to those which Bach used in his "operas" – which, of course, are the Passions. What he did in the *St Matthew Passion* has absolutely nothing to do with the psychological operas of the 19th century. What Bach did was to write closed forms – a chorus or an aria or a recitative – in which there is a dramatic development which is actually the beginning of sonata form. (p. 82)

And Andrew Ford confirmed that 'the Greenaway/Andriessen opera will consist (as in the Bach Passions) only of closed forms; Andriessen says he is not interested in writing narrative music' (p. 24).

Andriessen's angle on Bach here sets up interesting analogies with Kagel, even though, in the event, the opera *Rosa* is rather more distant from baroque models than Kagel's *Sankt Bach Passion*. In particular, *Rosa* is more through-composed than a Bach Passion – and also less inclined to portray its protagonist as a model for the emulation of ordinary mortals. But even if *Rosa* is more in the tradition of Brechtian epic theatre than of post-medieval mystery play, it is resourceful and consistent in its sidelining of romantic narrative music, and Andriessen's avowed dislike of these traditions fits with his preference for the kind of aesthetic tone he finds in Stravinsky, and in jazz:

in the end I like jazz because it's cold...Charlie Parker...had an enormous distance from his musical material. I call that classicism, in that it's contradictory to romanticism. Romanticism takes you by the hand and leads you to another world; classicism has a certain distance always from the musical object, and that's what interests me in music. (p. 82)

The detachment of that 'certain distance' calls Stravinskian declarations to mind, and in particular the passage from the ghosted *Autobiography* of 1936, with its comments on Apollo and Dionysus, whose aesthetic opposition has formed a prominent *Leitmotiv* throughout this book. In the *Autobiography*, Stravinsky expressed his admiration for 'the aristocratic austerity' of classical ballet, which

so closely corresponds with my conception of art. For here, in classical dancing, I see the triumph of studied conception over vagueness, of the rule over the arbitrary, of order over the haphazard. I am thus brought face to face with the eternal conflict in art between the Apollonian and the Dionysian principles. The latter assumes ecstasy to be the final goal – that is to say, the losing of oneself – whereas art demands above all the full consciousness of the artist. There can, therefore, be no doubt as to my choice between the two.[6]

Stravinsky's concern with such 'full consciousness' led him to underwrite the further declaration in *Poetics of Music*, also discussed in Chapter 4: Apollo's demand is that, 'for the lucid ordering of the work...all the Dionysian elements which set the imagination of the artist in motion must be properly subjugated before they intoxicate us, and must finally be made to submit to the law', with the consequence that 'variety is valid only as a means of attaining similarity'.[7] But, as suggested in Chapter 4, it is questionable whether even Stravinsky's most determined attempts at musical Apollonianism were capable of reducing out contrasting, conflicting feelings to the extent that absolutely no challenge to the rule of Apollo could be sensed. To this extent, subjugating Dionysus is a particular problem for musical languages in which dissonance remains emancipated and modal ambiguity rules. Subduing Dionysus is easier for such wholeheartedly holy minimalists as Arvo Pärt and John Tavener.

The Andriessen/Greenaway *Rosa* is quite unlike Stravinskian neoclassical opera. With its comic/sinister surrealism it is closer in spirit, if not musical style, to Poulenc's *Les Mamelles de Tirésias*. And it confronts the problem of all non-narrative dramatic works: what, in the absence of traditional character development, of the dynamic evolution of events and emotions, should the audience care about? Should it care about the cultural/political allegory of an oppressive composer (Juan Manuel de Rosa) who prefers horses to women, and is shot dead – the victim of a conspiracy? Should the rare reality of twentieth-century shootings of composers (Webern, Lennon) be enough to legitimise such a fantastically loose construction around the theme? No one who has experienced *Rosa* only by way of CDs and vocal score can attempt a definitive answer to these questions. But what it is possible to care about, given this level of contact with the work, is the universalising, mythicising force of the music, a force that probably has more to do with Andriessen's sense of history, and his ability to offer new perspectives on the on-going confrontation between Apollo and Dionysus, than with notions of the music meekly setting scenes and words.

The 'distance' the CD listener is likely to feel from the work as staged fits well with that 'certain distance...from the musical object' which signifies classicism for Andriessen: and the use of 'closed' forms in *Rosa* achieves the objective of stopping any possible flow of psychological development in its tracks. In its place there is the aesthetic satisfaction of hearing how more measured lyricism interrupts extended, apparently unstoppable Dionysian outpourings. This is a lyricism subject to the constraints of subject-matter from which serenity, and ritual ceremonial, are excluded. As Example 10.1 shows – it comes from the third of three strophes in an aria (Scene 7) for Rosa's wife Esmeralda – the warm formality of the melodic writing is darkened by dissonant accompanying chords, which fit with the bitterness expressed in the text. Yet because there is no happy ending, lyric warmth cannot prosper. It always struggles to make its presence felt: the opera explodes

Ex. 10.1   Andriessen, *Rosa*, from Scene 7, bars 63–73

into a bizarrely stylised presentation of the investigation into Rosa's death, and this is followed by an open-ended, rap-style burlesque of the work's content and language, word-dependent yet as far as possible from conventional operatic song. On the recording, certainly, the so-called Index Singer is Dionysus personified – or rather, Dionysia.

As a jet-black comedy about death and non-transfiguration, *Rosa* can, without excessive musicological contrivance, be said to lie behind both *The Trilogy of the Last Day* and *Writing to Vermeer*: while the former continues to celebrate death, with graveyard if not gallows humour, the latter goes to the opposite extreme, ending with declarations of undying love for the absent genius from his female relatives. As a concert work, the *Trilogy* brings ceremony and ritual (if not, exactly, religion) back to the heart of the musical event. It contrasts, in the most starkly defined fashion, the turbulence of the first part, 'The Last Day', with the more restrained lament of the second, 'Tao': then, the renewed dynamism of the 'diabolic' scherzo 'Dancing on the Bones' – tuneful but not lyrical – connotes defiant rather than resigned acceptance of the inevitable. Ascent to Paradise is evidently not an option, and if, as suggested above, the 'Postlude' of Stravinsky's *Requiem Canticles* was indeed in Andriessen's mind at the end of the *Trilogy*, he distanced himself from its ethos while echoing its technical character: an undeniably classicising move, despite the valid remark by Frits van der Waa that 'the music's jagged construction and climactic effects produce a sort of rapture that at the very least suggests the passion for expression that was brought to a head in nineteenth-century music'.[8] But Andriessen's allusion to Saint-Saëns's 'Danse Macabre' (and to Ravel's *La Valse*?) in 'Dancing on the Bones' is more Bruegelesque than Baudelairean. Even nineteenth-century connections can be classicised in Andriessen's later musical world, as the deliciously mordant allusions to Brahms in *Rosa* confirm.

That lyricism – even romanticism – reassert themselves in *Writing to Vermeer* might be deduced from the prevalence of markings like 'tranquillo' and 'dolce' in the score, and the archaising modal purity of the opening. But this has less to do with the kind of late romantic recreation of renaissance polyphony found at the start of Pfitzner's *Palestrina* than with the chaste patterns of John Cage's *Six Melodies* (1950), which 'provide the durational outline for the opera'.[9] If Cage is one source, Sweelinck (most prominently, 'Mein junges Leben hat ein End') is another, and this connection could be the most fundamental of all, given Andriessen's declaration that ' "irony now replaced dialectics" as his basic philosophical framework in this opera, and that "irony and melancholy are the same" – both relating to the awareness of alienation and loneliness' (p. 48).

Such qualities are quite different from the exuberantly crude fantasies of *Rosa*. Yet *Writing to Vermeer*'s tendency to lyric restraint is subverted in at least two respects: by the occasional electronic interruptions[10] – depicting the social 'violence and destruction' threatening the 'tranquil domesticity' of Vermeer's female relatives, whose letters to the absent painter provide the work's material; and also by the tendency of the lyricism to turn more ecstatic than restrained, with dance-like celebration sidelining more solemn, processional genres. While *Writing to Vermeer* has many of the attributes of a consciously contrived contrast to *Rosa*, for example, in the way the central character of an idealised, real painter valued extremely highly by present-day culture replaces the degraded fictional composer who is *Rosa*, it remains questionable whether it manages that pure, distancing classicism that we might presume to be its intention. Andriessen draws attention to the opera's constructivist, palindromic routines and hints of Cageian detachment

Ex. 10.2   Andriessen, *Writing to Vermeer*, ending

in order to underline what he describes as 'a certain degree of contradiction between the non-developmental stasis in the music of Cage and the dramatization
of the music. This antithesis is in fact the area that has preoccupied me for twenty
years'.[11] The ending of *Writing to Vermeer* (Ex. 10.2), in which the radiant higher
consonances of the women's declarations of devotion are finally drowned out by

Ex. 10.2 (cont.)

'flood' sounds on tape, embodies contained ecstasy rather than unbridled abandon. Yet the effect is still to question, if not contradict, the purest Apollonian values: the serenity is more earthy, more fervent, than detached or elevated.

What does Andriessen really think of Vermeer, a painter of sublimely ambiguous understatement who chose not to represent any of the violence and destruction which afflicted his country in 'the Dutch year of disasters, 1672', when the opera is set? Andriessen's attitude is, presumably, 'ironic', since the opera contrasts the atmosphere surrounding the painter with intimations of catastrophe, and allows the electronic representations of that catastrophe to move from the margins to the centre, having the 'last word'. The sense of encroaching revolution is palpable, as is the comparable (though non-electronic) effect at the end of Henze's secular oratorio *The Raft of the Medusa* (1968/1990). And revolutionary force is not heard as wholly destructive in these works of high art: Dionysus is reborn as a political Lord of Misrule, not concerned with replacing something bad with something better, but leaving the question of what comes next to be decided by those who survive. Put in this way, Andriessen's agenda seems potentially Wagnerian: after all, *Parsifal* is a work in which, among other things, bells summon the faithful to celebrate the curing of their sick society.

Ways, means, materials

Andriessen's compositions of the 1990s follow on from his major work of the 1980s, the four-part theatre-piece *De Materie* (1984–88), which was his first project after the publication of *The Apollonian Clockwork*, and redolent with the attributes of Stravinsky, whom Andriessen (in 1994) declared to be '*the* composer for the future'.[12] Those combinations (in *The Rite of Spring*) of 'pulsed rhythms and diatonic melodies, which are elements from folk music, with highly chromatic harmony', which Andriessen then saw as 'an example for me of how to deal with material', undoubtedly persist into the works of the 1990s. But have the problems of *De Materie* been solved?

One of those problems was a result of pursuing the 'classical' ideal of distancing. *De Materie* ends with the recitation of a text suggested by Robert Wilson, a monologue in which the scientist Marie Curie speaks to her dead husband, and also refers to the speech she made on receiving the Nobel Prize for chemistry in 1911. So, intensely personal comments – 'Your coffin is closed and I will never see you again. I forbid them to cover it with the terrible black drapes. I cover it with flowers and sit near it' – are followed by unemotional scientific declarations: 'the importance of radium from the point of view of theories in general has been decisive'. Andriessen might be thought to have kept pathos at bay, by the simple device of not setting Curie's words to music. But by preceding this downbeat response with a fulsome, even romantic choral celebration of love – 'united with you, journeying with you to eternity' – the composer sets up a contrast from which the distancing hand of irony seems absent: unless, that is, it can be read into the mere juxtaposition of spoken lament and statements about science.

The ending of *Writing to Vermeer*, with its progression from the ecstatically lyrical (the music) to the contextually destructive (the electronic flood), is comparable in its motion from upbeat to downbeat, though there is a stronger sense in the opera than in *De Materie* of society as a collective entity (the three women), less emphasis on the heroically achieving, heroically suffering individual woman. Like

De Materie, *Writing to Vermeer* may just escape that deplorable tendency of senti-mental romanticism to 'take you by the hand and lead you to another world' – by implication, a false world in which art offers escape from reality. In both works the consolations of art and the encroaching pains of reality are juxtaposed: the two complement each other, but the former cannot eliminate the latter. Nevertheless, for the consolation that comes from depicting suffering *through* art, the central movement of Andriessen's *Trilogy of the Last Day*, 'Tao', is more satisfying.

The title 'Tao' – 'the way' – refers to one of the texts involved, 'The classic of the way and its virtue' by the sixth-century BC Chinese writer Lao Tze. Characteristically, Andriessen juxtaposes this, with its emphasis on 'calm, emptiness and invulnerability', with a twentieth-century Japanese poem, 'Knife-Whetter', by Kotaro Takamura, in which the main mood is 'ominous'.[13] The com-poser reinforces the contrast by setting the Lao Tze text for four women's voices, and the Takamura for a vocalist who is given pitched recitation rather than fully fledged melody, and who also plays piano and koto.

'Tao' is the 'cool' slow movement of the *Trilogy*. Nevertheless, it centres on a human presence, anonymous yet vulnerable, an individual quite lacking the heroic aura of Marie Curie. The use of the Chinese language is also a distancing device, but the music is devoid of exoticising 'otherness'. Andriessen says that 'I have made no attempt to relate to what is known as "music from the Far East", or, even worse, "world music".' Instead, he takes a cue from the first text's reference to thirteen companions and bases the music on 'a series of thirteen chords' (ibid.). Quite how these are to be identified is not entirely clear from the score. But the pe-riodic simultaneities which underpin the melodic, contrapuntal lines evolve from an initial 'higher consonance' (F, G, C) similar to the B♭, C, E, F which generates *De Materie*, through a succession of pentachords and hexachords to climax (Fig. 27) on a dense octachord before dissolving onto a pair of bell-like trichords. The persistent dissonance of these sonorities acts as a check on lyric warmth and expansiveness ('romanticism'): and that 'check' is even more potently embodied in the earlier music for the soloist, whose piano-playing entry – *fff*, 'as if crying' – is an unambiguous manifestation of the lament topos, formalised as a mechanism, yet searingly immediate in its emotional impact (Example 10.3).

This entry is the second time that the austere detachment of the delicately accompanied Lao Tze setting has been broken – the first (Fig. 6) is a severe, Stravinskian incantation which anticipates the 'Lacrimosa'-style ritual of what is to come. A decorated version of the incantation is combined with the solo pi-ano lament as it expands and intensifies. Then, from Fig. 20, as the instrumental ensemble takes over aspects of the lament idea, the Lao Tze setting continues in a darker tone. At its climax, after Fig. 24, bells ring out the admonitory minor third F to D, and this is taken up by the voice during the setting of the Takamura poem which serves as a counter-structural conclusion to the main body of the work.

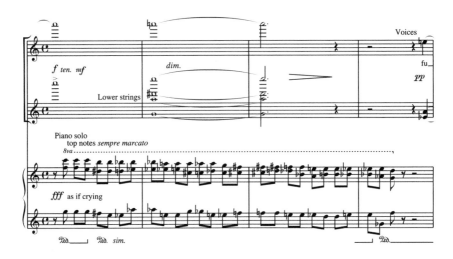

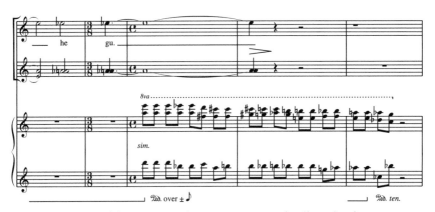

Ex. 10.3   Andriessen, 'Tao', bars 132–45 (some details omitted)

The G-based octachord (Fig. 27) which seems to be the harmonic goal of the piece is framed by quiet chanting, the voice supported by the unearthly koto and the severely cadential chimes of the ensemble. The tone of the poem is enigmatic: why is the knife-grinder so assiduously at work? One implication is that the continuous activity keeps him alive, even as he ages. In a sense, therefore, the knife-grinder 'knows how to live', like the subject of Lao Tze's text: 'it is said that he who knows well how to live meets no tigers or wild buffaloes on his road, and comes out from the battle-ground untouched by the weapons of war... How is this? Because there is no room for Death in him.' There are worse images of the nature and value of artistic creativity, and worse explanations for its social worth.

Andriessen finds the tone of Takamura's poem ominous, and his music stresses the vulnerability, the sorrow, of the half-singing, koto-and-piano-playing protagonist. As with some other late-twentieth-century musical laments (Ligeti, Birtwistle), there is a strength to the structure which lends positive substance to the images evoked. But in the context of *Trilogy*, 'Tao' is on the way to the 'diabolical' defiance of 'Dancing on the Bones'. This is not a world in which a 'Lacrimosa' yields to a serene 'In paradisum', and the classicising Andriessen is never so detached from his materials or his subject-matter as to suggest that all contact with the immediacy of late-modern reality is in danger of being lost. Fortunately, perhaps, Andriessen in the 1990s was no more successful than the neoclassical Stravinsky forty and more years before in submerging the human in the mechanical.

Mechanical and spiritual

Minimalist composers have always risked accusations of celebrating the mindlessly mechanistic, and the main way in which they seem to have tried to give depth and humanity to their music is by rejecting the aura of alienation and frustration central to modernism and the avant-garde. Just as Andriessen directly, and rather awkwardly, explored the conjunctions between science and humanity in *De Materie*, so Steve Reich has aimed to incorporate the 'real world', and not only its aesthetic elements, in his compositions. From the transformations of speech on tape that underpin early pieces like *It's Gonna Rain* (1965) and *Come Out* (1966) to *Three Tales*, a 'three act digital video opera' (first complete performance, 2002), Reich has been increasingly absorbed by the challenge of exploiting multi-media technology to dramatise contemporary issues. Of the three tales, 'Hindenburg', 'Bikini' and 'Dolly', he says that 'each of these reflects on the growth and implications of technology during the 20th century from early air transport and world wars to the current ethical debate about the future of our species. This debate about the physical, ethical and religious nature of the expanding technological environment has continued and grown pervasive since 1945.'[14]

Such preoccupations help to explain that 'darkening' of Reich's expressive world, noted by Paul Griffiths,[15] which emerged after *The Desert Music* (1982–4), and which has overridden the more exuberantly expressed spirituality of the Hebrew psalm settings in *Tehillim* (1981). With its onomatopoeic rendering of train-like sounds, and use of real speech fragments, *Different Trains* (1988) is a very different response to the Holocaust than Birtwistle's *Pulse Shadows* (see Chapter 9). *Different Trains* is more immediately evocative of reality, more directly expressive of the anxieties of those living in times of persecution, and shunning the distancing, and – it might be argued – deepening, which results from mythicising and transforming reality into a musical treatment of the felt structures of a poetic language from which semantic worldliness has been largely erased. Reich's rituals are potently explicit, not so much transcending the secular as validating its ability to match the spiritual in force of expression. With Reich, the technological, the mechanical, is offered as the true voice of modern times. The danger is that, in so resourcefully holding up a mirror to reality, he risks accusations of banality from those who believe that music itself has more richness and subtlety than his motoric pattern-making allows for. The greater distancing from such 'reality', and from the documentary, found in Andriessen's later dramatic works does not undermine their emotional impact.

At the end of the twentieth century the purer manifestations of minimalism continued to provide a source of timeless religious – and specifically Christian – meditation and worship. Only rarely – as in John Tavener's powerful *Total Eclipse* (2000), where environmental upheaval is portrayed as a symbol of divine intervention in the lives of men – does such music break free of its liturgical, contemplative constraints: and rightly so, since all else is mere aesthetics. In the secular world the apotheosis of the mechanical will be electronic or electroacoustic composition, and here it is the human interaction with the machine which creates worthwhile aesthetic results. As the emphatically non-minimalist music of Jonathan Harvey shows, such works can be no less potent in their immediate spirituality than the purely acoustic works of Tavener or Pärt. But with John Adams (b. 1947), the question of 'compromises' with minimalism has opened out into the wider topic of reliance on contemporary subject-matter which is not just political, but also religious.

Adams is a decade or so younger than Glass, Reich and their fellow pioneers La Monte Young and Terry Riley,[16] and he has commonly been seen as replacing their relative 'purity' with brash, exuberant impurity. In K. Robert Schwarz's diagnosis, Adams 'inherited the minimalist vocabulary and enriched it with a new expressive power and an impudent delight in stylistic juxtapositions'.[17] With all the conviction of a serious-minded New Englander converted to West Coast hedonism, Adams was prepared at one stage to assert: 'in the serious contemporary music that I was being taught [essentially as a pupil of the Schoenbergian Leon Kirchner at

Harvard], feeling had become extremely refined and so restrained and so sub-limated and so complicated' that for the expression of 'our Dionysian side, our spiritual side, and our convivial, social side' he had to turn to rock music (p. 175).

Perhaps only a Harvard undergraduate, bored with counting note rows, and spending most of his time 'getting high and listening to Cecil Taylor and John Coltrane and the Rolling Stones', could ever have entertained such simplistic notions. But any early element of defiant defensiveness for the benefit of interviewers in Adams's self-construction has long since been eroded by the sincere admission, in 1985, that 'I'm trying to embrace the tragic aspects of life in my work'. The truth of the claim that this was something 'that minimalism has not really succeeded in doing yet' (p. 177) is questionable. As seen earlier in this chapter, Philip Glass regards *Akhnaten* (1983) as 'tragic', but it seems unlikely that Adams would agree. While accepting that his own music 'suggests a very strong evolution away from what Glass has done', and that the earlier opera *Satyagraha* (1980) 'worked very well because the plain, spare, repetitive musical language...was so perfectly appropriate to the theme of passive resistance', Adams argues that Glass 'never seems to challenge himself with creating more than one layer of music, hence the music gets tiresome very quickly'.[18] In contrast to Glass, Adams aims to bring 'greater intricacy to the elegant simplicity of minimalism' (Schwarz, *Minimalists*, p. 179). And one aspect of that 'greater intricacy' is evident in Adams's comment that 'I think I've always rested apart from the other minimalist composers in this desire to have a strong sense of pulse, but at the same time to confound the listener's expectations.'[19]

Adams has also declared that 'what sets me apart from Reich and Glass is that I am not a modernist. I embrace the whole musical past, and I don't have the kind of refined, systematic language that they have' (p. 179). This disclaimer can obviously be turned round, at least if one believes that the search for refinement and system is more a classical than a modernist impulse, and therefore tends to make 'an unpredictable music filled with emotive outbursts and stylistic disparities' – as Schwarz characterises Adams's at one point – more not less modernist. Yet Adams's resistance to being labelled a modernist makes sense: the more consistently he has pursued his embrace of 'the whole musical past' (p. 179), the more integrated, both stylistically and structurally, his compositions have become. Schwarz tacitly concedes this in his reference to the 'unlikely synthesis of minimalism and post-Romanticism – a merger so personal that it can be recognized as Adams's own after hearing only a few bars of music' (p. 182), which Schwarz detects in both *Harmonium* (1981) and *Harmonielehre* (1985). And while there is certainly an element of 'polarity' between such 'dark, introspective, "serious"' pieces and a 'garish, ironic wild card' like *Grand Pianola Music* (1981–2) (p. 183), that demonstrates the composer's ability to 'vary the song', rather than any fundamental stylistic or structural fracturing within individual pieces. Schwarz puts this neatly in his remarks about Adams's 'multi-faceted musical personality', and 'his ability to integrate styles, not merely juxtapose them...More than any composer of his generation, Adams has achieved an accessible and genuinely American synthesis of serious classical ambition with the touch of the common man – a populism hardly heard since the heyday of Copland in the 1940s and Bernstein in the 1950s' (p. 187).

These claims will benefit from a modest degree of deconstruction. Yet it is undeniable that modernism as stylistic disparity is far less apparent in those later and more substantial works in which Adams engages directly with traditional genres, and moves closer to the compositional mainstream. Above all, he has relished the challenge of socially or politically charged, as well as religious subject-matter, if not as 'tragedy' then as modern mythology. The operas *Nixon in China* (1984–7) and *The Death of Klinghoffer* (1990–1) were not the first twentieth-century stage works to explore contemporary political and ideological themes, but in representing real people convincingly, even without strict adherence to 'documentary' values, they mark a significant advance on more purely allegorical attempts at comparable themes, whether in the Brecht/Weill 'epic' theatre in relatively popular style, or in the postwar avant-garde tendencies of Luigi Nono's *Intolleranza 1960* (1960–1) and Michael Tippett's *The Ice Break* (1973–6). With *El Niño* (first performed 2000) Adams moved even more decisively towards a compositional mainstream dominated by the large-scale dramatic forms of opera and oratorio.

El Niño can take the form of a 'multi-media theatre piece',[20] performed by acting singers, chorus, dancers, and accompanying (silent) film – made by the original director Peter Sellars – or it can be performed in concert as an oratorio. Given the composer's declaration that 'I wanted to write a *Messiah*',[21] the oratorio label has obvious salience. Yet *El Niño* is not a religious, devotional work, to be put alongside the large-scale contemporary scores of Pärt or Tavener. By their standards it is far from exclusively holy, and strains consistently against minimalist routines. Since Adams was apparently as interested in composing a response to 'the inexaustible miracle of birth' as of exploring his 'shaky and unformed' religious beliefs – or, indeed, of trying to discover whether he actually had such beliefs – it is to be expected that text and music will veer towards the more secular and social topics of oppression and persecution. Not since Tippett's *A Child of Our Time* (1939–41) has a modern oratorio dealt so powerfully with analogies between ancient and modern events: in the case of *El Niño*, between the massacre of the innocents, as ordered by King Herod, and the killings of students and civilians by soldiers and police in Mexico City on 2 October 1968. (This event had a more directly related ancient precedent in that the same Mexican district was the site for a battle between the Aztecs and Spanish conquistadors in August 1521.)

Ex. 10.4   Adams, El Niño, no. 20, 'Memorial de Tlatelolco', bars 104–11

In setting Rosario Castellanos's poem, 'Memorial de Tlatelolco', and framing it with biblical passages about Herod's wickedness and 'the day of the great slaughter' as foretold by the Old Testament prophet Isaiah, Adams leads a narrative dominated by the story of Mary's pregnancy, the birth of Christ and the flight into Egypt into regions far darker than any explored in *Messiah*, and the ferocious, quasi-canonic chorus for the Isaiah text (which includes the words, chilling in the wake of events in New York on 11 September 2001, 'in the day of the great slaughter, when the towers fall') ends on harsh dissonance. In all the sections of Part 2 concerned with Herod's edict and the flight into Egypt, Adams never compromises his post-minimalist credentials, given that the possibility of 'symphonic' dialogue and argument between voices and instruments is avoided. The orchestra creates and sustains atmosphere, and may have its own imitative ostinato patterns as well as repeated chords (Ex. 10.4), but even the work's most starkly dramatic effect, the sharp punctuating chords during the final stages of 'Memorial de Tlatelolco', doesn't suggest an orchestral 'voice' of greater awareness or profundity than the human narrative. Rather, Adams's style has something of the gravity and concentration of Stravinsky's in *Oedipus rex*, as well as reflecting

Ex. 10.5   Adams, El Niño, no. 24, 'A Palm Tree', ending

that work's aesthetic commitment to an 'anti-Wagnerian' avoidance of thematic dialogue between voices and orchestra.

It would have been a bold stroke to end *El Niño* at this point – to leave it open-ended, with the contact between Christian story and contemporary events unmediated. Yet, as if in conformity to the Christian belief that – despite the massacre of the innocents, and despite the Crucifixion – the story has a happy ending, the last three movements of *El Niño* turn to hopeful allegories of fruitfulness and rebirth, celebrating innocence and allowing a childrens's choir (for preference) to have the last word, the last song (Ex. 10.5). New Age preciousness is (just) avoided, as if Adams were recalling his remark to Edward Strickland that 'with some notable exceptions, most New Age music is soporific and basically tries to put its listener into a kind of gelatinous trance' (Strickland, *Dialogues*, p. 187). But the ending of *El Niño* is still a bit too sweet to be true, not least when compared to the way Tippett manages to be both upbeat and profound in the last part of *A Child of Our Time*.

In a more immediately contemporary comparison, the black comedy of Andriessen's 'dance of death' at the end of 'Dancing on the Bones' could be more appealing to modern-day agnostic tastes than Adams's gentle dance of life, with its politically correct attempt to infuse secular instincts with sacred overtones. Yet Adams manages an element of understatement, as well as of humour and sheer innocence, while retaining some dissonant spice in the harmony, so that his ending escapes banality. *El Niño* is never false to the balance of religious and mythic themes which give it its distinctive aura. It may be that Copland achieved a stronger sense of benediction, and a more profound feeling of oneness with the world of nature, in the sublime closing bars of his *Appalachian Spring* (1944). But Adams has brought off the particularly difficult task of acknowledging the capacity of religious feelings and beliefs to persist, even when the questioning of those feelings and beliefs becomes more and more insistent, and the Herods of history show no signs of losing their alarming power. Would Adams himself deny an element of escapism in those final stages? One hopes not, despite his claim, as 'a totally lapsed Episcopalian from New England', that 'even though [in 1989] I haven't gone to church in the last twenty-five years, I acknowledge the power of music to contact our innermost emotions, which I believe are religious' (p. 187).

11 Modernism in retreat?

What kind of century?

The twentieth century explored in this book is a period of musical history in which post-tonal modernism lay at the heart of a complex compositional web whose diverse stylistic and structural elements embraced or resisted that modernism to varying degrees. Nevertheless, analytical interpretation of this music dealing solely and exclusively with 'stylistic and structural elements' is, more often than not, unappealingly restrictive. The responses to twentieth-century works presented here operate — as verbal narratives — with mediations between formal and contextual, 'internal' and 'external', purely musical and immanently cultural. This final chapter will pursue the modernism-centred theme to a logical conclusion, asking whether the end of the twentieth century might not also mark the end of modernism. First, however, some significant attempts to simplify and summarise the century by equating that modernism with the example and influence of particular composers need to be addressed. I will also consider the view that a retreat from modernism in the twenty-first century is essential if serious music is to survive.

Richard Taruskin's eloquent salute to Stravinsky is one attempt to characterise the world of twentieth-century music in terms of one composer's influence:

> to the extent that terms like *stasis, discontinuity, block juxtaposition, moment* or *structural simplification* can be applied to modern music — a very great extent — and to the extent that Stravinsky is acknowledged as a source or an inspiration for the traits and traditions they signify — an even greater extent — the force of his example bequeathed a *russkiy slog* to the whole world of twentieth-century concert music. To that world Stravinsky related not by any 'angle'. He was the very stem.[1]

Taruskin seems to be on strong ground, in that Stravinsky's influence, on his contemporaries and on a multitude of later composers, has had consequences extending well beyond the style-specific sediment of that '*russkiy slog*', or Russian 'slant'. Yet, as one analyst of 'the Stravinsky legacy' has argued, Stravinsky's importance lay in offering one particularly potent response to the elements listed by Taruskin.[2] There were others, and Stravinsky's Russian (and neoclassical) angle on modernism was stylistically very different from the Viennese or Austro-German angle of the expressionist and early twelve-note composers: different again, for that matter, from the refined instabilities of Debussy, which Stravinsky himself, when seeking to play down his reliance on those 'Russian traditions', claimed as decisive in prompting radical developments.[3]

Such differences made it possible for later generations of composers to have strongly contrasted views about important precedents and models. For example, in direct opposition to Stravinsky's claim, from his own Webern-orientated twelve-note years, that Berg's legacy 'contains very little on which to build' (Stravinsky and Craft, *Conversations*, p. 72), Pierre Boulez in 1958 declared that

> it is likely that when the question of modern style becomes more settled Berg's influence will be able to make itself felt more profitably. It would in any case be superficial to see in Berg no more than a heroic figure rent by contradictions or to think of him merely as the culmination of romanticism on whom it would now be pointless to model oneself. On the contrary, by detaching the contradictions that are the key to his work from the particular context which gave them birth, it is possible to learn from Berg an extremely valuable lesson in aesthetics. His work retains intact all its potential for influence; and it is this which makes him indispensable to the musical domain of our time.[4]

Whether or not Berg's influence was of actual importance to Boulez himself, it is clear that many later twentieth-century composers found Berg's techniques, and the atmosphere of his music, stimulating and productive. Yet declaring Berg 'indispensable' need not involve dispensing with Stravinsky: and just as Taruskin's diagnosis of the Stravinskian stem can be mapped onto a broader modernist stem, so too can similar criteria be applied to Berg, while allowing due space for what Stravinsky claimed to be 'the barrier of style (Berg's radically alien emotional climate)' (Stravinsky and Craft, *Conversations*, p. 71). Elsewhere, I have compared the final stages of two operas from the 1920s – Berg's *Wozzeck* and Stravinsky's *Oedipus rex* – in order to open up the terms of a possible dialogue between 'expressionism' and 'neoclassicism' as opposite sides of the same modernist coin.[5] However, this is not to claim that a history of twentieth-century music which divides composers into Stravinskians and Bergians would be any better than one which funnelled all varieties of modernism into Taruskin's exclusively Stravinskian pigeon-hole. The problem with composer-centred encapsulations of twentieth-century developments remains. More appropriate, and far more difficult, is the attempt to calibrate composers' positions on the continuum between the extremes of 'pure' modernism and 'pure' classicism, in a complex ballet of advance and retreat. The main part of this chapter considers a group of compositions from the 1990s with this 'ballet', as well as with certain possibilities for the future, in mind. As always in current musicology, however, consideration of composition cannot be separated from concern with ways of writing, and with contextual verbal interpretation.

Theory, science, semiotics

Towards the end of 2001, books were published by two leading American musicologists: one, Lawrence Kramer, associated with the hermeneutically orientated interpretative musicology that emerged around 1980, and the other, Fred Lerdahl, an exponent of theoretical formalism at its most abstractly systematic.[6] Little common ground might be expected: but Kramer and Lerdahl converge – and concur with Philip Glass, among others (see above, p. 152) – on the judgement that art music lost its way during the twentieth century, and that modernism was to blame.

Kramer accepts that there was more to twentieth-century composition than 'high modernism', with its belief in 'originality as the indispensable sign of responsiveness to changing times, and therefore of seriousness and artistic integrity' (p. 260). Nevertheless, the dominance and persistence of modernism's 'cult of exclusion' (p. 267) has been so damaging that the 'efforts' of composers who write more 'accessibly' may have 'come too late': 'it may...be true that high modernism was the death knell of classical music' (p. 271). Lerdahl's primary topic is *how* music 'means', rather than *what* it means, but he comes to a broadly comparable conclusion:

> much twentieth-century music arose from compositional systems spawned not by knowledge of how the musical mind works (this knowledge is only now emerging) but by the ideology of historical progress. Schools of composition grew around various ideas of what the next historically significant step should be. These steps led to mutually incompatible and largely private compositional codes. Without guidance from study of music cognition, this result was in retrospect predictable, for the musical mind does not spontaneously learn arbitrary syntaxes. Cultural variation is infinite but constrained. (p. 381)

Putting Kramer and Lerdahl together, the verdict is that during the twentieth century 'the ideology of historical progress' spawned a high modernist 'cult of exclusion' which damaged – perhaps irreversibly – a classical-music culture centred on tonal compositions performed in churches, concert halls and opera houses to largely middle- and upper-class audiences, as well as enjoying a healthy domestic life within the same social classes.

Given the absence of ground-breaking shifts of social balance during the twentieth century, at least in the affluent West, it is perhaps not so surprising that the institutions associated with classical music did not change as radically as developments in technology and social practice might have facilitated. Nor, obviously enough, was there a shift away from the tonal, classical repertory decisive enough to call those nineteenth-century institutions of performance and dissemination seriously into question. Enthusiasts for high modernist music who declared a preference to hear that music in 'definitive' recordings through domestic loudspeakers rather than as part of heterogeneous and inconveniently located public concerts were therefore likely to be stigmatised as sadly anti-social in their failure to support the collective aural experience. The possibility that classical, and high modernist, music might find a more stable and sustained cultural position through the increasing use of 'private' technology and less reliance on old-style public socialising remains improbable, and even distasteful, but it should not be ruled out. Other social and cultural changes in the years ahead might render such a possibility far more plausible than it seems at the moment. But in any case, assumptions about the eternal rightness of cultural practices established during the tonal era, embracing as that did (from the time of late Beethoven) an emergent musical modernism, should no longer be offered as anything other than ripe for constant reinterpretation. For all the piety which continues to attend the phenomenon, live performance can be mindlessly mechanical, just as recordings can be endlessly revealing and absorbing.

In linking the persistence of modernist values with the possible 'death knell of classical music', Lawrence Kramer focuses on the difficulties modernism has allegedly placed in the way of the on-going evolution of 'accessible' serious composition, and the consequent emergence of a 'museum culture' in which the old is generally preferred to the new. The implication here, that modernism is asking more of performers and listeners than nature, as well as culture, has made it possible for them to provide, is brought fully into focus by Fred Lerdahl. Lerdahl's critique of modernism concerns the mental constraints of individual musical cognition, rather than the social observations of collective cultural practice, and his preference as a theorist is for the music that enables his theory to be exemplified most fully. Perhaps his definitive statement of principle is that 'a listener familiar with a musical idiom organizes its sounds into coherent structures' (p. 3). Lerdahl acknowledges historical evolution in compositional thinking – 'with the rise of chromaticism, tonal stability began to lose force, whether through ambiguity in projecting tonal orientation or though the use of symmetrical scales' (p. 315): and he declares that 'salience' fills the partial (syntactic) vacuum as the perceiver attempts to organise the sounds into coherent structures. But he relates his concept of coherence in post-tonal or atonal music to the kind of all-embracing designs he finds in diatonic tonal contexts, and says nothing about less hierarchic but still coherent transformational networks, such as are demonstrated by David Lewin in composers like Webern and Stockhausen[7] – networks which at the very least throw bald generalisations involving absolute distinctions between natural and 'arbitrary' syntaxes into question.

Controversy continues to rage as to what cognition, or reception, involves, and a critique of Lerdahl's earlier work, like Nicholas Cook's, which proposes two different types of reception, 'musical' and 'musicological',[8] suggests a less intractable basis for the practice of interactive hermeneutic and formalist analysis than Lerdahl himself provides. Yet Lerdahl's declaration that knowledge of how the musical mind works 'is only now emerging' is a salutary reminder that dogmatism in this area is unwise. The best case for the relevance and validity of music unconstrained by tonal principles comes in a study like David Clarke's monograph on Tippett, with its principled exploration of the 'profound discontinuity' between 'formalist discussion of music' and 'other modes of contextual discourse', and its concern with a music whose modernism inheres in the fact that it involves a range of signifiers which 'cannot be completely mapped by conventional harmonic understanding; hence they must be understood through feeling rather than through thought'.[9]

It is by way of such countering of purely syntactic analysis that the resistance to twentieth-century forms of musical expression represented by both Kramer and Lerdahl can most effectively be challenged. Understanding 'through feeling' is evidently a difficult concept to theorise, and most musicologists writing about twentieth-century music have preferred to offer interpretations in which matters formal remain at the forefront. For example, Robert Adlington has dealt with the problem of syntactic perception in Birtwistle by reading the composer's attitude to form as concerned with 'encouraging a limiting of formal awareness to the processes of the moment', and employing 'a focus on moment-to-moment fantasy rather than some evolving, obligatory larger form'. Yet Adlington is no more dedicated than any other serious writer to exclude matters of feeling and expression from his discourse, and it is when the consideration of signifiers in music begins to move between matters of form and matters of feeling that developments in the field of semiotics become most relevant.[10]

> A semiotic analysis does not start from ideas developed in cognitive psychology (for example, ideas of grouping), then seek to show how they can be musically instantiated. Nor does it start with presuppositions about the nature of 'mind'...then proceed to treat musical experience as entirely 'cerebral' (based on cognitive acts without bodily enactment). Instead, it starts with the terms used by musicians, and those in a musical community, to describe music-as-signifying, taking seriously the 'understanding' involved in kinesthetic activity, as well as that found in more abstract forms of pattern recognition.[11]

Naomi Cumming has provided a compelling statement of the case for musicology as a human science which uses interpretative strategies placed on a continuum linking perceptions about form and feeling:

> Instead of a polarization of sensuous qualities and formal relations, of feeling and thought, 'criticism' and 'analysis', what is needed is a recognition of continuity between these ways of understanding. Giving credence to a continuity between comments on the sensuous and the schematic might serve to dislodge any defensive avoidance of the former, or false sense of security in the latter. (p. 48)

The way in which interpretation of musical works can embody – but also question – a specifically modernist sense of tolerance emerges when Cumming quotes David Schroeder's view that 'the highest form of unity is not one which eliminates conflict. On the contrary, it is one in which opposing forces can coexist' (p. 257). Although the significance of this remark is the greater for being made about music – Haydn's – whose embodiment of tonal classicism makes the unifying control of the Schenkerian *Ursatz* an especially potent interpretative element, it can be read as an acknowledgement of the potential for modernist refraction in all music from the time of the Enlightenment, even if that potential was not fully realised until the early twentieth century. Contextual coexistence of 'opposing forces' means something rather different when tonality is absent. Yet the need for analysis to acknowledge 'the sensuous and the schematic' remains – at the same time as it continues the invaluable musicological work of urging the significance of the specific detail alongside the sweeping totality.

Resonance in space

Naomi Cumming's injunction to give 'credence to a continuity between comments on the sensuous and the schematic' will be a central factor in the sequence of commentaries which follows, on works from the 1990s which demonstrate different weightings between the modernist and the classic, as well as very different fields of feeling and expression. Furthest from any construction of alienated sadness and despair are the IRCAM works of Pierre Boulez, which celebrate sonic resonance and its power to imbue space with richness, depth and luminosity. Such man-made structures do not aspire to transcend materiality, or to generate intimations of the beyond. But they can create a poetic sense of mystery and majesty, by means of shaped gestures which evoke the dithyrambic ceremonies of human drama.

In Chapter 2, I cited Boulez's Debussian self-analysis: 'I need, or work, with a lot of accidents, but within a structure that has an overall trajectory – and that, for me, is the definition of what is organic.'[12] Boulez's IRCAM works embody precisely this shift of emphasis in favour of the organic, which gives new strength to classicising aspirations to integration, and moves the kind of modernistic tensions he once celebrated in Berg to the margins. Nowhere is this shift more potently explored than in Boulez's major work of the 1990s, which involved the elaboration of a short piano piece – *Incises* (1994) (itself expanded by Boulez in 2001) – into the forty-minute *Sur Incises* (1996–8) for three pianos, three harps and three percussionists playing pitched metal instruments. Though *Sur Incises* is not concerned with the interaction of live and electro-acoustic sounds, its protean allusions to notions of shadowing and mirroring are comparable to those found in *Répons* (1980–4) and ... *explosante/fixe* ... (1991–3). Typically, a temporal-spatial action – incision, cutting into – serves as a metaphor for the kind of interruptive splicings that were required in early tape-composition technique, and also for those explosive intrusions that can be so dramatic a part of human experience. Action creates reaction: in physical terms, a cut, however instantaneous, 'reverberates' as nerve-pain: so it is not the least of Boulez's achievements to make this nexus of images turn from the painful to the playful, by devising strategies which set intrusive gestures against reactions which contextualise and to some degree 'colonise' them. This role-playing is clear at the start of *Incises*, where a diversity of gestural types is orientated towards a basic rhetoric of fluidity and forcefulness. Even here, however, what could have been a simple opposition of materials exemplifying the 'explosante/fixe' principle[13] – for example, quiet sequences of hemidemisemiquavers, low in register, set against loud, sustained tremolandi of at least four notes, higher up – is moved in the direction of interactive dialogue by the actual sequence of materials. Even an initial segmentation into three gestural types, by reference to playing instructions – 'très rapide', 'souple' and 'tremolando' – is overridden by the fluid use of dynamics and register, suggesting that any one of these types is always moving away from or towards the other two (Ex. 11.1). The urgency and resourcefulness of dialogue renders the separate identities ambiguous and vulnerable. But it is in the principal section of *Incises*, a dance-toccata marked 'prestissimo possibile', that the drama of a dialogue dominated by the interaction of distinct yet relatable gestural types, line or arch on the one hand, reiterated chord or 'pedal' note on the other, becomes most intense. The piece can only end, giving the increasing aggressiveness of the interplay, with the assertion of a single type, line as flowing arch, and a final descent with rhythmic foreshortening which imposes a sufficient sense of closure by suggesting a reinvocation of the more expansive, reflective atmosphere of the piece's beginning.

As with Boulez's orchestral *Notations* in relation to their piano originals, *Sur Incises* is no simple 'arrangement' or orchestration of *Incises*, but an elaborate and complex expansion treating the original as a template or blueprint, a basic statement of principle whose substance remains to be fully realised. The overriding impulse behind the exercise of elaboration is nevertheless not to fragment that substance, placing it in a centrifuge which explodes its single sound source and takes delight in monitoring the separate development of thousands of musical shards and splinters. Instead, the ensemble devised for *Sur Incises* suggests a single super-instrument, masquerading as nine separate, acoustic sound-sources. *Sur Incises* moves inside that super-instrument, as if to model a music of the future which can recreate a classical equilibrium without mimicking the classical style. The fundamental distinctions taken from the solo piano piece *Incises*, between slow and fast, improvisatory and dance-like, exploding and 'fixated', are greatly expanded, but not to generate a more ramified diversity and separation. *Sur Incises* is nothing if not a celebration of common ground, of shared principles (Ex. 11.2, pp. 194–6, shows a short but representative passage). There is therefore

Ex. 11.1   Boulez, *Incises*, beginning

no dramatic crisis of identity, no build up threatening disintegration: there are no songs of sorrow. Even the increasing aggressiveness that brought the dance-section of *Incises* to its end is transformed here into an exuberant competitiveness which requires no warnings from the referee.

As with Conlon Nancarrow's *Studies for Player Piano*, which harness technology to promote a defiantly unresonant celebration of human enterprise and

Ex. 11.2   Boulez, *Sur Incises*, from 2 bars before Fig. 75

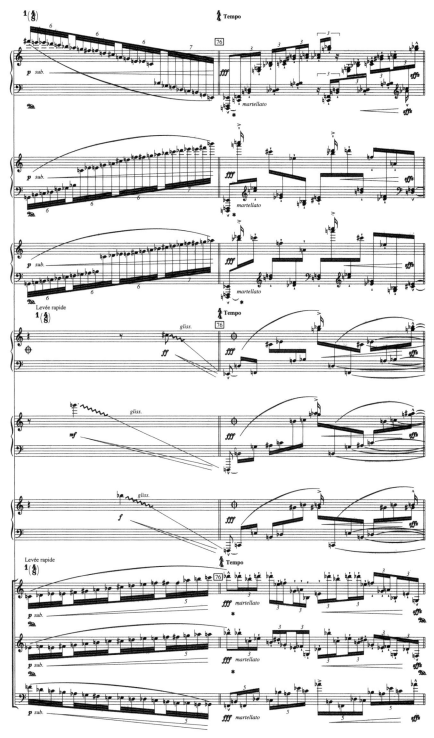

Ex. 11.2   (cont.)

Ex. 11.2   (cont.)

energy, the exuberance of *Sur Incises* is vital, since without it the risks of degenerating into soulless, mechanical pattern-making would be great. No less vital is a degree of eloquence, in which elegant shapes reveal an expressive depth to match the purely acoustic resonance of their ringingly sensuous sonorities. This, though Boulez would certainly not welcome the comparison, can even be thought of as a late-century equivalent to Stravinsky's 1920s 'sacrifice to Apollo', as represented most touchingly in the troubled yet wholly unexpressionistic serenity of *Apollo*'s 'Apothéose'. But *Sur Incises* avoids any hint of pathos, of tragedy or of the gently sorrowful spirit that steals into the final vocal passage of Stravinsky's *Les Noces*, or the chiming Postlude of *Requiem Canticles*. Boulez may come to this in time. But even if he does not, other contemporary composers who seem to acknowledge the turn from modernism to modern classicism have begun to show what its effects can be.

Echoes of voice

Like Boulez, Luciano Berio enjoys the process of elaborating templates, though not so much by transformation from the inside out as by 'the adding of extra layers to a pre-existent core so as to create new perspectives and balances'.[14] Berio is also unlike Boulez in retaining a degree of Bergian ambivalence, both structurally and expressively, to keep overtly classicising tendencies at bay. The result can vary greatly: at one extreme, there are the melodramatically disorientating collisions between radically contrasted elements (the scherzo from Mahler's Second Symphony as 'ground', with a wide range of fragments from across the orchestral repertory) which is found in the third movement of *Sinfonia* (1968–9); at the other extreme, the addition of textural layers to the solo instrumental *Sequenzas* in the *Chemins* series and other associated works, creating effects of interactive enrichment rather than confrontation. Berio has had no inhibitions about working with such found materials as Schubert's symphonic fragments (*Rendering*, 1989) or making arrangements of anything from folksongs to a Brahms sonata (the orchestration of Op. 120 No. 1, 1986). He is also very unlike Boulez in his willingness to work within traditional genres – most notably opera – though Berio prefers terms like 'azione scenica' or, in the case of the three substantial stage works written between 1979 and 1999, 'azione musicale', to signal his preference for avoiding traditionally operatic subject-matter and structure.

David Osmond-Smith has argued that Berio's 'understanding of the potential of musical theatre' demonstrates his 'fundamental and enduring mission to articulate and thus to place in the realm of the humanly shared, perceptions for which there is as yet no code' (p. 356). No less potent is the sense of music which builds on allusions to existing expressive codes. Many composers of opera and vocal music since Berg have not attempted to distance themselves from the kind of expressionistic lyricism which reaches its apotheosis in Countess Geschwitz's brief, ecstatic lament for Lulu, and Berio's music, whether fiercely active or meditatively melancholy, manages a remarkably personal tone of voice, especially when presenting instrumental 'song' in ways which challenge received modes of instrumental writing and playing. When coupled with an impulse that seems to represent a determined attempt to counter fragmentation — and even what Osmond-Smith defines, with reference to the earlier stage works, as showing how 'the most challenging diversities may be affirmed as "belonging together"' (p. 356) — a new concern with the drama of stretching continuity and connection to test its inner strength and durability can be detected.

There might even be a degree of fellow feeling with the more developed phases of minimalism, though the sympathy is aesthetic rather than technical. It emerges memorably in Berio's *Sequenza XII* for bassoon (1995), an extraordinary conception in which the player uses circular breathing to ensure over eighteen minutes of unbroken sound. That very basic physical unity and connectedness is certainly not paralleled by an utterly unvaried preservation of the initial texture and mood. But contrasts are introduced, quasi-classically, to enhance rather than to undermine the essential continuity — the 'circular structure', in Berio's phrase. A poetic aphorism provided by Edoardo Sanguineti (a writer set by Berio in several earlier compositions) captures this inexorably diversified unity: 'I move very slowly, I look at you from all sides, I explore your facets, I touch you, pensively: I turn you this way and that, transforming you, trembling: I torment you, terrifying.'[15] From pensive contemplation to terrifying torment suggests strong contrast, and a modulation from passive to active can be traced in the piece's materials: primarily, single notes, sustained for a long time, which gradually shade into other adjacent notes to form a line which slides slowly through the bassoon's four-octave registral space. Timbre and dynamic shaping make an aura of regretfulness and sorrow inescapable, even if there is also a sense of recalling such moods in relative tranquillity. It is the decorative antitheses of this slowly moving line — rapid repetitions of single pitches, explosive *gruppetti* in distant registers, as well as more elaborate melodic figures which can be either lyric or dramatic in character — that create the prospect of transformation, and even terror, as Sanguineti hears it.

Berio defuses what might otherwise hint at mawkishly unmediated pathos by moments of understatement, as with the final cadential jest of the barely articulated low B♭ (Ex. 11.3). The cliché of the bassoon's personification as sad clown is wryly touched in by such gestures. Shunning the ebulliently resonant sonic fireworks of Boulezian detachment and self-confidence, Berio suggests a compassionate response to alienation that has something of Berg's sympathy with the underdog and the socially deprived about it, even if Berio would never represent such characters directly in dramatic form. Proclaiming the lyric tradition in vocal writing, as Osmond-Smith sees it, while at the same time focusing on a

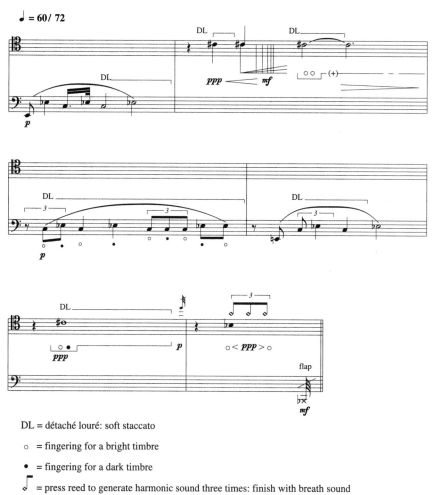

DL = détaché louré: soft staccato

o   = fingering for a bright timbre

●   = fingering for a dark timbre

♪   = press reed to generate harmonic sound three times: finish with breath sound

'flap': hard staccato on the reed without blowing (percussive effect)

Ex. 11.3   Berio, *Sequenza XII* for solo bassoon, ending

more modernist form of 'non-narrative counterpoint between word, music and vi-sual symbol', in *Outis* (1995–6) and *Cronaca del Luogo* (1998–9) (p. 356), Berio continues to test, and occasionally undermine, the ability of modernist technical strategies to embody a palpably human dimension for those codes which need to challenge as well as communicate. Such scepticism about modernism might well prove to be modernism's best defence, and best hope of survival.

Songs of ambivalence and experience

Towards the end of Berio's *Sequenza XII*, the melodic stratum is fined down to a minor-third oscillation (C/Eb). Berio alternates between these phrases and pro-longed C♯s: and if we think in pitch-class set terms, there is a relationship between

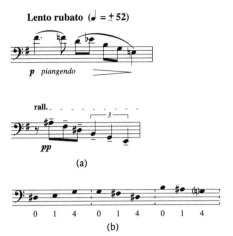

Ex. 11.4   (a) Britten, Suite for Cello, No. 1, 'Lamento', first and last bars
(b) Britten, Suite for Cello, No. 1, 'Lamento', pc set elements of final bar

the three-note collection formed by the melodic phrases (E, Eb, C) and that of the last three notes of the piece before the final 'flap' sound – C♯, D, Bb (see again Ex.11.3). Although the C/Eb oscillations contribute to the feeling of relative stability as the music winds down, the Eb can only be heard as a 'centre' in the most attenuated sense, and the realisation of the [014] set as the alternation of a major and minor third on C is even less explicit. There is nevertheless an appropriately mournful quality to the repetitions of the minor third, and Benjamin Britten, in music closer to tonality, is one composer who brought the major/minor third alternation into specific connection with lament. The opening phrase of the 'Lamento' movement from his First Suite for Solo Cello (1965) begins with a [014] trichord, but this is less salient in the movement as a whole than the linear alternation of the two thirds, as shown most conclusively in the final phrase. While this can also be parsed to reveal three intersecting [014]s, the sense of an unstable tonic triad (B/G/E) being shadowed, a half-step away, by another triad (A♯/F♯/D♯) seems more immediate, and more important (Ex. 11.4).

To argue that the sighing and falling which gives the [014] motive its lament-like quality is reason enough to connect the lyric styles of Britten and Berio, and to classify *Sequenza XII* as a lament, would be hyper-reductive. Music analysis observes such 'similarities' mainly in order to underline the corresponding differences, and to highlight the ambiguities of coincidence, especially with respect to encapsulations of harmonic characteristics which play vital expressive roles in earlier music. The play of comparison engages the faculty of memory, and it seems more than probable that music itself 'remembers' – offers the listener and analyst the opportunity for comparison – even when the composer was not consciously recalling a specific precedent. A case in point is Elliott Carter's

Ex. 11.5   (a) Schoenberg, 'Waltz' from *Five Piano Pieces*, Op. 23, 12-note set
(b) Carter, 'Inner Song', beginning
(c) Schoenberg, 'Waltz' from Op. 23, bars 100–1

'Inner Song' for solo oboe (1992), inscribed 'in memory of Stefan Wolpe', and Carter's use of a hexachord which was particularly significant for Wolpe himself was certainly not accidental. Yet there is another reminiscence in 'Inner Song', of the Waltz from Schoenberg's Op. 23, which is doubtless involuntary, but which it is nevertheless tempting to ascribe to mutual respect for the coherence-creating properties of developing variation.

This reminiscence involves another manifestation of the [014] trichord – a subset of the 'Wolpe' hexachord [012345]. Pitch-classes 3, 4 and 5 from Schoenberg's row for Op. 23 no. 5 are B, G, A♭ (Ex. 11.5a), and Carter begins 'Inner Song' with G, B and A♭ (Ex. 11.5b). Moreover, near the end of Op. 23 no. 5, Schoenberg treats the B and G to a brief, prolonging tremolando (Ex. 11.5c), and Carter's piece begins with the same effect, providing a link from the end of the previous piece for solo harp.[16]

From the beginning of 'Inner Song' to bar 8, G and B remain as fixed elements around which the melodic line evolves. Then, from bar 9, B and A♭ or G♯ take on this stabilising role. As is typical with Carter, this linear evolution can be perceived as a kind of developing variation, involving degrees of closeness and distance between successive phrases, and engaging the capacity of memory to recognise relationships and thereby create continuity. Like Schoenberg's Op. 23 in Charles Rosen's reading, that 'long-familiar compositional principle' of 'the unity of musical material'[17] is evident, even if the relationships Carter creates by such

Ex. 11.6   Carter, 'Inner Song', bars 59–67

'unity' are inherently less explicit than those found in the more concrete thematic processes of other styles, including Schoenberg's.

In pitch-class set terms, and using phrasing slurs as guides to segmentation, 'Inner Song' evolves from its initial [014] trichord into the pentachord of bars 2–6 [01245], and B♭ duly appears in bar 8 to complete the Wolpe hexachord. The pitch-class content of the whole piece can indeed be classified in relation to the Wolpe hexachord and its complement, but such abstraction sidelines much salient detail – for example, the arch-like shaping and pitch repetitions of bars 2 to 6, as well as the elements of compound melody: the way in which the motion in the upper register from A♭ in bar 2 to A and G♯ in bar 4 is complemented between bars 6 and 9 by the lower-register motion from C to B♭.

A close reading of 'Inner Song', in which set-class designation is complemented by developing variation, suggests a formal design which moves to a point of maximum stability towards the centre, between bars 59 and 67. In bars 59–61, there is a version of the generative [014] trichord – D♭, C, A – which spans the major sixth C to A in a shape which might be consciously designed to counter the lamenting quality of other possible orderings. This is followed by two more statements spanning C to A (bars 61–4 and 64–7) (Ex. 11.6). At this stage of the piece, the fixed A♮ and C act rather as G and B did at the beginning, as relatively stable elements to be retained in the memory while other things change gradually and coherently around them. This is Carter in the mode which, as noted in Chapter 9, David Schiff connects to an alleged 'classicizing' tendency. Yet here, as in all Carter's important later works, the tendency to classic, even Apollonian, poise and refinement is balanced by more volatile, more disruptive gestures.

At the end of 'Inner Song' the move to closure is projected through two complementary Wolpe hexachords, whose pitch-class content exhausts the total chromatic. The first extends from the low B at the end of bar 110 to the C in 113: the second from the D♯ in bar 113 to the end (Ex. 11.7). But the compositional treatment of these two hexachords is very diverse: the first is phrasally divided into two tetrachords – B, G, A♭, B♭: B, A, G, C – statements which involve a reminiscence of the piece's initial G, B, A♭ trichord, and include the repetition at pitch of both

Worte gehen noch zart am Unsäglichen aus . . . (Rilke)

Ex. 11.7   Carter, 'Inner Song', ending

B and G. The second hexachord is a single phrase, wedge-shaped in terms of its pitch-classes (D♯, E, F, D, F♯, C♯), and this contrast in basic presentation is matched by the wide intervals and varied rhythmic patterning. This ending is rather more brittle and edgy than the steady approach to that central phase of relative stability between bars 59 and 67: and those notoriously imprecise, evanescent multiphonics certainly do not bring the piece to a conclusion which reinforces the implications of its opening. This element of open-endedness is also touched on by the words from Rilke which Carter places at the end of 'Inner Song': 'words easily pass into what cannot be expressed'. What is left open is whether that acknowledgement of transcendence is to be welcomed, or whether, as the music seems to suggest, the existence of 'what cannot be expressed', whether by words or anything else, is not exactly a source of reassurance. Music, like humanity, is defined as much by its limitations as by its potentialities.

'Inner Song', in common with Carter's other memorial pieces, avoids the overtly sorrowing qualities of lament in favour of an incantatory, celebratory tone: it even hints at the dithyrambic spirit discussed in Chapter 9 with reference to *Syringa*. Carter here arguably alludes to – and therefore remembers – a more profoundly classical generic heritage than anything to do with the continuities and composed-out unities of traditional tonal structures. Those 'long-familiar principles of composition' which Rosen detects in Schoenberg are operative in Carter too: yet the modernist spirit of a work like 'Inner Song' happily transcends any yearning nostalgia for an ancient time that can never be recaptured. There is greater continuity than in the most radically fragmented and disjunctive works of Carter's earlier years – but the overall effect is of balanced diversities, not synthesis. It is the ability of modernism to accept and work with aspects of tradition which is the essential principle, and which makes the prospect of a new, modern classicism based, not on tonality, like Sibelius's, but on more equivocal ideas of stability and centredness, a real and attractive possibility for the music of the future.

A final focus

Writing of Ligeti in 1997, I said that 'no other contemporary composer has surpassed his capacity to alternate on more or less equal terms between exuberance and lamentation, turbulence and coherence', and that his 'reinvigorated modernism is tangible in his continued refusal to allow his music to settle down into unambiguously resolving, stable structures'.[18] To define this 'reinvigorated modernism' I evoked the by-now-familiar formula of 'a stylistic impurity', to use Ligeti's own term, creating 'textural stratifications which aspire to the status of an organic, homogeneous whole yet simultaneously resist such wholeness'. My earlier discussion of Piano Study 15, 'White on White',[19] continued along these lines, and it is a more substantial work from the same period, the Solo Viola Sonata (1991–4), that I have chosen as my final example. It would impose an unrealistic burden on any composition to suggest that it somehow stood for the whole of twentieth-century music, as if that hydra-headed phenomenon were plausibly reducible to a single concept. Yet representative the Ligeti sonata certainly is – and not simply of Ligeti's own development and sensibility. In the formal domain, there are obvious generic links with multi-movement instrumental works, although the sonata's six movements and sequence of generic titles suggest a more immediate connection with the suite. Syntactically, the music mirrors this ambivalence, employing a language whose pitch structures involve the kind of unstable centredness that can be found in much non-avant-garde twentieth-century music, particularly music which has associations with folk idioms: Janáček and Bartók immediately come to mind.

To extend the interpretative context from the formal and syntactic to the sensuous, the expressive, is to seek a formulation adequate to the music's voice, and here generic associations can help to bridge the gap, especially since they can be applied with the help of the composer's Preface to the score and his notes with the recording.[20] The primary voice is that of an instrument whose lowest string 'gives the viola a unique acerbity, compact, somewhat hoarse, with the aftertaste of wood, earth and tannic acid', and Ligeti couples this striking description with comments about the viola player Tabea Zimmermann, for whom the complete work was conceived, and 'her particularly vigorous and pithy – yet always tender – C-string'. The opposition offered here – acerbity and tenderness – can be seen as the force-field within which the music moves. But there is a further, more personal force-field, involving 'the spirit of Romanian folk music which, together with Hungarian folk music and that of the Gipsies, made a strong impression on me during my childhood'. This is seminal for the first movement, and brings with it broader ethnic, historical and personal features which ground other allusions: for

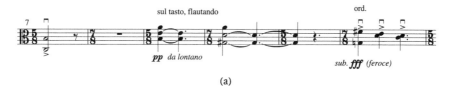

(a)

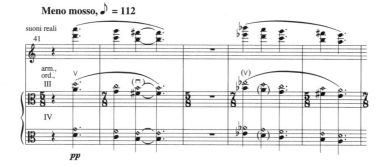

(b)

Ex. 11.8   Ligeti, Sonata for Viola Solo, 'Lamento', bars (a) 1–12 and (b) 41–49

example, the fifth movement's use of two-part writing in seconds similar to that 'found in the Balkan area…the Ivory Coast and Melanesia', or the third movement's tribute to Ligeti's teacher, Sándor Veress. The third movement's Hungarian title, 'Facsar', alludes to wrestling, distortion, and 'the bitter sensation felt in the nose when one is about to cry'.

As in other later works by Ligeti, the range of ethnic associations enters in dialogue with art-music perspectives reaching from early music to minimalism. In these terms, then, the sonata is typical of the twentieth century: music whose

Ex. 11.9 Ligeti, Sonata for Viola Solo, 'Chaconne chromatique', bars (a) 1–12, (b) 79–end

character derives from reactions to – and even evocations of – other musics. The predominant mood is that of lament, of a ferocity it is hard not to relate to the composer's experiences as a survivor of the Second World War and the political, psychological turmoil that followed it. As with Berio's *Sequenza XII*, there is a sense of a wordless, breathing human voice reasoning with the void, in a spirit which seeks to assuage the Dionysian turmoil of modernity in Orphic song.

There is no resolution of the conflict in Ligeti's sonata, however – no wry, rueful cadential gesture like Berio's, no Boulezian celebration of science, and little of Carter's poise and refinement. Any hint of nostalgia in the first movement is mediated by the increasing instability of the melodic line, and this instability mutates into the direct oppositions of anger and restraint which dominate the later movements. Indeed, the first movement is the only one to offer overt songfulness. The other five are fierce dances, obsessed with patterns which establish distinct identities while avoided the rooted security of tonal dance forms. The penultimate 'Lamento' presents a contrast between 'tempo giusto, intenso e barbaro' in the viola's lowest register, 'con tutta la forza, feroce', and a slower chorale in attentuated harmonics, a recurring cadence-figure, 'sul tasto, flautando', quietly adrift in the void between (Ex. 11.8, p. 205). By contrast, the concluding 'Chaconne chromatique' is as rhythmic and texturally continuous as its baroque model implies: but it is temperamentally disturbed from the outset – 'impetuous', also mysterious (Ex. 11.9a, p. 206) – and in its final stages it suddenly drifts into what sounds like an attempt at more lyrical resolution, from a distance, but fading, open-ended (Ex. 11.9b). Something of Tippett's characteristic opposition between the 'hard-headed' and the 'heart-easing' can be sensed here, and appropriately, given that the Ligeti sonata is a late work, in a style which – like Tippett's and that of other twentieth-century geniuses – confronts the abiding dilemma, 'of continuing to embrace modernist principles while also seeking to recover something from the past' (Clarke, *Tippett*, pp. 217, 213). Given such vital and moving results, it is by no means inevitable that the years ahead will see modernism in retreat in new compositions: rather, it could acquire new contexts, new perspectives. Twentieth-century modernism will not exactly become a tradition, but it could provide a standard of comparison for future innovations and experiments, and could also offer an invaluable yardstick against which to consider other twentieth-century initiatives. If so, exploring twentieth-century music will continue to be justified, and even necessary, as the twentieth century itself recedes in time, and new notions of the contemporary appear.

Notes

1 The work in the world

1 *Western Music and Its Others: Difference, Representation, and Appropriation in Music*, ed. Georgina Born and David Hesmondhalgh (Berkeley, Los Angeles and London: University of California Press, 2000), 5. Further page references in text.

2 Peter J. Martin, *Sounds and Society: Themes in the Sociology of Music* (Manchester and New York: Manchester University Press, 1995), 12.

3 Julian Johnson, *Webern and the Transformation of Nature* (Cambridge: Cambridge University Press, 1999), 14–15. Further page references in text.

4 Richard Taruskin, *Stravinsky and the Russian Traditions: A Biography of the Works through* Mavra (Berkeley, Los Angeles and London: University of California Press, 1996), 662.

5 The ending of *Petrushka* is illustrated and discussed in Arnold Whittall, *Musical Composition in the Twentieth Century* (Oxford: Oxford University Press, 1999), 39–40.

6 Judit Frigyesi, *Béla Bartók and Turn-of-the-Century Budapest* (Berkeley, Los Angeles and London: University of California Press, 1998), 88. Further page references in text.

7 Reich's notes are included with the 1996 CD recording. Nonesuch 7559-79430-2.

8 Lawrence Kramer, 'The Musicology of the Future', *repercussions*, 1 (1992), 9.

9 David Schiff, *The Music of Elliott Carter* (London: Faber and Faber, 1998), 300. Further page reference in text.

10 Roger Scruton, *The Aesthetics of Music* (Oxford: Oxford University Press, 1997), 494.

11 'Wide-spread they stand, the Northland's dusky forests / Ancient, mysterious, brooding savage dreams / within them dwells the forest's mighty God / And wood-sprites in the gloom weave magic secrets.'

12 See especially *Sibelius: Symphony No. 5* (Cambridge: Cambridge University Press, 1993), 11–15, and 'Sibelius', *The New Grove,* 2nd edn (London: Macmillan, 2001), vol. XXIII, 329–33. Further page references in text.

13 Timothy L. Jackson, 'Observations on Crystallization and Entropy in the Music of Sibelius and Other Composers', in *Sibelius Studies*, ed. Timothy L. Jackson and Veijo Murtomäki (Cambridge: Cambridge University Press, 2001), 225.

14 'Rotations, Sketches, and the Sixth Symphony', in *Sibelius Studies*, ed. Jackson and Murtomäki, 351.

15 See Arnold Whittall, 'Music–Discourse–Dialogue: Webern's Variations, Op. 30', in *Webern Studies*, ed. Kathryn Bailey (Cambridge: Cambridge University Press, 1996), 297.

16 Robert S. Hatten, *Musical Meaning in Beethoven: Markedness, Correlation, and Interpretation* (Bloomington and Indianapolis: Indiana University Press, 1994), 92, 96.

17 Hepokoski, 'Rotations', 351.

18 Geoffrey Chew, 'Pastoral and Neoclassicism: A Reinterpretation of Auden's and Stravinsky's *The Rake's Progress*', *Cambridge Opera Journal*, 5 (1993), 239–63 [p. 262].

19 Geoffrey Chew and Owen Jander, 'Pastoral', *The New Grove*, 2nd edn (London: Macmillan, 2001), vol. XIX, 217.

20 ' "Sibelius the Progressive" ', in *Sibelius Studies*, ed. Jackson and Murtomäki, 56.

21 See Jackson, 'Observations', 175–272.

22 Arnold Whittall, ' "A dance of the deadly sins": *The Beltane Fire* and the Rites of Modernism', in *Perspectives on Peter Maxwell Davies*, ed. Richard McGregor (Aldershot: Ashgate, 2000), 138–58.

2   Reflections, reactions

1 Roger Nichols, *The Life of Debussy* (Cambridge: Cambridge University Press, 1998), 163. Further page reference in text.

2 Craig Ayrey, 'Debussy's Significant Connections: Metaphor and Metonymy in Analytical Method', in *Theory, Analysis and Meaning in Music*, ed. Anthony Pople (Cambridge: Cambridge University Press, 1994), 128, 129, 131.

3 The epigraph of Schenker's *Der freie Satz* is 'Semper idem sed non eodem modo'.

4 Pierre Boulez, *Orientations*, ed. Jean-Jacques Nattiez, trans. Martin Cooper (London: Faber and Faber, 1986), 317.

5 Christophe Charle, 'Debussy in Fin-de-Siècle Paris', in *Debussy and His World*, ed. Jane Fulcher (Princeton and Oxford: Princeton University Press, 2001), 290.

6 See Simon Trezise, *Debussy: La Mer* (Cambridge: Cambridge University Press, 1994), 41–2.

7 Cited by Roger Nichols, 'Debussy', *The New Grove*, 1st edn (London: Macmillan, 1980), vol. V, 307.

8 Richard S. Parks, *The Music of Claude Debussy* (New Haven and London: Yale University Press, 1989), 37. Further page references in text.

9 This terminology derives from Edward T. Cone, 'Stravinsky: The Progress of a Method', *Perspectives of New Music*, 1 (1962), 18–26.

10 Cited in Richard Langham Smith, 'Pelléas et Mélisande', *The New Grove Dictionary of Opera* (London: Macmillan, 1992), vol. III, 934.

11 Leon Botstein, 'Beyond the Illusions of Realism: Painting and Debussy's Break with Tradition', in *Debussy and His World,* ed. Fulcher, 158. Elliott Carter, 'Two Sonatas, 1948 and 1952', in *Elliott Carter: Collected Essays and Lectures, 1937–1995*, ed. Jonathan W. Bernard (Rochester, NY and Woodbridge: University of Rochester Press, 1997), 229.

12   David Lewin, *Musical Form and Transformation: 4 Analytic Essays* (New Haven and London: Yale University Press, 1993), 97–159.

13   Matthew Brown, 'Tonality and Form in Debussy's *Prélude à "L'Après-midi d'un faune"*', *Music Theory Spectrum*, 15/2 (1993), 128–43. Marie Rolf, 'Semantic and Structural Issues in Debussy's Mallarmé Songs', in *Debussy Studies,* ed. Richard Langham Smith (Cambridge: Cambridge University Press, 1997), 179–200.

14   Rocco di Pietro, *Dialogues with Boulez* (Lanham, MD and London: Scarecrow Press, 2001), 25, 69, 70.

15   Boulez, *Orientations*, 371.

16   Cited in Hans Moldenhauer with Rosaleen Moldenhauer, *Anton von Webern: A Chronicle of His Life and Work* (London: Victor Gollancz, 1978), 104.

17   Kathryn Bailey, *The Life of Webern* (Cambridge: Cambridge University Press, 1998), 191. Further page references in text.

18   Julian Johnson, *Webern and the Transformation of Nature* (Cambridge: Cambridge University Press, 1999), 211, 224–5. Further page references in text.

19   J. P. Stern, *Nietzsche* (Glasgow: Fontana/Collins, 1978), 44.

20   The technical terminology used in this discussion is introduced by Allen Forte in *The Atonal Music of Anton Webern* (New Haven and London: Yale University Press, 1998), 5–20. Forte's discussion of Webern's Op. 16 no. 2 is on pp. 351–3. See also *The New Grove*, 2nd edn (London: Macmillan, 2001), under 'Pitch Class' and 'Set'.

21   For a detailed demonstration, see Jonathan Dunsby and Arnold Whittall, *Music Analysis in Theory and Practice* (London: Faber Music, 1988), 192–200.

22   Kathryn Bailey, *The Twelve-Note Music of Anton Webern* (Cambridge: Cambridge University Press, 1991), 215–22. Further page references in text.

23   Anton Webern, *Letters to Hildegard Jone and Josef Humplik*, ed. Josef Polnauer, trans. Cornelius Cardew (Bryn Mawr: Presser, 1967), 37.

24   Arnold Whittall, 'Webern and Multiple Meaning', *Music Analysis*, 6 (1987), 336–7. Further page references in text.

25   Kyle Gann, *The Music of Conlon Nancarrow* (Cambridge: Cambridge University Press, 1995), 175–6.

26   Roger Scruton, 'True Authority: Janáček, Schoenberg and Us', in *Reviving the Muse: Essays on Music after Modernism*, ed. Peter Davison (Brinkworth: Claridge Press, 2001), 29.

27   David Clarke, 'Parting Glances', *The Musical Times* (December 1993), 684.

28   'Sprich auch du/Speak you also', in Paul Celan, *Selected Poems*, trans. Michael Hamburger (London: Penguin Books, 1996), 100–1.

3   Rites of renewal and remembrance

1   *Intimate Letters: Leoš Janáček to Kamila Stösslová*, ed. and trans. John Tyrrell (London: Faber and Faber, 1994), 281.

2   'True Authority: Janáček, Schoenberg and Us', in *Reviving the Muse: Essays on Music after Modernism*, ed. Peter Davison (Brinkworth: Claridge Press, 2001), 7–30. Further page references in text.

3   The allusion is to Richard Taruskin's essay 'Stravinsky and the Subhuman', in *Defining Russia Musically: Historical and Hermeneutical Essays* (Princeton and Oxford: Princeton University Press, 1997), 360–467. See Chapter 4 below.

4   'Janáček, Musical Analysis, and Debussy's "Jeux de vagues"', in *Janáček Studies*, ed. Paul Wingfield (Cambridge: Cambridge University Press, 1999), 270.

5   '"Nothing but pranks and puns": Janáček's Solo Piano Music', in *Janáček Studies*, ed. Wingfield, 18.

6   Paul Griffiths, *The String Quartet* (London: Thames and Hudson, 1983), 186. Further page references in text.

7   Igor Stravinsky and Robert Craft, *Dialogues* (London: Faber and Faber, 1982), 128.

8   *Schoenberg, Berg, Webern: The String Quartets: A Documentary Study*, ed. Ursula von Rauchhaupt, trans. Eugene Hartzell (Hamburg: Deutsche Grammophon Gesellschaft, 1971), 52.

9   Arnold Schoenberg, *Fundamentals of Musical Composition*, ed. Gerald Strang and Leonard Stein (London: Faber and Faber, 1967), 58–9.

10 Carl Dahlhaus, *Realism in Nineteenth-Century Music*, trans. Mary Whittall (Cambridge: Cambridge University Press, 1985), 102.

11 Judit Frigyesi, *Béla Bartók and Turn-of-the-Century Budapest* (Berkeley, Los Angeles and London: University of California Press, 1998), 271–3. Further page references in text.

12 Halsey Stevens, *The Life and Music of Béla Bartók*, 3rd edn, prepared by Malcolm Gillies (Oxford: Oxford University Press, 1993), 189–90.

13 *Béla Bartók Essays*, ed. Benjamin Suchoff (London: Faber and Faber, 1976), 121–2.

14 See Elliott Antokoletz, 'Middle-Period String Quartets', in *The Bartók Companion*, ed. Malcolm Gillies (London: Faber and Faber, 1993), 267.

15 Taruskin, 'Stravinsky and the Subhuman', 453.

16 Rachel Beckles Willson, 'Vocal Music: Inspiration and Ideology', in *The Cambridge Companion to Bartók*, ed. Amanda Bayley (Cambridge: Cambridge University Press, 2001), 90–1. Further page references in text.

17 See Julie Brown, 'Bartók, the Gypsies, and Hybridity in Music', in *Western Music and Its Others: Difference, Representation, and Appropriation in Music*, ed. Georgina Born and David Hesmondhalgh (Berkeley, Los Angeles and London: University of California Press, 2000), 119–42.

18 Theodor W. Adorno, cited in Max Paddison, *Adorno's Aesthetics of Music* (Cambridge: Cambridge University Press, 1993), 41.

19 David Cooper, *Bartók: Concerto for Orchestra* (Cambridge: Cambridge University Press, 1996), 84.

20 Richard Cohn, 'Bartók's Octatonic Strategies: A Motivic Approach', *Journal of the American Musicological Society*, 44 (1991), 298.

21 Stephen Downes, 'Eros in the Metropolis: Bartók's *The Miraculous Mandarin*', *Journal of the Royal Musical Association*, 125 (2000), 42. Further page reference in text.

22 György Lukács, cited in Downes, 'Eros in the Metropolis', 43.

23   Elliott Antokoletz, 'Modal Transformation and Musical Symbolism in Bartók's *Cantata Profana*', in *Bartók Perspectives: Man, Composer, and Ethnomusicologist*, ed. Elliott Antokoletz, Victoria Fischer and Benjamin Suchoff (Oxford: Oxford University Press, 2000), 74–5. Further page reference in text.

24   Benjamin Suchoff, 'Structure and Concept in Bartók's Sixth Quartet', *Tempo*, 83 (Winter 1967–8), 10. Further page references in text.

25   László Somfai, *Béla Bartók: Composition, Concepts, and Autograph Sources* (Berkeley, Los Angeles and London: University of California Press, 1996), 109.

26   For a detailed exploration of this concept, see Paul Wilson, *The Music of Béla Bartók* (New Haven and London: Yale University Press, 1992).

4   Transcending the secular

1   Malcolm Gillies, *Bartók Remembered* (London and Boston: Faber and Faber, 1990), 130. Further page references in text.

2   Paul Wilson, *The Music of Béla Bartók* (New Haven and London: Yale University Press, 1992), 190.

3   Richard Taruskin, 'Stravinsky and the Subhuman', in *Defining Russia Musically: Historical and Hermeneutical Essays* (Princeton and Oxford: Princeton University Press, 1997), 360–467.

4   Igor Stravinsky and Robert Craft, *Dialogues* (London: Faber and Faber, 1982), 124–5. Further page references in text.

5   Stephen Walsh, *Stravinsky: Oedipus rex* (Cambridge: Cambridge University Press, 1993), 65.

6   Igor Stravinsky, *Poetics of Music in the Form of Six Lessons,* trans. Arthur Knodel and Ingolf Dahl (New York: Vintage, 1947), 83. Further page references in text.

7   Taruskin, 'Stravinsky and the Subhuman', 390. Further page references in text.

8   For detailed statements of this position, see Paul Lawrence Rose, *Wagner: Race and Revolution* (London: Faber and Faber, 1992), and Marc A. Weiner, *Richard Wagner and the Anti-Semitic Imagination* (Lincoln, NE: University of Nebraska Press, 1995).

9   Taruskin uses this term 'as a convenient way of conveying a sense of *ur*-Russianness', and 'to denote the imaginary *ur*-Russia that Stravinsky conjured up in the music of his "Swiss" period'. See *Stravinsky and the Russian Traditions: A Biography of the Works through* Mavra (Berkeley, Los Angeles and London: University of California Press, 1996), 1127. 'Anhemitony' refers to the use of modal segments which lack semitones.

10   Naomi Cumming, *The Sonic Self: Musical Subjectivity and Signification* (Bloomington and Indianapolis: Indiana University Press, 2000), 145.

11   Walsh, *Oedipus rex*, 34. Further page references in text.

12   Igor Stravinsky, *Themes and Conclusions* (London: Faber and Faber, 1972), 27–8.

13   Paul Griffiths, 'Messiaen', *The New Grove*, 2nd edn (London: Macmillan, 2001) vol. XVI, 491. Further page references in text.

14   For a detailed commentary, see Anthony Pople, *Messiaen: Quatuor pour la fin du Temps* (Cambridge: Cambridge University Press, 1998).

15   Anthony Pople, 'Messiaen's Musical Language: An Introduction', in *The Messiaen Companion*, ed. Peter Hill (London: Faber and Faber, 1995), 16.

16   Wilfrid Mellers, 'Mysticism and Theology', in *The Messiaen Companion*, ed. Hill, 225.

17   Richard Steinitz, '*Des canyons aux étoiles*', in *The Messiaen Companion*, ed. Hill, 484. Further page references in text.

18   Notes with CD recording DG439 929-2 (1994), 5.

19   Robert Worby, 'An Introduction to Stockhausen's *Light*', Barbican Hall programme book (2001), 12–13.

5   Overlapping opposites: Schoenberg observed

1   Arnold Schoenberg, *Structural Functions of Harmony* [completed 1948], ed. Leonard Stein (London: Ernest Benn, 1969), 193. In a rather cryptic late note, 'My Technique and Style' (c. 1950), Schoenberg wrote that his style took 'a turn – perhaps you would call it to the Apollonian side – in the *Suite for Seven Instruments*, Op. 29 [1925–6]'. See *Style and Idea*, ed. Leonard Stein, trans. Leo Black (London: Faber and Faber, 1975), 110. This chapter derives from my article 'Overlapping Opposites: Schoenberg since 1951', *The Musical Times* (Autumn 2000), 11–20.

2   Theodore W. Adorno, 'Arnold Schoenberg 1874–1951', in *Prisms*, trans. Samuel and Shierry Weber (London: Neville Spearman, 1967), 151.

3   Roberto Gerhard, 'Reluctant Revolutionary', in *The London Sinfonietta Schoenberg/Gerhard Series*, ed. David Atherton (London: London Sinfonietta Productions, 1973), 43. Reprinted in *Gerhard on Music: Selected Writings*, ed. Meirion Bowen (Aldershot: Ashgate, 2000), 112–13.

4   See *Gerhard on Music*, especially 103–13. See also Joaquim Homs, *Roberto Gerhard and His Music*, ed. Meirion Bowen (Sheffield: Anglo-Catalan Society, 2000), 112.

5   Schoenberg, *Style and Idea*, 174.

6   See *The Musical Times* (September 1974), 739–43.

7   Igor Stravinsky and Robert Craft, *Conversations with Igor Stravinsky* (London: Faber and Faber, 1979), 71.

8   Hans Keller, 'Perspective', *Music Survey*, 4 (October 1951). Reprinted in *Music Survey: New Series 1949–1952*, ed. Donald Mitchell and Hans Keller (London: Faber and Faber, 1981), 315.

9   Hans Keller, 'Schoenberg and the Crisis of Communication', in *The London Sinfonietta Schoenberg/Gerhard Series*, ed. Atherton, 47–8.

10   Milton Babbitt, 'Memoir' in 'Hans Keller (1919–1985): A Memorial Symposium', ed. Christopher Wintle, *Music Analysis*, 5 (1986), 376.

11   Within this particular region of formalistic enquiry I would single out the following: Jack Boss, 'Schoenberg on Ornamentation and Structural Levels', *Journal of Music Theory*, 38 (1994), 187–216; David S. Lefkovitz, 'Listening

Strategies and Hexachordal Combinatorial "Functions" in Schoenberg's Op. 23 no. 4', *Music Analysis*, 16 (1997), 309–48. For a rather different context see Lefkovitz, 'Schoenberg and His Op. 23 No. 4: A Functional Analysis' and 'The Composer as Jew: A Homage', *Music Analysis*, 18 (1999), 375–85.

12 Hans Keller, 'Schoenberg: The Future of Symphonic Thought', in *Essays on Music*, ed. Christopher Wintle (Cambridge: Cambridge University Press, 1994), 179–91. Further page references in text. Originally published in *Perspectives of New Music*, 13 (1974).

13 Hans Keller, 'Principles of Composition', in *Essays on Music*, 212–32. Further page references in text. Originally published in *The Score*, 26 and 27 (1960).

14 Christopher Wintle, editorial note to Keller, 'Schoenberg', in *Essays on Music*, 260.

15 Martha M. Hyde, 'Neoclassic and Anachronistic Impulses in Twentieth-Century Music', *Music Theory Spectrum*, 18 (1996), 200–35. Further page references in text.

16 Joseph H. Auner, 'Schoenberg's Handel Concerto and the Ruins of Tradition', *Journal of the American Musicological Society*, 49 (1996), 264–313; 'Schoenberg and His Public in 1930: The Six Pieces for Male Chorus, Op. 35', in *Schoenberg and His World*, ed. Walter Frisch (Princeton: Princeton University Press, 1999), 85–125. Further page references in text.

17 Bryan Simms, *The Atonal Music of Arnold Schoenberg, 1908–1923* (New York and Oxford: Oxford University Press, 2000), 105, 177. For a thorough discussion of the possible relationships between these Nietzschean categories and musical analysis, see Richard Kurth, 'Music and Poetry, a Wilderness of Doubles: Heine–Nietzsche–Schubert–Derrida', *19th Century Music*, 21 (1997), 3–27. See also Alan Street, '"The Ear of the Other": Style and Identity in Schoenberg's Eight Songs Op. 6', in *Schoenberg and Words: The Modernist Years*, ed. Charlotte M. Cross and Russell A. Berman (New York and London: Garland, 2000), 103–37, and William E. Benjamin, 'Abstract Polyphonies: The Music of Schoenberg's Nietzschean Moment', in *Political and Religious Ideas in the Works of Arnold Schoenberg*, ed. Charlotte M. Cross and Russell A. Berman (New York and London: Garland, 2000), 1–39.

18 Adorno, 'Schoenberg', 171.

19 See *Schoenberg, Berg, Webern: The String Quartets: A Documentary Study*, ed. Ursula von Rauchhaupt, trans. Eugene Hartzell (Hamburg: Deutsche Grammophon Gesellschaft, 1971), 52.

20 Michael Cherlin, 'Dialectical Opposition in Schoenberg's Music and Thought', *Music Theory Spectrum*, 22 (2000), 175, 176.

21 Michael Cherlin, 'Memory and Rhetorical Trope in Schoenberg's String Trio', *Journal of the American Musicological Society*, 51 (1998), 559–602. Further page references in text.

22 Silvina Milstein, *Arnold Schoenberg: Notes, Sets, Forms* (Cambridge: Cambridge University Press, 1992), 157–84.

23 Theodor W. Adorno, *Quasi una fantasia*, trans. Rodney Livingstone (London and New York: Verso, 1994), 152–3.

24   Christopher Hasty, 'Form and Idea in Schoenberg's *Phantasy*', in *Music Theory in Concept and Practice*, ed. James M. Baker, David. W. Beach and Jonathan W. Bernard (Rochester, NY and Woodbridge: University of Rochester Press, 1997), 461.

25   Arnold Whittall, *Schoenberg Chamber Music* (London: BBC, 1972), 60.

26   Schoenberg, *Style and Idea*, 136.

27   Steven J. Cahn, 'The Artist as Modern Prophet: A Study of Historical Consciousness and Its Expression in Schoenberg's "Vorgefühl", Op. 22 No. 4', in *Schoenberg and Words*, ed. Cross and Berman, 264.

28   Reinhold Brinkmann, 'Schoenberg the Contemporary: A View from Behind', in *Constructive Dissonance: Arnold Schoenberg and the Transformations of Twentieth-Century Culture*, ed. Juliane Brand and Christopher Hailey (Berkeley, Los Angeles and London: University of California Press, 1997), 214.

29   Alexander L. Ringer, 'Assimilation and the Emancipation of Historical Dissonance', in *Constructive Dissonance*, ed. Brand and Hailey, 33.

30   Arnold Whittall, 'Uncertain Reconciliations', *The Musical Times* (August 1997), 30.

31   Bluma Goldstein, 'Schoenberg's *Moses und Aron*: A Vanishing Biblical Nation', in *Political and Religious Ideas,* ed. Cross and Berman, 187, 189. Further page references in text. Among Richard Taruskin's writings on Schoenberg, see 'Back to Whom? Neoclassicism as Ideology', *19th Century Music*, 16 (1993), 286–302, 'Revising Revision', *Journal of the American Musicological Society*, 46 (1993), 114–38, and *Rethinking Russia Musically* (Princeton and Oxford: Princeton University Press, 1997), 349–59. In considerable contrast, David S. Lefkovitz's Functional Analysis of Op. 23 No. 4 (see note 11 above) unequivocally celebrates Schoenberg's project for asserting authority over the Jewish nation.

32   Camille Crittenden, 'Texts and Contexts of *A Survivor from Warsaw*, Op. 46', in *Political and Religious Ideas*, ed. Cross and Berman, 246, 247. Further page references in text.

33   David Isadore Lieberman, 'Schoenberg Rewrites His Will: *A Survivor from Warsaw*, Op. 46', in *Political and Religious Ideas,* ed. Cross and Berman, 212. Further page references in text.

34   William E. Benjamin, 'Abstract Polyphonies: The Music of Schoenberg's Nietzschean Moment', in *Political and Religious Ideas*, ed. Cross and Berman, 1–39. Further page references in text.

35   See Robert Falck, 'Schoenberg in Shirtsleeves: The Male Choruses, Op. 35', in *Political and Religious Ideas*, ed. Cross and Berman, 117.

36   See Naomi André, 'Returning to a Homeland: Religion and Political Contexts in Schoenberg's *Dreimal tausend Jahre*', in *Political and Religious Ideas*, ed. Cross and Berman, 274.

37   Peter Franklin, review of Alexander L. Ringer, *Arnold Schoenberg: The Composer as Jew* (Oxford: Oxford University Press, 1990), *Music and Letters*, 72 (1991), 630.

6   The subject of Britten

1   Benjamin Britten, *On Receiving the First Aspen Award* (London: Faber Music, 1964), 14. Further page references in text.

2   *New York Times*, 16 November 1969: quoted in Humphrey Carpenter, *Benjamin Britten: A Biography* (London: Faber and Faber, 1992), 441. Further page references in text.

3   'The Musical Character', in *Benjamin Britten: A Commentary on His Works from a Group of Specialists*, ed. Donald Mitchell and Hans Keller (London: Rockliff, 1952), 350.

4   See *Times Literary Supplement*, 28 June 1991, 15. The discussion at this point is drawn from my essay 'Along the Knife-Edge: The Topic of Transcendence in Britten's Musical Aesthetic', in *On Mahler and Britten: Essays in Honour of Donald Mitchell on His Seventieth Birthday*, ed. Philip Reed (Woodbridge: Boydell Press/Britten–Pears Library, 1995), 290–8.

5   Robin Holloway, 'The Prince of the Pagodas', *Tempo*, 176 (March 1991), 32.

6   'Britten's Dream', in *Musicology and Difference: Gender and Sexuality in Music Scholarship*, ed. Ruth A. Solie (Berkeley, Los Angeles and London: University of California Press, 1993), 263.

7   See Whittall, 'Along the Knife-Edge', 292.

8   Carpenter, *Benjamin Britten*, 133.

9   Whittall, 'Along the Knife-Edge', 297.

10   *Music Survey*, 2/4 (Spring 1950), 227–36.

11   Mitchell and Keller, *Commentary*, 350–1.

12   Mervyn Cooke, *Britten and the Far East: Asian Influences in the Music of Benjamin Britten* (Woodbridge: Boydell Press/Britten–Pears Library, 1998), 248–9.

13   Edward T. Cone, 'Attacking a Brahms Puzzle', *The Musical Times* (February 1995), 72.

14   Gary Tomlinson, *Metaphysical Song: An Essay on Opera* (Princeton: Princeton University Press, 1999), 4. All other quotations from Tomlinson are from pp. 154–6.

15   For further critique of Tomlinson's reading, see Philip Rupprecht, *Britten's Musical Language* (Cambridge: Cambridge University Press, 2001), 185–6.

16   See Arnold Whittall, 'Britten's Lament: The World of *Owen Wingrave*', *Music Analysis*, 19 (2000), 145–66.

17   Lawrence Kramer, *Franz Schubert: Sexuality, Subjectivity, Song* (Cambridge: Cambridge University Press, 1998), 164–5.

18   Philip Brett, 'Britten's Dream', in *Musicology and Difference*, ed. Solie, 267. Brett also discusses this topic in 'Grimes and Lucretia', in *Music and Theatre: Essays in Honour of Winton Dean*, ed. Nigel Fortune (Cambridge: Cambridge University Press, 1987), 353–65, and 'Eros and Orientalism in Britten's Operas', in *Queering the Pitch: The New Gay and Lesbian Musicology*, ed. Philip Brett, Elizabeth Wood and Gary C. Thomas (New York: Routledge, 1994), 235–56.

19   Rupprecht, *Britten*, 163.

20   Brett, 'Britten's Dream', 267.

21   Craig Ayrey, 'Debussy's Significant Connections: Metaphor and Metonymy in Analytical Method', in *Theory, Analysis and Meaning in Music*, ed. Anthony Pople (Cambridge: Cambridge University Press, 1994), 131, 129.

22   Roy Travis, 'The Recurrent Figure in the Britten/Piper Opera *Death in Venice*', in *The Music Forum*, 6/1, ed. Felix Salzer and Carl Schachter (New York: Columbia University Press, 1987), 129–346.

7   Engagement or alienation?

1   Michael Burleigh, *The Third Reich: A New History* (London: Macmillan, 2000), 812. Further page reference in text.

2   James Pritchett, *The Music of John Cage* (Cambridge: Cambridge University Press, 1993), 192–3. Further page references in text.

3   For a documentary study, see Georgina Born, *Rationalizing Culture: IRCAM, Boulez, and the Institutionalization of the Avant-Garde* (Berkeley, Los Angeles and London: University of California Press), 1995.

4   Richard Taruskin, 'Hearing Cycles', Aldeburgh Festival Programme Book (2000), 67.

5   See Igor Stravinsky, *Themes and Conclusions* (London: Faber and Faber, 1972), 47–51.

6   *Tippett on Music*, ed. Meirion Bowen (Oxford: Oxford University Press, 1995), 6. Further page references in text.

7   'Kagel', *The New Grove*, 2nd edn (London: Macmillan, 2001) vol. XIII, 309.

8   Björn Heile, 'Collage vs. Compositional Control: The Interdependency of Modernist and Postmodernist Approaches in the Work of Mauricio Kagel', in *Postmodern Music/Postmodern Thought*, ed. Judy Lochhead and Joseph Auner (New York and London: Routledge, 2002), 295. Further page references in text.

9   Notes with Winter & Winter CD, 910 035-2, 1998.

10   I discuss this topic more fully in my essay 'Resisting Tonality: Tippett, Beethoven and the Sarabande', *Music Analysis*, 9 (1990), 267–86.

11   Michael Tippett, *Moving into Aquarius* (St Albans: Paladin Books, 1974), 155.

12   Nicholas Cook, *Beethoven: Symphony No. 9* (Cambridge: Cambridge University Press, 1993), 101.

13   Taruskin, 'Hearing Cycles', 67.

14   Laurel E. Fay, *Shostakovich: A Life* (New York and Oxford: Oxford University Press, 2000), 52.

15   *Testimony: The Memoirs of Dmitri Shostakovich, as Related to and Edited by Solomon Volkov*, trans. Antonina W. Bouis (London and Boston: Faber and Faber, 1981), 127.

16   'Schnittke', *The New Grove*, 2nd edn (London: Macmillan, 2001) vol. XXII, 566.

17   Richard Taruskin, *Defining Russia Musically: Historical and Hermeneutical Essays* (Princeton and Oxford: Princeton University Press, 1997), 101. Further page references in text.

18   Alexander Ivashkin, *Alfred Schnittke* (London: Phaidon Press, 1996), 31–2. Further page references in text.

19   See above, p. 80.

20   See above, p. 83.

21   For extensive and invaluable discussion of the philosophical and cultural context of Tippett's work, see David Clarke, *The Music and Thought of Michael Tippett: Modern Times and Metaphysics* (Cambridge: Cambridge University Press, 2001).

8   Rites of transformation

1   'Requiem Mass', *The New Grove*, 2nd edn (London: Macmillan, 2001) vol. XXI, 208.

2   Hans Werner Henze, *Bohemian Fifths: An Autobiography*, trans. Stewart Spencer (London: Faber and Faber, 1998), 57. Further page references in text.

3   See Igor Stravinsky, *An Autobiography* (New York: Steuer, 1958), 38–40.

4   Notes with 1977 LP recording, DG 2530 834.

5   Nicholas Baragwanath, 'Alban Berg, Richard Wagner, and Leitmotivs of Symmetry', *19th Century Music*, 23 (1999), 83.

6   One of the most significant contributions to a steadily expanding literature is Richard Cohn, 'Maximally Smooth Cycles, Hexatonic Systems, and the Analysis of Late-Romantic Triadic Progressions', *Music Analysis*, 15 (1996), 9–40.

7   Pierre Boulez, 'Approaches to *Parsifal*' and '*The Ring*: A Performer's Notebook', in *Orientations*, ed. Jean-Jacques Nattiez, trans. Martin Cooper (London and Boston: Faber and Faber, 1986), 254 and 290.

8   Timothy L. Jackson, *Tchaikovsky: Symphony No. 6 (Pathétique)* (Cambridge: Cambridge University Press, 1999), 4. Further page references in text.

9   Hans Werner Henze, 'Language, Music and Artistic Invention', trans. Mary Whittall (Aldeburgh: Britten–Pears Library, 1996), 22–3. Further page reference in text.

10   Thomas Mann, *Pro and Contra Wagner*, trans. Allan Blunden (London and Boston: Faber and Faber, 1985), 128.

11   Joseph Kerman, *Opera as Drama* (New York: Vintage, 1956), 194–5.

12   Michael Tanner, 'The Total Work of Art', in *The Wagner Companion*, ed. Peter Burbidge and Richard Sutton (London and Boston: Faber and Faber, 1979), 188.

13   Wagner's notes can be found in *Richard Wagner: Prelude and Transfiguration from Tristan und Isolde*, ed. Robert Bailey (New York and London: Norton, 1985), 48.

14   Robert Gutman, *Richard Wagner: The Man, His Mind and His Music* (Harmondsworth: Penguin Books, 1968), 359.

15   John Deathridge, 'Post-Mortem on Isolde', *New German Critique*, 69 (1996), 116.

16   Arthur Groos, 'Wagner's "Tristan und Isolde": In Defence of the Libretto', *Music and Letters*, 69 (1988), 472.

17   Ian Pace, 'Positive or Negative 2', *The Musical Times* (February 1998), 16–17.

18 Jürg Stenzl, 'York Höller's *The Master and Margarita*', *Tempo*, 179 (December 1991), 15.

19 'All Contradictions Reconciled? Perspectives on York Höller', *The Musical Times* (Autumn 1998), 11–19.

20 These comments derive from my review of the Hänssler Classic recording in *Gramophone* (August 2001), 86.

21 See Chapter 9 below for a discussion of Harrison Birtwistle's Celan settings.

9   Modernism, lyricism

1   'where we stay awake all night,/where the heavens are shallow as the sea/is now deep, and you love me.'

2   For further analysis, see Brenda Ravenscroft, 'The Moon and the Insomniac: Musical Personae in Elliott Carter's "Insomnia"', *South African Journal of Musicology*, 19/20 (1999–2000), 57–70.

3   John Felstiner, *Paul Celan: Poet, Survivor, Jew* (New Haven and London: Yale University Press, 1995), 167. Further page reference in text.

4   Birtwistle used Michael Hamburger's English translations: *Poems of Paul Celan* (London: Anvil Press, 1988).

5   Allen Edwards, *Flawed Words and Stubborn Sounds: A Conversation with Elliott Carter* (New York: Norton, 1971), 61.

6   See Robert Coe, 'Philip Glass Breaks Through', *New York Times Magazine*, 25 October 1981, cited in John Richardson, *Singing Archeology: Philip Glass's Akhnaten* (Hanover, NH and London: Wesleyan University Press), 22.

7   'Shop Talk by an American Composer', in *Elliott Carter: Collected Essays and Lectures, 1937–95*, ed. Jonathan W. Bernard (Rochester, NY and Woodbridge: University of Rochester Press, 1997), 217.

8   See Carter's comments in 'Double Concerto, 1961, and Duo, 1974 (1975)', in *Essays and Lectures*, 260–1. Carter has also described his Piano Concerto as representing 'a kind of remembrance of war and all its victims' and reflecting 'the climate of tragedy that still hung over those years'. See *Elliott Carter: In Conversation with Enzo Restagno for Settembre Musica 1989*, interview by Enzo Restagno trans. Katherine S. Wolfthal, I.S.A.M. Monographs, no. 32 (Brooklyn, NY: Institute for Studies in American Music, 1989), 68–9.

9   David Schiff, *The Music of Elliott Carter* (London: Faber and Faber, 1998), 123, 254. Further page references in text.

10 'Modernist Aesthetics, Modernist Music: Some Analytical Perspectives', in *Music Theory in Concept and Practice*, ed. James M. Baker, David W. Beach and Jonathan W. Bernard (Rochester, NY and Woodbridge: University of Rochester Press, 1997), 157–80.

11 David Schiff, 'Carter's New Classicism', *College Music Symposium*, 29 (1989), 119.

12 David Schiff, 'Elliott Carter's Harvest Home', *Tempo*, 167 (December 1988), 6.

13 Introduction, *Syringa* (New York and London: Associated Music Publishers, 1980), iii.

14 Lawrence Kramer, *Music and Poetry: The Nineteenth Century and After* (Berkeley, Los Angeles and London: University of California Press, 1984), 208. Further page references in text.

15 Robert Adlington, *The Music of Harrison Birtwistle* (Cambridge: Cambridge University Press, 2000), 66.

16 Jonathan Cross, *Harrison Birtwistle: Man, Mind, Music* (London: Faber and Faber, 2000), 114–15.

17 Michael Hall, *Harrison Birtwistle in Recent Years* (London: Robson Books, 1998), 132. Further page references in text.

18 Michael Hall, *Harrison Birtwistle* (London: Robson Books, 1984), 117.

19 See Michael Hall's quotations from Jane Harrison, *Prolegomena to the Study of Greek Religion* (London: Merlin Press, 1962), in *Birtwistle* (1984), 126–8.

20 Stephen Pruslin, notes with Teldec CD, 3984-26867-2 (2001).

21 This discussion derives from my review-article, 'The Mechanisms of Lament: Harrison Birtwistle's "Pulse Shadows"', *Music and Letters*, 80 (1999), 86–102.

22 Michael Hamburger, *Paul Celan: Selected Poems* (Harmondsworth: Penguin Books, 1990), 24.

23 Michael Hall, 'Birtwistle's *Pulse Shadows*', *Tempo*, 204 (1998), 13.

10 Experiment and orthodoxy

1 Keith Potter, 'Minimalism', *The New Grove*, 2nd edn (London: Macmillan, 2001), vol. XVI, 716.

2 Edward Strickland, 'Glass', *The New Grove*, 2nd edn (London: Macmillan, 2001), vol. IX, 934.

3 John Richardson, *Singing Archeology: Philip Glass's* Akhnaten (Hanover, NH and London: Wesleyan University Press, 1999), 66. Further page references in text.

4 Louis Andriessen and Elmer Schönberger, *The Apollonian Clockwork: On Stravinsky* (Oxford and New York: Oxford University Press, 1989), 273. My discussion of Andriessen derives from my article 'Three for All: Andriessen's Recent Music', *Musical Times* (Summer 2001), 9–20.

5 Andrew Ford, *Composer to Composer: Conversations about Contemporary Music* (London: Quartet Books, 1993), 81. Further page references in text.

6 Igor Stravinsky, *An Autobiography* (New York: Steuer, 1958), 100.

7 Igor Stravinsky, *Poetics of Music*, trans. Arthur Knodel and Ingolf Dahl (New York: Vintage, 1947), 83–4.

8 From notes with Donemus CD CV79 (1999).

9 Maria Anne Harley in *Tempo*, 212 (April 2000), 48. Further page reference in text.

10 The electronic material was devised by Michel van Aa.

11 Andriessen quoted in programme book essay for *Writing to Vermeer* by Frits van der Waa.

12 Gavin Thomas, 'Life Downtown: Conversation with Louis Andriessen', *The Musical Times* (March 1994), 139.

13   From 'Composer's Note' in study score of 'Tao' (London: Boosey & Hawkes, 1999). Further reference in text.

14   See *Quarternotes* (London: Boosey & Hawkes, October 2001), 4.

15   Paul Griffiths, 'Reich', *The New Grove*, 2nd edn (London: Macmillan, 2001), vol. XXI, 127.

16   For a close study of these pioneers, see Keith Potter, *Four Musical Minimalists* (Cambridge: Cambridge University Press, 2000).

17   K. Robert Schwarz, *Minimalists* (London: Phaidon Press, 1996), 175. Further page references in text.

18   Edward Strickland, *American Composers: Dialogues on Contemporary Music* (Bloomington and Indianapolis: Indiana University Press, 1991), 179–80. Further page references in text.

19   Rebecca Jemain and Anne Marie de Zeeuw, 'An Interview with John Adams', *Perspectives of New Music*, 34 (1996), 94.

20   Robert Stein, 'First Performances: Adams's *El Niño*', *Tempo*, 216 (April 2001), 37.

21   See Michael Steinberg, 'A Nativity for a New Century', booklet with Nonesuch CD 7559-79634-2 (2001), 14–15.

11   Modernism in retreat?

1   Richard Taruskin, *Stravinsky and the Russian Traditions: A Biography of the Works through* Mavra (Berkeley, Los Angeles and London: University of California Press, 1996), 1675.

2   Jonathan Cross, *The Stravinsky Legacy* (Cambridge: Cambridge University Press, 1998).

3   'The musicians of my generation and I myself owe the most to Debussy.' Igor Stravinsky and Robert Craft, *Conversations with Igor Stravinsky* (London: Faber and Faber, 1959), 30. Further page references in text.

4   Pierre Boulez, *Stocktakings from an Apprenticeship*, trans. Stephen Walsh (Oxford: Oxford University Press, 1991), 257–8.

5   'Stravinsky in Context', in *The Cambridge Companion to Stravinsky*, ed. Jonathan Cross (Cambridge: Cambridge University Press), forthcoming.

6   Lawrence Kramer, *Musical Meaning: Toward a Critical History* (Berkeley, Los Angeles and London: University of California Press, 2002). Fred Lerdahl, *Tonal Pitch Space* (New York and Oxford: Oxford University Press, 2001). Further page references in text.

7   David Lewin, *Musical Form and Transformation: 4 Analytic Essays* (New Haven and London: Yale University Press, 1993).

8   Nicholas Cook, *Music, Imagination, and Culture* (Oxford: Oxford University Press, 1990), especially 152–60.

9   David Clarke, *The Music and Thought of Michael Tippett: Modern Times and Metaphysics* (Cambridge: Cambridge University Press, 2001), 9, 62. Further page references in text.

10   Robert Adlington, *The Music of Harrison Birtwistle* (Cambridge: Cambridge University Press, 2000), 151–2.

11 Naomi Cumming, *The Sonic Self: Musical Subjectivity and Signification* (Bloomington and Indianapolis: Indiana University Press, 2000), 16. Further page references in text.

12 Rocco di Pietro, *Dialogues with Boulez* (Lanham, MD and London: Scarecrow Press, 2001), 25.

13 For useful comments, see Paul Griffiths's notes with DG CD 445 833-2 (1995).

14 David Osmond-Smith, 'Berio', *The New Grove*, 2nd edn (London: Macmillan, 2001), vol. III, 354. Further page references in text.

15 Sanguineti's texts are printed in the booklet with the DG recording, 457 038-2 (1998).

16 *Trilogy* (1992) was written for Heinz and Ursula Holliger, and comprises 'Bariolage' for harp, 'Inner Song' for oboe, and 'Immer neu' for oboe and harp.

17 Charles Rosen, *Schoenberg* (London: Marion Boyars/Fontana, 1976), 82.

18 Arnold Whittall, *Musical Composition in the Twentieth Century* (Oxford: Oxford University Press, 1999), 299–300.

19 See pp. 31–3.

20 The score of the Sonata for Viola Solo is published by Schott, ED 8374 (2001). Notes with Sony Classical CD 01-062309-10 (1998).

Bibliography

Adès, Thomas, '"Nothing but pranks and puns": Janáček's Solo Piano Music', in *Janáček Studies*, ed. Paul Wingfield (Cambridge: Cambridge University Press, 1999), 18–35.

Adlington, Robert, *The Music of Harrison Birtwistle* (Cambridge: Cambridge University Press, 2000).

Adorno, Theodor W., *Prisms*, trans. Samuel and Shierry Weber (London: Neville Spearman, 1967).

Quasi una fantasia, trans. Rodney Livingstone (London and New York: Verso, 1994).

André, Naomi, 'Returning to a Homeland: Religion and Political Context in Schoenberg's *Dreimal tausend Jahre*', in *Political and Religious Ideas*, ed. Cross and Berman, 259–88.

Andriessen, Louis and Elmer Schönberger, *The Apollonian Clockwork: On Stravinsky* (Oxford and New York: Oxford University Press, 1989).

Antokoletz, Elliott, 'Middle-Period String Quartets', in *The Bartók Companion*, ed. Malcolm Gillies (London: Faber and Faber, 1993), 257–77.

'Modal Transformation and Musical Symbolism in Bartók's *Cantata Profana*', in *Bartók Perspectives: Man, Composer, and Ethnomusicologist*, ed. Elliott Antokoletz, Victoria Fischer and Benjamin Suchoff (Oxford: Oxford University Press, 2000), 61–76.

Atherton, David (ed.), *The London Sinfonietta Schoenberg/Gerhard Series* (London: Sinfonietta Productions Limited, 1973).

Attinello, Paul, 'Kagel', *The New Grove*, 2nd edn (London: Macmillan, 2001), vol. XIII, 309–12.

Auner, Joseph H., 'Schoenberg's Handel Concerto and the Ruins of Tradition', *Journal of the American Musicological Society*, 49 (1996), 264–313.

'Schoenberg and His Public in 1930: The Six Pieces for Male Chorus, Op. 35', in *Schoenberg and His World,* ed. Walter Frisch (Princeton: Princeton University Press, 1999), 85–125.

Ayrey, Craig, 'Debussy's Significant Connections: Metaphor and Metonymy in Analytical Method', in *Theory, Analysis and Meaning in Music*, ed. Anthony Pople (Cambridge: Cambridge University Press, 1994), 127–51.

Babbitt, Milton, 'Memoir', in 'Hans Keller (1919–1985): A Memorial Symposium', ed. Christopher Wintle, *Music Analysis*, 5 (1986), 376.

Bailey, Kathryn, *The Twelve-Note Music of Anton Webern* (Cambridge: Cambridge University Press, 1991).

The Life of Webern (Cambridge: Cambridge University Press, 1998).

Bailey, Robert (ed.), *Richard Wagner: Prelude and Transfiguration from* Tristan und Isolde (New York and London: Norton, 1985).

Baragwanath, Nicholas, 'Alban Berg, Richard Wagner, and Leitmotivs of Symmetry', *19th Century Music*, 23 (1999), 62–83.

Beckles Willson, Rachel, 'Vocal Music: Inspiration and Ideology', in *The Cambridge Companion to Bartók*, ed. Amanda Bayley (Cambridge: Cambridge University Press, 2001), 78–91.

Benjamin, William E., 'Abstract Polyphonies: The Music of Schoenberg's Nietzschean Moment', in *Political and Religious Ideas*, ed. Cross and Berman, 1–39.

Bernard, Jonathan W. (ed.), *Elliott Carter: Collected Essays and Lectures, 1937–95* (Rochester, NY and Woodbridge: University of Rochester Press, 1997).

Born, Georgina, *Rationalizing Culture: IRCAM, Boulez, and the Institutionalization of the Avant-Garde* (Berkeley, Los Angeles and London: University of California Press, 1995).

Born, Georgina and David Hesmondhalgh (eds.), *Western Music and Its Others: Difference, Representation, and Appropriation in Music* (Berkeley, Los Angeles and London: University of California Press, 2000).

Boss, Jack, 'Schoenberg on Ornamentation and Structural Levels', *Journal of Music Theory*, 38 (1994), 187–216.

Botstein, Leon, 'Beyond the Illusions of Realism: Painting and Debussy's Break with Tradition', in *Debussy and His World*, ed. Fulcher, 141–79.

Boulez, Pierre, *Orientations*, ed. Jean-Jacques Nattiez, trans. Martin Cooper (London: Faber and Faber, 1986).

    Stocktakings from an Apprenticeship, trans. Stephen Walsh (Oxford: Oxford University Press, 1991).

Bowen, Meirion (ed.), *Tippett on Music* (Oxford: Clarendon Press, 1995).

    Gerhard on Music: Selected Writings (Aldershot: Ashgate, 2000).

Brand, Juliane, and Christopher Hailey (eds.), *Constructive Dissonance: Arnold Schoenberg and the Transformation of Twentieth-Century Culture* (Berkeley, Los Angeles and London: University of California Press, 1997).

Brett, Philip, 'Grimes and Lucretia', in *Music and Theatre: Essays in Honour of Winton Dean*, ed. Nigel Fortune (Cambridge: Cambridge University Press, 1987), 353–65.

    'Britten's Dream', in *Musicology and Difference: Gender and Sexuality in Music Scholarship*, ed. Ruth A. Solie (Berkeley, Los Angeles and London: University of California Press, 1993), 259–80.

    'Eros and Orientalism', in *Queering the Pitch: The New Gay and Lesbian Musicology*, ed. Philip Brett, Elizabeth Wood and Gary C. Thomas (New York: Routledge, 1994), 235–56.

Brinkmann, Reinhold, 'Schoenberg the Contemporary: A View from Behind', in *Constructive Dissonance*, ed. Brand and Hailey, 196–219.

Britten, Benjamin, *On Receiving the First Aspen Award* (London: Faber Music, 1964).

Brown, Julie, 'Bartók, the Gypsies, and Hybridity in Music', in *Western Music and its Others*, ed. Born and Hesmondhalgh, 119–42.

Brown, Matthew, 'Tonality and Form in Debussy's *Prélude à "l'Après-midi d'un faune"*', *Music Theory Spectrum*, 15 (1993), 128–43.

Burleigh, Michael, *The Third Reich: A New History* (London: Macmillan, 2000).

Cahn, Steven J., 'The Artist as Modern Prophet: A Study of Historical Consciousness and Its Expression in Schoenberg's "Vorgefühl", Op. 22 No. 4', in *Schoenberg and Words*, ed. Cross and Berman, 243–71.

Carpenter, Humphrey, *Benjamin Britten: A Biography* (London: Faber and Faber, 1992).

Carter, Elliott, *Elliott Carter: In Conversation with Enzo Restagno for Settembre Musica 1989*, interview by Enzo Restagno, trans. Katherine S. Wolfthal, I.S.A.M. Monographs, no. 32 (Brooklyn, NY: Institute for Studies in American Music, 1989).

Celan, Paul, *Poems*, trans. Michael Hamburger (London: Anvil Press, 1988).

Selected Poems, trans. Michael Hamburger (Harmondsworth: Penguin Books, 1996).

Charle, Christophe, 'Debussy in Fin-de-siècle Paris', in *Debussy and His World*, ed. Fulcher, 271–95.

Cherlin, Michael, 'Memory and Rhetorical Trope in Schoenberg's String Trio', *Journal of the American Musicological Society*, 51 (1998), 559–602.

'Dialectical Opposition in Schoenberg's Music and Thought', *Music Theory Spectrum*, 22 (2000), 157–76.

Chew, Geoffrey, 'Pastoral and Neoclassicism: A Reinterpretation of Auden's and Stravinsky's *The Rake's Progress*', *Cambridge Opera Journal*, 5 (1993), 239–63.

Chew, Geoffrey with Owen Jander, 'Pastoral', *The New Grove*, 2nd edn (London: Macmillan, 2001), vol. XIX, 217–25.

Clarke, David, 'Parting Glances', *The Musical Times* (December 1993), 680–4.

The Music and Thought of Michael Tippett: Modern Times and Metaphysics (Cambridge: Cambridge University Press, 2001).

Cohn, Richard, 'Bartók's Octatonic Strategies: A Motivic Approach', *Journal of the American Musicological Society*, 44 (1991), 262–300.

'Maximally Smooth Cycles, Hexatonic Systems, and the Analysis of Late-Romantic Triadic Progressions', *Music Analysis*, 15 (1996), 9–40.

Cone, Edward T., 'Stravinsky: The Progress of a Method', *Perspectives of New Music*, 1 (1962), 18–26.

'Attacking a Brahms Puzzle', *The Musical Times* (February 1995), 72–8.

Cook, Nicholas, *Music, Imagination, and Culture* (Oxford: Oxford University Press, 1990).

Beethoven: Symphony No. 9 (Cambridge: Cambridge University Press, 1993).

Cooke, Mervyn, *Britten and the Far East: Asian Influences in the Music of Benjamin Britten* (Woodbridge: Boydell Press/Britten–Pears Library, 1998).

Cooper, David, *Bartók: Concerto for Orchestra* (Cambridge: Cambridge University Press, 1996).

Crittenden, Camille, 'Texts and Contexts of *A Survivor from Warsaw*, Op. 46', in *Political and Religious Ideas*, ed. Cross and Berman, 231–58.

Cross, Charlotte M. and Russell A. Berman (eds.), *Political and Religious Ideas in the Works of Arnold Schoenberg* (New York and London: Garland, 2000).

Schoenberg and Words: The Modernist Years (New York and London: Garland, 2000).

Cross, Jonathan, *The Stravinsky Legacy* (Cambridge: Cambridge University Press, 1998).

Harrison Birtwistle: Man, Mind, Music (London: Faber and Faber, 2000).

Cumming, Naomi, *The Sonic Self: Musical Subjectivity and Signification* (Bloomington and Indianapolis: Indiana University Press, 2000).

Dahlhaus, Carl, *Realism in Nineteenth-Century Music*, trans. Mary Whittall (Cambridge: Cambridge University Press, 1985).

Deathridge, John, 'Post-Mortem on Isolde', *New German Critique*, 69 (1996), 99–126.

Downes, Stephen, 'Eros in the Metropolis: Bartók's *The Miraculous Mandarin*', *Journal of the Royal Musical Association*, 125 (2000), 41–61.

Dunsby, Jonathan and Arnold Whittall, *Music Analysis in Theory and Practice* (London: Faber Music, 1988).

Edwards, Allen, *Flawed Words and Stubborn Sounds: A Conversation with Elliott Carter* (New York: Norton, 1971).

Falck, Robert, 'Schoenberg in Shirtsleeves: The Male Choruses, Op. 35', in *Political and Religious Ideas*, ed. Cross and Berman, 111–30.

Fay, Laurel E., *Shostakovich: A Life* (New York and Oxford: Oxford University Press, 2000).

Felstiner, John, *Paul Celan: Poet, Survivor, Jew* (New Haven and London: Yale University Press, 1995).

Ford, Andrew, *Composer to Composer: Conversations about Contemporary Music* (London: Quartet Books, 1993).

Forte, Allen, *The Atonal Music of Anton Webern* (New Haven and London: Yale University Press, 1998).

Franklin, Peter, review of Alexander L. Ringer, *Arnold Schoenberg: The Composer as Jew* (Oxford: Oxford University Press, 1990), *Music and Letters*, 72 (1991), 628–30.

Frigyesi, Judit, *Béla Bartók and Turn-of-the-Century Budapest* (Berkeley, Los Angeles and London: University of California Press, 1998).

Fulcher, Jane (ed.), *Debussy and His World* (Princeton and Oxford: Princeton University Press, 2001).

Gann, Kyle, *The Music of Conlon Nancarrow* (Cambridge: Cambridge University Press, 1995).

Gerhard, Roberto, 'Reluctant Revolutionary', in *The London Sinfonietta Schoenberg/ Gerhard Series*, ed. Atherton, 43.

Gillies, Malcolm, *Bartók Remembered* (London and Boston: Faber and Faber, 1990).

Goldstein, Bluma, 'Schoenberg's *Moses und Aron*: A Vanishing Biblical Nation', in *Political and Religious Ideas*, ed. Cross and Berman, 159–92.

Griffiths, Paul, *The String Quartet* (London: Thames and Hudson, 1983).

'A Mind Withdrawing: Britten's Music and the Lure of Might-have-beens', *Times Literary Supplement*, 28 June 1991, 14–15.

'Messiaen', *The New Grove*, 2nd edn (London: Macmillan, 2001), vol. XVI, 491–504.

'Reich', *The New Grove*, 2nd edn (London: Macmillan, 2001), vol. XXI, 124–9.

Groos, Arthur, 'Wagner's "Tristan und Isolde": in Defence of the Libretto', *Music and Letters*, 69 (1988), 465–81.

Gutman, Robert, *Richard Wagner: The Man, His Mind and His Music* (Harmondsworth: Penguin Books, 1968).

Hall, Michael, *Harrison Birtwistle* (London: Robson Books, 1984).

  Harrison Birtwistle in Recent Years (London: Robson Books, 1998).

  'Birtwistle's *Pulse Shadows*', *Tempo*, 204 (April 1998), 12–13.

Harley, Maria Anne, 'Andriessen's *Writing to Vermeer*', *Tempo*, 212 (April 2000), 47–8.

Hasty, Christopher, 'Form and Idea in Schoenberg's *Phantasy*', in *Music Theory in Concept and Practice*, ed. James M. Baker, David W. Beach and Jonathan W. Bernard (Rochester, NY and Woodbridge: University of Rochester Press, 1997), 459–79.

Hatten, Robert S., *Musical Meaning in Beethoven: Markedness, Correlation, and Interpretation* (Bloomington and Indianapolis: Indiana University Press, 1994).

Heile, Björn, 'Collage vs. Compositional Control: The Interdependency of Modernist and Postmodernist Approaches in the Work of Mauricio Kagel', in *Postmodern Music/Postmodern Thought*, ed. Judy Lochhead and Joseph Auner (New York and London: Routledge, 2002), 287–99.

Henze, Hans Werner, 'Language, Music and Artistic Invention', trans. Mary Whittall (Aldeburgh: Britten–Pears Library, 1996).

  Bohemian Fifths: An Autobiography, trans. Stewart Spencer (London: Faber and Faber, 1998).

Hepokoski, James, *Sibelius: Symphony No. 5* (Cambridge: Cambridge University Press, 1993).

  'Sibelius', *The New Grove*, 2nd edn (London: Macmillan, 2001), vol. XXIII, 319–47.

  'Rotations, Sketches, and the Sixth Symphony', in *Sibelius Studies*, ed. Jackson and Murtomäki, 322–51.

Hill, Peter (ed.), *The Messiaen Companion* (London: Faber and Faber, 1995).

Holloway, Robin, 'The Prince of the Pagodas', *Tempo*, 176 (March 1991), 31–2.

Homs, Joaquim, *Roberto Gerhard and His Music*, ed. Meirion Bowen (Sheffield: Anglo-Catalan Society, 2000).

Howell, Tim, '"Sibelius the Progressive"', in *Sibelius Studies*, ed. Jackson and Murtomäki, 35–57.

Hyde, Martha M., 'Neoclassic and Anachronistic Impulses in Twentieth-Century Music', *Music Theory Spectrum*, 18 (1996), 200–35.

Ivashkin, Alexander, *Alfred Schnittke* (London: Phaidon Press, 1996).

Jackson, Timothy L., *Tchaikovsky: Symphony No. 6 (Pathétique)* (Cambridge: Cambridge University Press, 1999).

  'Observations on Crystallization and Entropy in the Music of Sibelius and Other Composers', in *Sibelius Studies*, ed. Jackson and Murtomäki, 175–272.

Jackson, Timothy L. and Veijo Murtomäki (eds.), *Sibelius Studies* (Cambridge: Cambridge University Press, 2001).

Jemain, Rebecca and Anne Marie de Zeeuw, 'An Interview with John Adams', *Perspectives of New Music*, 34/2 (Summer 1996), 88–104.

Johnson, Julian, *Webern and the Transformation of Nature* (Cambridge: Cambridge University Press, 1999).

Keller, Hans, 'Perspective', in *Music Survey. New Series 1949–1952*, ed. Donald Mitchell and Keller (London: Faber Music/Faber and Faber, 1981), 315.

   'The Musical Character', in *Benjamin Britten: A Commentary*, ed. Mitchell and Keller, 319–51.

   'Schoenberg and the Crisis of Communication', *London Sinfonietta Schoenberg/ Gerhard Series*, ed. Atherton, 44–8.

   Essays on Music, ed. Christopher Wintle (Cambridge: Cambridge University Press, 1994).

Kerman, Joseph, *Opera as Drama* (New York: Vintage Books, 1956).

Kramer, Lawrence, *Music and Poetry: The Nineteenth Century and After* (Berkeley, Los Angeles and London: University of California Press, 1984).

   'The Musicology of the Future', *repercussions*, 1 (1992), 5–18.

   Franz Schubert: Sexuality, Subjectivity, Song (Cambridge: Cambridge University Press, 1998).

   Musical Meaning: Towards a Critical History (Berkeley, Los Angeles and London: University of California Press, 2002).

Kurth, Richard, 'Music and Poetry, a Wilderness of Doubles: Heine–Nietzsche–Schubert–Derrida', *19th Century Music*, 21 (1997), 3–27.

Langham Smith, Richard, 'Pelléas et Mélisande', *The New Grove Dictionary of Opera* (London: Macmillan, 1992), vol. III, 934–9.

Lefkovitz, David S., 'Listening Strategies and Hexachordal Combinatorial "Functions" in Schoenberg's Op. 23 No. 4', *Music Analysis*, 16 (1997), 309–48.

   'Schoenberg and His Op. 23 No. 4: A Functional Analysis', and 'The Composer as Jew: A Homage', *Music Analysis*, 18 (1999), 375–85.

Lerdahl, Fred, *Tonal Pitch Space* (New York and Oxford: Oxford University Press, 2001).

Lewin, David, *Musical Form and Transformation: 4 Analytic Essays* (New Haven and London: Yale University Press, 1993).

Lieberman, David Isadore, 'Schoenberg Rewrites His Will: *A Survivor from Warsaw*, Op. 46', in *Political and Religious Ideas,* ed. Cross and Berman, 193–229.

Mann, Thomas, *Pro and Contra Wagner*, trans. Allan Blunden (London and Boston: Faber and Faber, 1985).

Martin, Peter J., *Sounds and Society: Themes in the Sociology of Music* (Manchester and New York: Manchester University Press, 1995).

Mellers, Wilfrid, 'Mysticism and Theology', in *The Messiaen Companion*, ed. Hill, 220–33.

Milstein, Silvina, *Arnold Schoenberg: Notes, Sets, Forms* (Cambridge: Cambridge University Press, 1992).

Mitchell, Donald and Hans Keller (eds.), *Benjamin Britten: A Commentary on His Works from a Group of Specialists* (London: Rockliff, 1952).

Moldenhauer, Hans with Rosaleen Moldenhauer, *Anton von Webern: A Chronicle of his Life and Work* (London: Victor Gollancz, 1978).

Moody, Ivan with Alexander Ivashkin, 'Schnittke', *The New Grove*, 2nd edn (London: Macmillan, 2001), vol. XXII, 564–8.

Nichols, Roger, 'Debussy', *The New Grove*, 1st edn (London: Macmillan, 1980), vol. V, 292–314.

    The Life of Debussy (Cambridge: Cambridge University Press, 1998).

Osmond-Smith, David, 'Berio', *The New Grove*, 2nd edn (London: Macmillan, 2001), vol. III, 350–8.

Pace, Ian, 'Positive or Negative 2', *The Musical Times* (February 1998), 4–15.

Paddison, Max, *Adorno's Aesthetics of Music* (Cambridge: Cambridge University Press, 1993).

Parks, Richard S., *The Music of Claude Debussy* (New Haven and London: Yale University Press, 1989).

Pietro, Rocco di, *Dialogues with Boulez* (Lanham, MD and London: Scarecrow Press, 2001).

Pople, Anthony, 'Messiaen's Musical Language: An Introduction', in *The Messiaen Companion*, ed. Hill, 15–50.

    Messiaen: Quatuor pour la fin du Temps (Cambridge: Cambridge University Press, 1998).

Potter, Keith, *Four Musical Minimalists* (Cambridge: Cambridge University Press, 2000).

    'Minimalism', *The New Grove*, 2nd edn (London: Macmillan, 2001), vol. XVI, 716–18.

Pritchett, James, *The Music of John Cage* (Cambridge: Cambridge University Press, 1993).

Rauchhaupt, Ursula von (ed.), *Schoenberg, Berg, Webern: The String Quartets: A Documentary Study*, trans. Eugene Hartzell (Hamburg: Deutsche Grammophon Gesellschaft, 1971).

Ravenscroft, Brenda, 'The Moon and the Insomniac: Musical Personae in Elliott Carter's "Insomnia"', *South African Journal of Musicology*, 19/20 (1999–2000), 57–70.

Richardson, John, *Singing Archeology: Philip Glass's* Akhnaten (Hanover, NH and London: Wesleyan University Press).

Ringer, Alexander L., 'Assimilation and the Emancipation of Historical Dissonance', in *Constructive Dissonance*, ed. Brand and Hailey, 23–34.

Roeder, John, 'Pitch Class', *The New Grove*, 2nd edn (London: Macmillan, 2001), vol. XIX, 804.

    'Set', *The New Grove*, 2nd edn (London: Macmillan, 2001), vol. XXIII, 164–8.

Rolf, Marie, 'Semantic and Structural Issues in Debussy's Mallarmé Songs', in *Debussy Studies*, ed. Richard Langham Smith (Cambridge: Cambridge University Press, 1997), 179–200.

Rose, Paul Lawrence, *Wagner: Race and Revolution* (London: Faber and Faber, 1992).

Rosen, Charles, *Schoenberg* (London: Marion Boyars/Fontana, 1976).

Rupprecht, Philip, *Britten's Musical Language* (Cambridge: Cambridge University Press, 2001).

Schiff, David, 'Elliott Carter's Harvest Home', *Tempo*, 167 (December 1988), 2–13.

   'Carter's New Classicism', *College Music Symposium*, 29 (1989), 115–22.

   The Music of Elliott Carter (London: Faber and Faber, 1998).

Schoenberg, Arnold, *Fundamentals of Musical Composition*, ed. Gerald Strang and Leonard Stein (London: Faber and Faber, 1967).

   Structural Functions of Harmony, ed. Leonard Stein (London: Ernest Benn, 1969).

   Style and Idea, ed. Leonard Stein, trans. Leo Black (London: Faber and Faber, 1975).

Schwarz, K. Robert, *Minimalists* (London: Phaidon Press, 1996).

Scruton, Roger, *The Aesthetics of Music* (Oxford: Oxford University Press, 1997).

   'True Authority: Janáček, Schoenberg and Us', in *Reviving the Muse: Essays on Music after Modernism*, ed. Peter Davison (Brinkworth: Claridge Press, 2001), 7–30.

Shostakovich, Dmitri, *Testimony: The Memoirs of Dmitri Shostakovich, as Related to and Edited by Solomon Volkov*, trans. Antonina W. Bouis (London and Boston: Faber and Faber, 1981).

Simms, Bryan, *The Atonal Music of Arnold Schoenberg* (New York and Oxford: Oxford University Press, 2000).

Smallman, Basil, 'Requiem Mass', *The New Grove*, 2nd edn (London: Macmillan, 2001), vol. XXI, 203–8.

Somfai, László, *Béla Bartók: Composition, Concepts, and Autograph Sources* (Berkeley, Los Angeles and London: University of California Press, 1996).

Stein, Robert, 'First Performances: Adams's *El Niño*', *Tempo*, 216 (April 2001), 37–8.

Steinitz, Richard, '*Des canyons aux étoiles*', in *The Messiaen Companion*, ed. Hill, 460–87.

Stenzl, Jürg, 'York Höller's *The Master and Margarita*', *Tempo*, 179 (December 1991), 8–15.

Stern, J. P., *Nietzsche* (Glasgow: Fontana/Collins, 1978).

Stevens, Halsey, *The Life and Music of Béla Bartók*, 3rd edn, prepared by Malcolm Gillies (Oxford: Oxford University Press, 1993).

Stravinsky, Igor, *Poetics of Music in the Form of Six Lessons*, trans. Arthur Knodel and Ingolf Dahl (New York; Vintage, 1947).

   An Autobiography (New York: Steuer, 1958).

   Themes and Conclusions (London: Faber and Faber, 1972).

Stravinsky, Igor and Robert Craft, *Conversations with Igor Stravinsky* (London: Faber and Faber, 1959).

   Dialogues (London: Faber and Faber, 1982).

Street, Alan, ' "The Ear of the Other": Style and Identity in Schoenberg's Eight Songs Op. 6', in *Schoenberg and Words*, ed. Cross and Berman, 103–37.

Strickland, Edward, *American Composers: Dialogues on Contemporary Music* (Bloomington and Indianapolis: Indiana University Press, 1991).

   'Glass', *The New Grove*, 2nd edn (London: Macmillan, 2001), vol. IX, 932–6.

Suchoff, Benjamin, 'Structure and Concept in Bartók's Sixth Quartet', *Tempo*, 83 (Winter 1967–8), 2–11.

Suchoff, Benjamin (ed.), *Béla Bartók Essays* (London: Faber and Faber, 1993).

Tanner, Michael, 'The Total Work of Art', in *The Wagner Companion*, ed. Peter Burbidge and Richard Sutton (London and Boston: Faber and Faber, 1979), 140–224.

Taruskin, Richard, *Stravinsky and the Russian Traditions: A Biography of the Works through* Mavra (Berkeley, Los Angeles and London: University of California Press, 1996).

Defining Russia Musically: Historical and Hermeneutical Essays (Princeton and Oxford: Princeton University Press, 1997).

'Hearing Cycles', Aldeburgh Festival programme book (2000), 60–9.

Thomas, Gavin, 'Life Downtown: Conversation with Louis Andriessen', *The Musical Times* (March 1994), 138–41.

Tippett, Michael, *Moving into Aquarius* (St Albans: Paladin Books, 1974).

Tippett on Music: see under Bowen.

Tomlinson, Gary, *Metaphysical Song: An Essay on Opera* (Princeton: Princeton University Press, 1999).

Travis, Roy, 'The Recurrent Figure in the Britten/Piper Opera *Death in Venice*', in *The Music Forum*, 6/1, ed. Felix Salzer and Carl Schachter (New York: Columbia University Press, 1987).

Trezise, Simon, *Debussy: La Mer* (Cambridge: Cambridge University Press, 1994).

Tyrrell, John (ed. and trans.), *Intimate Letters: Leoš Janáček to Kamila Stösslová* (London: Faber and Faber, 1994).

Walsh, Stephen, *Stravinsky: Oedipus rex* (Cambridge: Cambridge University Press, 1993).

Webern, Anton, *Letters to Hildegarde Jone and Josef Humplik*, ed. Josef Polnauer, trans. Cornelius Cardew (Bryn Mawr: Presser, 1967).

Weiner, Marc A., *Richard Wagner and the Anti-Semitic Imagination* (Lincoln, NE: University of Nebraska Press, 1995).

Whittall, Arnold, *Schoenberg Chamber Music* (London: BBC, 1972).

'Webern and Multiple Meaning', *Music Analysis*, 6 (1987), 333–53.

'Resisting Tonality: Tippett, Beethoven and the Sarabande', *Music Analysis*, 9 (1990), 267–86.

'Along the Knife-Edge: The Topic of Transcendence in Britten's Musical Aesthetic', in *On Mahler and Britten: Essays in Honour of Donald Mitchell on his Seventieth Birthday*, ed. Philip Reed (Woodbridge: Boydell Press/Britten–Pears Library, 1995), 290–8.

'Music–Discourse–Dialogue: Webern's Variations Op. 30', in *Webern Studies*, ed. Kathryn Bailey (Cambridge: Cambridge University Press, 1996), 264–97.

'Uncertain Reconciliations', *The Musical Times* (August 1997), 29–32.

'All Contradictions Reconciled? Perspectives on York Höller', *The Musical Times* (Autumn 1998), 11–19.

Musical Composition in the Twentieth Century (Oxford: Oxford University Press, 1999).

'The Mechanisms of Lament: Harrison Birtwistle's *Pulse Shadows*', *Music and Letters*, 80 (1999), 86–102.

'"A dance of the deadly sins": *The Beltane Fire* and the Rites of Modernism', in *Perspectives on Peter Maxwell Davies*, ed. Richard McGregor (Aldershot: Ashgate, 2000), 138–58.

'Britten's Lament: The World of *Owen Wingrave*', *Music Analysis*, 19 (2000), 145–66.

'Three for All: Andriessen's Recent Music', *The Musical Times* (Summer 2001), 9–20.

'Overlapping Opposites: Schoenberg since 1951', *The Musical Times* (Autumn 2001), 11–20.

Wilson, Paul, *The Music of Béla Bartók* (New Haven and London: Yale University Press, 1992).

Wingfield, Paul, 'Janáček, Musical Analysis, and Debussy's "Jeux de vagues"', in *Janáček Studies*, ed. Wingfield, 183–280.

Wingfield, Paul, (ed.), *Janáček Studies* (Cambridge: Cambridge University Press, 1999).

Worby, Robert, 'An Introduction to Stockhausen's *Light*' (Barbican Hall programme book, 2001), 12–13.

Index